WILD CAPITAL

Praise for *Wild Capital*

'A call to notice, to cherish and to protect, *Wild Capital* is for anyone who has ever found solace in the shade of a tree on a crowded city street, or marvelled at the tenacity of life sprouting through cracked concrete. This beautifully written book is a reminder that even in the heart of a city, wonder is waiting to be rediscovered.'

—Amitav Ghosh, author of *The Great Derangement: Climate Change and the Unthinkable*

'*Wild Capital* is a bold and glorious book about humans, cities and the wild lives of the beings—from fireflies to rivers—with whom we share the habitats we have built. It is brilliantly crafted at the level of the sentence and image, adventurous in its forms and tones, and its themes—memory, love, loss, care, value—are as embracing and urgent as they come. It's magnificent.'

—Robert Macfarlane, author of *Is a River Alive?*

'A triumph and a miracle—*Wild Capital* invites you to explore the living city hidden in plain sight, from ronjh and jaal to barbets and bats. Neha Sinha writes with deep, unsentimental love and wisdom about how we might recover and celebrate wildness, and dream of healing Delhi: ancient, ravaged, but teeming with life.'

—Nilanjana Roy, author of *Black River*

‘In *Wild Capital*, Neha Sinha returns to what she does best—catching a world between “forgotten” and “found”, flight and forest, she shares with us a city whose living history is the history of its plant and animal lives.’

—Sumana Roy, author of *How I Became a Tree*

‘A very original, lyrical but scientifically erudite hymn to the nature still flourishing in this most urban of urban environments, and a beautifully evocative reminder for a capitalist society of what capital really is: what we are all living off.’

—Ruth Padel, author of *Tigers in Red Weather* and *Where the Serpent Lives*

WILD CAPITAL

Discovering Nature in Delhi

Neha Sinha

HarperCollins *Publishers* India

First published in India by HarperCollins *Publishers* 2026
HarperCollins *Publishers* India, Cyber City, Building 10-A,
Gurugram, Haryana – 122002, India
www.harpercollins.co.in

2 4 6 8 10 9 7 5 3 1

Illustrations by Rituparna Sarkar
Photographs by Neha Sinha

P-ISBN: 978-93-6989-177-1
E-ISBN: 978-93-6989-346-1

Typeset in 12/16.2 Sabon LT Std
by HarperCollins *Publishers* India Pvt. Ltd

Printed and bound at
Manipal Technologies Limited, Manipal

MIX
Paper | Supporting responsible forestry
FSC www.fsc.org FSC™ C043100

This book is produced from independently certified FSC® paper
to ensure responsible forest management.

*

HarperCollins Publishers, Macken House, 39/40 Mayor Street Upper, Dublin 1,
D01 C9W8, Ireland

For Gypsy, the sweetest boy, my best friend,
the tenderest part of me:
You will always be the best person in the world.

Wazirabad (Yamuna river)
N
W
E
S
Yamuna
GAUTAM BUDDH NAGAR
Bhalaswa Lake
Sahibi-Yamuna Confluence
Naini Lake
Tagore Park
Northern Ridge
Sahibi
Delhi Heart and Lung Hospital
Central Ridge
Old Fort
Sanjay Lake
Mitraon Forest
Safdarjung Tomb
Aravalli Biodiversity park
Hauz Khas Lake
Southern Ridge (Sanjay Van)
Vasant Kunj
Najafgarh Jheel
Tughlaqabad Fort
Aravali Biodiversity park (Gurugram)
Southern Ridge
FARIDABAD
Asola wildlife Sanctuary
GURUGRAM
Mangar Bani Forest
Map not to scale

Contents

Introduction

What do you see out of your window as you read this? If you're in New York, perhaps you see a Common starling, pesky and invasive, but shining like glitter. In Sydney, maybe you hear rather than see a lorikeet screeching, full-throated, full-hearted and vivid. In London, perhaps you look out at a street which has the singular memory of a fox loping through at dusk. In Delhi, I see a thick-leafed tree with a red-eyed, mischievous Indian koel, a cuckoo, waiting to lay eggs in an unsuspecting crow's nest.

Cities are places for action and imagination. And a great city, as E.B. White wrote in his 1949 essay 'Here is New York', 'blends the gift of privacy with the excitement of participation'. We come to cities for anonymity but also recognition—we come to work, but we stay for the life they offer. Cities are like palimpsests, worlds set upon worlds, text upon text. Great cities wear history lightly, and sometimes, in the right light, you can see the past emerge from the present, or watch the present get subsumed into the past. In his book *City of Djinns: A Year in Delhi*, William Dalrymple writes on how some places in the city still remain as they were: mystics singing in the Nizamuddin dargah, a tradition of 700 years, Nilgai antelope roaming the Sanjay Van forest, having been here for even longer.

I'd like to argue that great cities are also indistinguishable from their natural histories. Cities like Delhi and London, that came up on the banks of great rivers, have lived in the space between fog-on-the-river and land, between the knowable and the unknowable, between the tepid and the exciting. More recent green interventions—Central Park in New York, the deftly curated gardens of Tokyo and Kyoto, Singapore's zoo and safari—are places not just to wander in, but to locate meaning in. And sometimes, a great bird flaps into these spaces. Recently, citizens of New York were enamoured by Flaco, a Eurasian eagle-owl who escaped the New York zoo and lived freely for an entire year in the city. Flaco had devoted fans who followed his every move, several newspaper articles on him, and an Instagram page. His life of celebrity began as his life of 'freedom' started—in him, New Yorkers perhaps sensed a mirror for what they wanted: free will combined with a homing instinct. Because that is what cities do to us, in the manner of kites on a headwind: they let us go, they let us be, but also let us come back to them.

But freedoms in cities are also negotiated spaces. Flaco died in 2024 because of the peculiarities of human density, and the way people construct lives in a crowded city—he collided into a building, and he also carried high levels of rat poison in his blood. Scientists have described the 'landscape of fear'[1] that birds can have in noisy urban areas, in which the fear of predation reduces nestling weight. This isn't just for birds: it is also true for women and the poor and marginalized in a metropolis, trying to live despite dangers, trying to belong, to thrive, even as fear pervades their life.

Wild Capital uncovers the great city of Delhi, enmeshed with nature, even as fear and challenges run through urban and neural networks. I go in the belly of mines, the slopes of the Aravalli hills, on the ramparts of forts, and into the depths of deciduous forests to find how wilderness thrives in the city, and also what wilderness means for the spirit of the extraordinary people who live here. I find things that slip in and out of our consciousness, London foxes at night. A mongoose mother, that creature of opportunity, crossing a road and disappearing into a hole whose position you forget as soon as her tail swishes away; a jackal laughing in the night next to an eleventh century monument; an Indian eagle-owl, much like Flaco, blinking solemnly at the world; a firefly flashing for a mate, just like the rest of us. Everyone looking to belong.

'What if our networks for joy included birdsong, the crescendo of crickets on a summer evening, and neighbours calling to each other across the road?' writes the wonderful

Robin Wall Kimmerer in *The Serviceberry: Abundance and Reciprocity in the Natural World*. 'I've long believed that those who have more joy win,' she writes. I agree, and while those with joy win, winning joy is a tough task in crowded cities. As the great poet J. Drew Lanham writes: 'Joy is the sharp eye/watching little brown sparrows,/and the kind one, focused/on little brown children too ... Joy is the justice we give ourselves.'[2]

And so, in *Wild Capital*, I search for places that have meaning for both the human and the more-than-human. Timeless places, such as an overlooked grove of centuries-old trees; imperilled places, such as a tree in the middle of a road; places that have been refound and rewilded: modern biodiversity parks that look to the past for resilience at a time of climate change. I parse through memories to understand how entangled we once were with rivers (there are two big rivers in Delhi, the Yamuna and the lesser-known Sahibi), search for oft-overlooked birds (there are over 400 bird species in Delhi, some crossing the tallest mountain range on earth, the Himalayas, to migrate to Delhi) and see how we might rediscover old words and wildernesses in our hearts. I meet people who have found joy, kept it and spread it, candles in the wind, a resistance to the cruelties of the world, an act of community.

'Umwelt' is a word to describe the particular way an organism sees the world—butterflies and birds have UV vision, ants sense things from their feet, some beetles use the stars to navigate. Expanding our umwelt to one that accommodates wildlife can be a radical act of seeing.

In the hundreds of hours that I have spent walking and clambering over the city—Delhi and the National Capital Region (or NCR) of Gurugram and Faridabad[3]—I include all that I see, with people being a single thread in a vast tapestry of plant, animal and rock. The palimpsest is now not just of the past and present, but of night and day, and the human and more-than-human.

In his book *Is a River Alive?* Robert Macfarlane leans on Maori philosophy to ask: Who are your waters? He suggests that rivers and clouds co-author each other. I find this is true for the trees we stand under, the soil we smell, the sunbird on the flower, the landscape we see every day, both concrete and cloud. The co-authors of our life are many.

My waters are of the Yamuna, my soil is the Aravalli hills. These are texts and beings begging to be read, to be felt, smelt and seen for what they are. This is their story as much as of those who live with them; the beginning of an idea that capital isn't just money, but a mingling of our lives with nature.

I hope the water colour illustrations in this book will help you sense nature. They are designed to leave an impression, to leave you with the feeling of the creature or plant, rather than recreate an exact photographic rendition. For instance, the impression that owlets leave on me is that they are rotund and friendly, and I hope the illustrations convey that.

As I write this in September, the air is turning in Delhi. Soon the time of festivities will take over, the wildflower calendar synchronizing their blooming with traditional ceremonies—grass flowers, sapphire blue-pea flowers, the bewitching *Alstonia scholaris* flowers. I hope you like the flower calendar in this book and liken it to ecological cosmologies from where you live. I have also provided ecological concepts and approaches to make our lives a little bit better, a 'little richer and rawer', as George Monbiot suggests in his book *Feral*. *Wild Capital* is thus a book about one great city, but it is seeded with ideas for all great cities.

PART 1

The Forgotten

'All flourishing is mutual.' *The Serviceberry*, Robin Wall Kimmerer

'But there is another, possibly deeper, limitation to the legend's mystical conception of balance: it is a contract drawn up and signed by a single party, and it provides for no mechanism through which to understand the needs of the other protagonists; in this scheme of things, the forest has no means of articulating its interests.' *Wild Fictions*, Amitav Ghosh

Forgotten Gardens

This little girl didn't like playing with dead dolls. She preferred her playmates to be living. A line of black ants, a bright-eyed bird that never came too close, a mongoose[1] that nibbled at something she couldn't see at the very boundary of her empire—a garden with a little wall around it. These playmates would walk into her games like human players and then amble off in the way of wild animals. She would sit in the garden talking to them, and they would appear into her line of sight or hearing. She realized later that they were co-creating the games—when ants marched forth over her feet, it would be all about tip-toeing so no one got hurt. When a bulbul picked up an insect to feed a chick, the game would tilt from loud kitchen-play to breath-withheld wild safari, and when a squirrel pranced amidst the yellow sorrel blossoms, it was hide-and-seek. She was learning how to notice things without hurting them, learning how to pursue without a chase. There was excitement without violence.

In her cupboards indoors, there were dolls. They were neatly arranged, because they were unused: she didn't play with them. Dolls never did anything more than open their eyes and then shut them. They were either asleep, or worse, awake with a single, frozen expression. Animals, though, had so much animation. Ants did things which defied how adults perceived insects to be. They didn't have eyebrows or voices like people did. But they certainly had expressions. When an ant walked down a path and met another one, she reached over and felt her friend. And she seemed to jump in surprise.[2] If you looked again you would realize they *both* jumped: it was a joyous greeting that just happened to be mute.[3] A silent shout through the grasses. The ants also carried things together, and the little girl had noticed how they seemed to feel for each other before they started their joint tasks—a '*Hello, how do you do*', and then: '*We can do this*.'[4] There were many kinds of ants in that garden in North Delhi. Large black ants with big mouth pincers, looking like scale models of sharply intelligent aliens,[5] becoming active after the rains. Small red ones that seemed to be angry all the time, because they bit the inside of her elbows and the backs of her knees. Ants with heads larger than their bodies. Small black ants that always drowned in the water she put out for birds.

There were other beings too, not as gleamingly sanitary as ants. There was one type which she could smell before she saw. It had a sour, forbidding scent, the smell of bad places—corners of walls where people urinated, unwashed toilets, forgotten buildings. The smell came from something with many stripes and many legs. This being liked the corners of walls meeting the ground and lay in heaps in those moist places. She would poke one to watch what happened next. The lithe, numerous-limbed body would abruptly slacken and then just as suddenly curl up into a tight ball, trembling with a desire to get away. It wasn't just the face of the animal: the entire body of the millipede was an expression when touched. And then there were dragonflies that landed on shards of grass, their wings gleaming like broken glass with veined cracks shining through. They were alert and muscular—their entire being was a stern, military expression. On the flowers, particularly the roses, there was a large, bright red-and-black insect. This was the blister beetle, and something about its body language—perhaps its slow, nearly overconfident steps over petals—told her the blister beetle should not be touched.

She had only seen one more thing that was as expressive as insects in the garden. It was a plant with a pink, dramatic poof of a flower and feathery leaves. When you as much as grazed the spine of the leaf with your smallest finger, the leaves shut themselves tightly, as if closing their eyes in protest. This was the touch-me-not or the mimosa plant.[6] She could almost see electric signals firing and synapses snapping in the plants and bugs—the aliveness of these organisms took her breath away. Snails glid forth from a bunch of shankhapushpi flowers, like stately ships in a sea with a destination only they knew. Soft-bodied slugs left silvery trails in the grass. Beetles shared secrets with each in their private world under fallen leaves below the row of football lilies. On the roses, ladybugs dived. And always, eternally, the ants greeted each other. The air fizzed with things that could not be heard in English or Bengali but were clearly happening right in front of her. There was a language being spoken here, without any words, but leaving its mark nonetheless. The signals were clear: life was here, right here.

On one side of the grasses, the garden contained a rose quarter with fifty rose shrubs planted in a circle. The flowers were strongly fragrant, but they fell apart the moment they were touched. Sometimes, she could tell if a desi (Indian) rose had been visited by a particular kind of insect, because it looked blowsy, about to tremble and fall to the ground. She knew then that in the garden, even insects left footprints. And the various signals and imprints—silver trails left by slugs, the nearly-fallen-apart roses, little round balls of earthworm waste, presented a neat lettering in front of her: Small is B.I.G.

That little girl was me. I had grown up in a house surrounded by a garden in Tagore Park, a small residential colony in North Delhi. The garden, too, had grown in me, putting forth shoots and branches: so much so that I remembered some things to the detriment of others. I forgot uncles and aunts, but I remembered plants and animals. Some plants had become giants, taking up all the space in my mind.

One such giant was a cactus that sprang up like a tree in a corner of the garden, though I didn't know its name. I often think about this cactus. And what were the names of the various yellow wildflowers in the grass? Which was the graceful orange bird with a long tail that visited on occasion? I didn't know the formal names of these visitors.

And then, as I grew up, I lost the sense of abandon of the little girl.

When I see a garden today, things hold me back in a vice. Embarrassments spring up around me in a sharp, thick knot of grasses. There is always somewhere else to go, an appointment to keep. The clock ticks with errands and impatience, both chains of their own kind. If I'm on my way to work, I can't muddy my knees and clothes. I can't bend over and run my hands through a clump of shrubs, fearing I will be pricked by something new I can't recognize. But more than anything, I wonder: Am I safe? Adulthood signifies a depletion of the cozy familiar. The unknown stretches wide and perilous, informed by the abstract horrors of the world, and by lived experience. The unknown sucks up everything, leeching into the boundaries of safe places. Adulthood is realizing the unknown *is* the world, and what we call safe are just little islands, lighthouses that signify the harbour but also the perils of getting there. Life gets defined not by its safe spots and harbours but by how the sea of the unsafe will be negotiated, every day, every hour. Every park and stretch of road can be a danger, especially in the dark. Is the prickle at the back of my neck because someone is watching? Whose garden am I in? Does the garden belong to the state? To a person? To no one? Is it sub-judice? The simple act of rifling through the grass growing on the ground is interrupted by these qualifications. That is how freshness can die, taking innocence with it. This is how caution makes cuts on fingers, grass-blade cuts, silently bleeding into the daily, leading to an attrition of energy and attention.

In my mind though, my cactus tree is still strong. The footprints of the insects of the subterranean and overground soil world are deep and dark. Even though the edges of the garden are tinged with danger, I know small is big. And you don't need a written language to be expressive. I must recreate these memories. I must find and name the plants and animals of the garden and revel again in their non-verbal sense-scape. I must translate what they tried to tell me.[7] In essence, I know the task in front of me: I must reclaim the garden of my childhood.

I must regrow its wild, strong sense of abandon. I must join hands with all the other misfits who hike up their skirts, trousers and saris to look through grasses and unknown flowers to understand our place in the world. And we must be resilient in the ancient, sentient and connected ways ecosystems are, while facing the great city of Delhi.[8]

Forgotten Trees

The Name of This Tree Is My Tree

Next to the house of my teenage years, there stood a tree. It was a twisted image from a clever carnival mirror—it looked like a doppelganger of the neem. But it wasn't the neem—not quite. Its proportions were a little different, a little more refined. The neem tree was ubiquitous[1]—everyone loved it and spoke of it like a rich, generous aunt: an entity that had passed on a gift to each family member at some point or the other. In my neighbourhood in the 1990s, people broke off neem twigs to clean their teeth with in the early mornings, leaving their teeth frothy and sparkling. My mother crushed the leaves, mixing them with honey to give us a truly eye-watering, tongue-curling daily tonic. Others used the baby pink leaves in early summer for chutneys and fries. The tree in front of my house resembled the neem. But it was subtly different. Its trunk had waving whorls, and the bole in the tree had such complex wrinkles that it looked like a mouth in a pout. The leaves were prettier than the neem's, a little less serrated, a little broader, overall more photogenic. Pale yellow fruit clustered on the tree, like it was wearing beaded earrings. When the wind blew, fractals of leaves would sway up and down, up and down. It was a mesmeric, eternal dance. Watching from the second-floor balcony, I felt like I was watching waves. The tree looked very old (would it be about thirty years old?—thirty felt positively ancient to my eleven-year-old self), but it also seemed very young, because of the new nubs of leaves, its round cheeks of fruit.

I didn't know the name of the tree, but I gave it a name. *Sea-tree.* Citri for short.

Looking at the Citri, I felt fiercely, and all over me, that this tree was mine. There would surely be better and bigger and more familiar trees that felt like generous aunts or waves of the sea. But this one was mine, and that counted. In its quiet but roiling waves, it made my life count. I never enjoyed mathematics and I'd look at my Citri when I was stuck with homework that paralysed me with tedium. A wind would spring up, and the tree's waves would hypnotize me. The tree was my weathervane, and my harbour—I always knew when a storm was coming because I would watch the tree from my study table. I wanted to be in the Citri, to feel leaf-waves around me, to feel like a tree, to experience rich green life beyond the blue lines of my maths notebook.

In the manner of what happens with great, beloved trees, other tree fans arrived too. A Rose-ringed parakeet pair wanted to take up residence in the bole and they fought with a pair of Common mynas over the space. No one got it in the end. Squirrels scampered up and down, horizontally and vertically, like they had everywhere to be all at once. If two parakeets take one fruit every two hours, how many does the squirrel have, I asked myself, in a crude parody of a maths problem. I didn't care much for the maths, but ecological questions, on relationships between animals and trees, were beginning to tunnel into my head.

I decided to ask the tree some questions. Maybe I could leave a message in that bole.

'What is your name? Do you want to stand in a forest, or are you fine here?'

The tree didn't respond. In my pre-teen impatience, I waited for waves that would present an immediate response to my deep, intelligent questions. The waves didn't come.

I understood something that day, though. The Citri, my tree, had to be *here*, where I was. It could not be elsewhere. Its placement as something I could see and access was of prime and urgent importance. The same rush may have informed those fighting for Sarojini Nagar trees in South Delhi.[2] Those trees were to be cut down for 'redevelopment' of government colonies. Tree lovers protested: why did the trees need to go, why couldn't new buildings be made with the existing neems, gulmohars and sausage trees on the sidewalk? Dreams of afforestation on the border of the city would never be the same as trees next to windows.

In the last house my parents had rented, another nameless tree had dripped mystery on the sidewalk.

This tree had feathery, romantic leaves and short, wicked thorns. It seemed a good personality balance as long as you didn't try to touch it. The first time I met Shakuntala, I was standing on the terrace and gazing at the tree and its green pods hanging in twisted spirals.

'Jalebi. The tree will give us jalebi,'[3] a girl's voice said. I turned to look at her. Shakuntala had almond-shaped eyes which were the colour of chocolate nutties. Her clothes were old and worn. But her eyes glinted with knowing, and an open challenge. The information had been offered as a gift, but the next line was a provocation. 'You can eat the fruit,' she said, 'if you know how to get it.' There was a challenge in that last line, a passive style of aggression that immediately called out to me. I had to know more.

Shakuntala didn't introduce herself. But I knew of her. She was the daughter of the chowkidar, who doubled as the handyman of the house. He had mournful eyes and a slow, somnolent voice. His daughter was just the opposite: her eyes sparkled with life and rebellion. Her story was just starting.

I considered what she had just said about the jalebi. The dense tree did not look like it wanted to part with anything, let alone sweetmeats. I decided I would be coolly detached and incredulous.

'I don't believe you.'

'We will see.'

Every evening, I would watch a peacock come and perch on another tree outside my house. As the sky turned darker, he would flap noisily towards a tall, straight tree with silvery bark. That tree was a solitary eucalyptus, standing straight and tall, its breadth making it look like a fair-skinned NRI who was proud of his Australian heritage. The peacock never came to the jalebi tree. In my mind this was because the tree's prickles were too intense and forbidding. It had none of the comfort or elegance that other trees did.

Hanging out with Shakuntala was like that too—there was never any comfort, elegance or any of the other qualities I had been taught to cherish at home or school. Instead, it meant stomping around the garden and climbing trees in my nice clothes. Shakuntala's family lived on our terrace. They never came into our rooms or gardens, so the terrace was her turf, and she knew every crevice of it. In a crack in the wall, she hid a special laminated picture that meant something to her, but which she never allowed me to see. She would caper up to the unfenced terrace above her room, her feet finding footholds only she knew about. She stood in the rain on this private little terrace, letting the water run through her while I waited in an alcove.

I was stabbed with jealousy as I watched—she always, always looked like she was willing to take risks, and she inherently understood that rewards chase risk-takers.

We had a begrudging friendship. She thought I was too rich and too soft, I thought she was too rude. She never said hello to me when I met her. I would stand in front of her, wanting to say something, and she would just say, 'We will get papayas today' or 'Today we are bringing down jalebis from the tree'. She set the rules for where we could go, because she took the risks, and I took only calculated risks. She said only the essential things, her mouth being occupied with a hunger and sharpness that I lacked. Every day I met her, I felt like I was handling thorns.

So when Shakuntala reminded me that the jalebi tree would give us fruit in a week, I believed her. On the day she decided the fruit was ripe enough to pluck, she went inside the room her family lived in and came back with a bamboo stick. Then, she palmed a stone and cracked the head of the bamboo open. The bamboo tore in a long, straight line. Its splinter was neat, remembering that it was grass, not wood. I had seen Baya weaver birds notch grass in a similar manner: they cocked their heads, and pulled thin, straight strips from the main blade of grass. These strands were easier to work with, and perhaps this also reduced the knife-like sharpness of the grass. Like the Baya, Shakuntala knew the way of the grass, and the rules it followed. She handled the bamboo deftly, with no runaway splinters piercing her fingers. Notch made, she then took the split head of the bamboo and lodged a pebble in it. What she now had—what *we* now had, I told myself—was something like a pair of bamboo pliers.

'I'm going to use this to get the jalebi,' Shakuntala announced, sweat beading her face. She stood on the veranda, leaning over with her bamboo-tool, her arms quivering with effort. Then, she craned further, her bare toes moving to grip the guardrail. She fastened the tool around the stem with the reddest fruit. She clamped down. Then, she started twisting.

I did nothing but watch. She wouldn't let me touch her weapon. Ten minutes later—she grunting with effort, and me sweating with the anxiety of paying attention—a jalebi lay on the ground, its stem lacerated by the twisting bamboo.

We raced downstairs to pick up the fruit which promised to be dessert.

'I'll get there first,' Shakuntala said as she panted down the stairs.

'No, it will be me,' I said. 'Silly witch,' I sniped in my mind.

She got there first, as I had known she would, and scooped up the prize. It was a long line of fruit, packed in a red pod. It fell in a spiral: sensuous and loose, like the sinuous body of a python packed with muscle. You had to use your nails to peel the pods, and then a litchi-white pulp, veined with red, emerged. We broke pieces of the jalebi, flung away the seeds, and then smashed the prize into our mouths to chew. We each wanted to be the first to deliver the verdict.

I masticated, waiting for my mouth to be suffused with flavour, syrup and achievement. I waited a beat more for comprehension, and disappointment flooded me. The taste was terrible. The fruit was stringy, and instead of a juicy sweetness, it had an astringent-like quality—like its sweetness had been diluted with each new pod taking birth.

'*Bllll* ... I hate this!' I said.

'It's not that bad,' she replied. *'I worked for it,'* was her implication.

'But it *is* that bad! Even a banana is better.'

'Well,' she rolled her shoulders and looked at me sideways. 'This is free.'

I stopped, ashamed. Shakuntala seemed to have said something of immense importance. For those who didn't have a centre-bowl of the season's latest fruit, foraged fruit was a reward. In her thorny, incisive way, Shakuntala had spoken the bare truth. Trees line tasteful avenues, something just to look at for the rich. For the less fortunate, they can be an afternoon of fun—and nutrition.

I ate some more jalebis that day, more to give my friend company than anything else. But indignation burned at me. The fruit made me uncomfortable somehow. It was like an untamed relative of all the kiwis, peaches and custard apples I ate at home. The incursion of a jungle jalebi felt like I was eating storms and wild sunrays which had somehow made themselves smaller for my weak, soft mouth.

Years later, I met Shakuntala again. On a school night, she had come to visit along with her sister. They were in the drawing room of our new house: we had shifted out from the old property. I hadn't thought about the jalebi tree in years. Or of her. Shakuntala sat in a chair, dressed in a salwar kameez, her eyes and lips lined with colour. Her gaze was lowered, and when she spoke to my father, her voice was a conscious whisper. All her thorns seemed to have turned inwards, like they had needled reality into her body. She looked like any other girl, not my rude, proud friend. She seemed to have learned that she must soften her voice, her hard edges, the fire of her defiance, and become an easily quietened woman. A sweet woman. We made polite conversation as evening fell.

I didn't realize it then, but the jalebi tree had been telling me something. It had stringy, tough fruit for stringy, tough women. If the fruit had been sweet, it would have been unmemorable. It would have been like a store-bought banana, not a hard-won battle prize. The jungle jalebi had the wildness that came before polite society bludgeoned us to conform.

Shakuntala left, her eyes still lowered, the fight gone out of her. I was in class XII, studying all the time. She didn't offer me her number. I didn't ask for it. We knew this was the last time we were seeing each other. I didn't have the heft, or the power, to help, or to change her life, if she wanted my assistance.

But through the tree, I remembered always: two wild women, sour-bitter, thorny and triumphant, free.

Later, in my college years, I began visiting my old house, not for the property, but for the tree.

And I learned something, almost as if the tree had texted me with a message.

Trees don't have to be elegant, and the truly memorable is often not sweet. Just like us, or the memories of us. For the first time, I left a tree with a message, not a question.

Thank you for the thorns.

Years later, armed with mobile applications and with a little money in hand that allowed me to buy Pradip Krishen's wonderful *Trees of Delhi*, I watched a Citri in a little park near Malcha Marg. The park was a neat square I had been birdwatching in. Like my Citri, this tree also hung with globules of fruit. There were so many it was clear they didn't get eaten as swiftly as the figs of other trees, like the peepals or banyans that grew through the walls of places one noticed only because of the trees—old houses, public toilets, a neighbour's roof. A pair of Grey hornbills flapped noisily towards the Citri,[4] their wings moving together. One of the birds landed, cocked its head, and plucked a drupe. These are some of the best things to see as a nature-lover: a full-grown tree, spread out beautifully like the arrangement of lines in a poem, and a mature bird on its branches, there for the fruit, there to give the poem a poignant ending. I expected the hornbill to throw its head back and toss the fruit into its huge bill. Instead, it hopped over to its partner. Tenderly, and with great focus, it fed its partner instead.

Hornbills nest in holes in large trees. To bring up their chick, the male seals the female in the hole. She takes care of the chick, and he takes care of the menu—bringing meals for both mother and chick. Even when they are not rearing their young, the male hornbill will feed the female so she can get accustomed to the period when she won't have the liberty to find her own food. What I was looking at then was the insight of a male caring for his mate and his future family, and the female accepting his gifts.[5] It was as a ritual on a dining table—when something hand-stirred and hand-measured is offered, you understand implicitly that it is special, regardless of whether it is staid khichdi for children or an exciting, spicy curry for adults. Whether stirred by hand, or carried in a hornbill's impressive beak, such food is regard. And the female accepting this regard comes with an implicit understanding: she knows food which is carried to her is food that scaffolds bonds. As an eleven-year-old, I had known that the Citri held nests of smaller parakeets. That day I learnt trees like Citri shelter and feed larger birds too. I knew that the Citri was mine, but it was theirs too. And because they didn't get to write books, it felt right that the tree was more theirs than mine. I searched for the formal name of the tree then. The Citri was called bakain, *Melia azedarach*. A cousin of the neem.

The bakain is not native to India, but it has threaded its quiet ways through our lives, and more importantly, into the lives of birds.

In the summer, the bakain produces a kind of magic. Usually, you can smell it before you see it. It is a subtle flower, unlike the ones we usually tend to notice. You have noticed a rose received on Valentine's Day, grown under precise conditions. You have seen the vinca or sada bahar flower (whose literal translation is: 'always blooming'), which grows and blossoms under any condition: in dry drains, on walls where water dribbles out of leaky pipes, on an inch of soil between bricks. You have noticed flowers in the garden that your family has tended to—marigolds, strung in necklaces and in songs, and tulsi, grown for its leaves but also possessing small, scented flowers. To see flowers we look downwards, and sideways. Towards the mulch of the garden, towards a man selling a bouquet next to a crumbling public market which features standard photocopy stores. Perhaps we don't always look up. We may be missing mature trees with crowns of small flowers. Especially if they are flowers like the neem or bakain, falling softly on the senses, small and delicate. The bakain, like the neem, produces a profusion of tiny, star-shaped flowers. The neem has white flowers, the bakain tender, lavender ones. Their petals are like the first flush of sunrays across the sky—a colour touched by soft beginnings. And in all, the flowers are unobtrusive. When you walk below the tree, the scent will come to you as a gentle suggestion, the kind of luxuriating fragrance that doesn't prickle your nostrils but opens a tunnel to another world, a particular memory. To me, the Citri's flowers are the smell of my grandmother's Pond's talcum powder—a fragile smell, meant to perfume miasmas of sickness and pat away the wrinkles of old age.

Despite their star-shaped beauty, bakain blooms are so small that you may easily miss them. They're tinier than your fingernails, more flecks than flowers, with their numbers giving them heft. When the tree fills with tens of hundreds of flowers, it's like the wind has fondled the tree's leaves and tossed them here and there, showing lighter backs and sides, like a trick of the wind and light. You can't really tell there's a flower unless you are paying close attention. And so, bakain flowers have forced me to pay attention, to them, and to the world—to my grandmother who does her hair in the same way every day; to a Rufous tree-pie that flies over a line of goods vehicles, one of which says 'Dekho magar pyar se';[6] at Citri clusters breaking the smog line.

Meanwhile, the Grey hornbill continues his love story on the bakain, even as I write mine with the Citri. There is no Shakuntala now, but there will always be affection for trees, for prickles, for cherishing the odd ones, the misfits.

I understand now: the name of the tree is not the most important thing. Memories could be more important, and the tree being where we are. Twenty years later, I find a tree with small leaves and a warty bark outside my office on Lodhi Road. It looks familiar. It looks like childhood, like fairy tales with teeth. It looks like a jungle jalebi.

I am a conservation biologist now, but I still know the formal name of a tree is not the most important thing. What matters is that you notice the tree, and that you allow it to tunnel into your life, to open new neural pathways. The jungle jalebi tree is called *Pithecellobium dulce*. But for me it will always be the jalebi tree from the summers spent with Shakuntala, sister to the Citri that had found me.

After years, I left a text for the office tree.

The name of this tree is my tree.

Forgotten Forests

Jaal

It is over an hour and a half from any place we recognize. As we come to Mitraon, all known symbols of Delhi recede into the background. The road descends into a series of potholes, and oddly enough, speed breakers—as if the potholes are not enough to jar the progress of our car. The dominant feeling is that of a noisy town jostling against large, silent wheat fields—behind the road and buildings, noise vanishes into the wheat, like someone smudged out the city and eased it into the bucolic. The April sun is a scuffed coin in the sky. Dust from the potholes and the fields is thick in the air, a thing the tongue can touch.

We are not far from the (relatively) better-known Najafgarh. This is a part of Delhi that lives at a different pace, and perhaps in a different time. Men walk around in white kurta-pajamas, an excellent shield from the heat, a common sight in Haryana. From little shops, a bonanza of chips, replicas of better-known brands, wink at us. 'Fun Fine', 'Sona Chandi', 'Karare', and my favourite: 'Paisa Vasool', *get your money's worth*. People stand outside the chips shops, puffing away at beedis and cigarettes. I watch the smoke curl through the air; suddenly, the mad pace of the city seems behind us, replaced by the long-drawn-out patience that is a sign of rural life.

Our destination is the city forest of Mitraon. We reach it after some confusion and many failed cartographic attempts. Outside the forest, there is a nice gate. We park and walk in. There are several people inside, morning walkers, people doing yoga, playing games, men walking their sons. It is a place where things happen in the morning. Next to the walking tracks, the soil is fine, lying in small undulating mounds; the ground resembles the surface of a giant golf ball. Clumps of broad grass grow in the depressions between the mounds. This grass is thick and spiky, the kind which needs moisture, and it spears upwards,[1] hungry for life. The ground's humps and cavities look like they have been moulded by something even greater than soil. Perhaps by water. We are on land that has the memory of water; that wants to hold on to water for as long as it can.

Years ago, Mitraon village was part of the Sahibi river flood plain.[2] I am reminded of the flood plains of the Brahmaputra river in Assam. The huge, roaring

Brahmaputra lies like a grey tongue, giving expression and animation to the area. The flood plains are the cheeks that hold the tongue—they swallow all that the river says in both anger and love. The catchment area is often water, sometimes land, occasionally something in-between, solid but swampy. On a blazing April day, I walked along the flood plain of the Brahmaputra. On the banks, wind sang as it mercilessly teased tall trees, echoing notes from the gushing sound of the water. The river was so big, and the roaring of the wind so loud, that I felt I was looking at the sea. The 'beach'—the flood plain—was sandy and brown, looking deceptively simple. But there hardly are any simple things in nature. One just needs to look closer. That day we bent, spines curved, palms on soil, and really looked. Holes dotted the ground. Some of them flickered with life—a gecko inside a hole, hiding from the merciless sun, its eyes roving the area like a heartbeat. Jhau plants grew restlessly tall. In other places, little yellow and pink wildflowers flecked the ground. The flood plain looked like our fingers do when kept under water for a long time, calloused and grooved. The fine soil laid itself in wave-like formations: this was land that felt the pressure of hundreds of litres of water each year. And thousands of kilometres away, on the edge of Delhi, Mitraon felt the same—like it had known water well.

In the *Delhi Gazetteer* of 1883–84, the portion on Najafgarh throws some light on the temperament of the Sahibi river:[3]

> The Dábar lies to west of the hills, and consists of low ground or basin scooped out by their westward drainage, and the floods of the Sahibi naddi, which comes down through Gurgaon from Alwar. In the rainy season, the country is under water for many miles round Chhaolah and the villages near it: as the rains subside and the cold weather comes on, the greater part of the floods is carried off into the Jamna by the Najafgarh jhil escape, but the jhil itself, except in years of drought, covers a great many acres with the residuum, which lies in a hollow south of the villages of Bahlolpur, Dahri and Zainpur.

Jainpur (or Zainpur) and Chhawla (Chhaolah) are next to Mitraon. Today, Aravalli's Sahibi river is cut off from Mitraon, and the latter no longer gets flooded by the river. In fact, the very name Sahibi is alien to most people in the city. The channelled course of Sahibi river is known more infamously as the Najafgarh drain, the greatest source of water pollution and effluents in the Yamuna. The *Gazetteer of Delhi*, 1912, notes that the Najafgarh jheel (lake) flooded as much as 80 square miles. In 1838, the British cut a channel into the jheel to prevent flooding. The cut was made at Chhawla, and the resultant Najafgarh drain passes Hastal, Basai and Kakraula and falls into the Yamuna river at Wazirabad.

In Mitraon, I am with Sohail Madan, an ecologist who spent many years restoring Asola Bhatti sanctuary. In Asola, he learnt how to nest plants in dry, often degraded soil. By the time he came to Mitraon, he had the experience of growing forests in lands that have faced the worst of human attention—mining, garbage and invasive species. Today, Asola has a thriving butterfly park, small water catchments and the overall idea that the native palash tree is better than the invasive *Neltuma juliflora* tree. Armed with this experience, he worked briefly in Mitraon. The purpose was to identify tree species and create a biodiversity and butterfly park. In the course of his planning, he encountered something unexpected—trees of the past, those that had lived hundreds of years. He wants to show me his special tree, the one he saw first. We walk through the area, through the people who are playing and walking. They turn around to look at us and our cameras.

'It's here, it's here … I hope it's still here,' Sohail says, with the wildly swinging pendulum of hope that all urban ecologists carry.

Sometimes, all your work disappears overnight as a road or a metro expands, crushing seedlings, and your spirit, completely and absolutely. A new restoration plan can get waylaid by cosmetic ideas of what a park should be—a place with swings and selfie points, concrete fountains and carpet grass, not tangles of spiky, scary-looking natives, not wild places. And at other times a new butterfly sails into the city, breaking a new record when you weren't even looking, buoying you with the headwind of hope. On the day of our walk, a new Swift butterfly, the Large-branded Swift, has been added to Delhi's butterfly list; so the pendulum swings that day towards hope. We reach the place the tree is supposed to be and stand with our feet firmly planted on the ground. The tree is not there.

Sohail swings his head from side to side, his forehead furrowed, a grief moving through his limbs. I understand his loss at not being able to see 'his' tree. He doesn't say it, but it's clear that he has a bond with the tree he found, one deeply felt, its lines scored into his skin. This tree is his tree the way the Citri was mine. A Brown-headed barbet calls near us, breaking our inner conversations. 'Did they cut it? Why would they?' he says. We don't want to acknowledge the enormity of never again being able to see something we valued. 'Oh, maybe it's not this place, but a little ahead,' he says. He exhales, his gait picking up. We walk on, in a trance that's familiar—the trance in which your body is preparing for the worst, the feeling when something which can't speak is taken away from you: silently, so swiftly the cut doesn't hurt at first.

And then, it's there. The trance snaps, and the tree is in front of us. He doesn't need to tell me, because I can see him standing there, his gaze like a bright vajradanti flower[4] looking towards the sun. He is looking at his tree. The tree looks down at our faces, a lord that has waited patiently. It has an immensely complex trunk, deeply grooved, as if runnels of lava have run down its shaft, changing it with each pulse of touch. It is milk-chocolate brown with filaments of dark chocolate in it. The bottom of the trunk has a muscular grip on the earth. The grips look like lion paws. At the very centre, the trunk parts. It holds what looks like an enchanted, cavernous doorway. This door is framed by leaves which are long and merry, dark green, almost grey. The dominant feeling is of great age and experience. This complex monument is a jaal tree. The *Salvadora oleoides*.[5] Sohail is reaching out to touch the trunk, his fingers reverent. 'This is an old tree. It must be 350 years old at the very least,' he breathes. His voice has dropped to a whisper, like we are in a church or temple. He takes a twig lying on the ground and snaps it into a tiny fragment. 'Jaal doesn't even grow that much in a year,' he says, pointing at the short length of twig. 'It starts off as a bush, and it takes decades till it can even look like a tree. Just imagine how many years this tree, which looks like a tree, has seen.' We are absorbing the feeling of standing next to something that is so old, so old but still growing. There are such few opportunities to be close to centuries-old living things. The other comparable entities in the living kingdoms would be Greenland sharks, Galapagos giant tortoises, perhaps a baobab tree in an African desert. I wonder if I have stood close to something so old, yet so alive, in Delhi. For Sohail, it's a homecoming. It's keeping a promise made with a friend to meet at the same spot seven years later, the kind of thing you watch in movies. For me, it feels like the beginning of a pilgrimage.

The 1912 *Gazetteer of Delhi* describes the jaal as bringing life to 'waste'.

> This tree is also indigenous and is to be found in large groves giving an appearance of verdure to

> tracts of country which would otherwise be sterile wastes: it is a stiff stunted tree rarely exceeding 15 feet in height with small linear dull green leaves much resembling those of the olive, from which it derives its specific name. It thrives well in a saline soil and its fruit, which ripens during the hot season, is much appreciated.[6]

Someone has carved tiny names into the trunks. VS loves SK. I wonder if VS and SK ever got together, whether they broke up, and how time hasn't erased their names. Situated in a city forest—one that is stewarded by the forest department—one would assume the tree would be safely preserved (ironically, so would the vandalism on the trunk). But as we look around, we realize the tree is not safe, and the primary problem is not people who scratch trunks, but other trees. Sohail is looking next to the tree with something like rising panic. His eyes dart at the skyline, left, right, up and down. He gulps. He points at one corner of the panopticon he is drawing with his eyes. A ring of vilayati, or *Neltuma juliflora*, stand around the old jaal. These trees are the vermin of the plant world: deadly invasives from Mexico that over-compete with other trees, eventually killing them.[7] 'I can't believe these are still here,' he says, a sentiment which is the complete opposite of him fervently wishing for the jaal to be there still. Sohail tried to get the trees removed, it didn't work. If the jaal has to survive the next few centuries, the vilayati kikars have to go. Below the larger vilayati kikar, smaller seedlings push up. There are more invasives here than on his last visit. They look robust, healthy and at home. And when I look closer, I see the ground is covered in a wash of fine golden dust—the fragments of the kikar's clustered, finger-like flowers. The invasive tree is a problem that grows bigger because it is invisible to others. Where people see green trees, ecologists see enemies. Three hundred and fifty years ago, there weren't so many vilayati kikars. Aided by human assistance, these trees have colonized entire forests, erasing what a natural landscape can and should look like. Perhaps the generational memory of the 1990s is vilayati kikar—with their anyhow growing branches, their fine golden dust, their inability to die. The image is charming but deceptive, and the situation requires intelligent and informed interventions—invasives must be removed so that natives can flourish. The canopy of the young invasive kikars must be broken so sunlight can reach the old, the rare.

A little ahead, we find one more jaal tree. This one is also ringed by vilayati kikar and looks visibly stunted. It's like watching a horror movie. In some films, the hills have eyes. In others, there are bad intentions in cornfields. Here, the invasive trees seem to have wings and feet and toothy mouths, gobbling land and sky. Mitraon has begun to feel bittersweet now—we have found the tree, but we have also found villains around it. Like the pendulum of hope and despair, this feeling too, is familiar—of mixed victories, a kind of solastalgia, a mourning for something not fully defined, and a foresight that the future will bring loss. We decide to walk to the other side of the forest. The day is becoming cloudy, and there is the hint of a fragrant wind. I wish I could smell a river of yesteryears, before it got drowned by sewage and construction.

On a nearby shahtoot tree, the Brown-headed barbet has found what she was looking for, and her neck is straining so she can tear at and gulp ripe purple mulberries. We walk on. As we reach, we find there are more trees and less paths. Here too, the land undulates. It's like looking at a hundred sand-coloured camels sitting down, their humps peering out at us. A woman is sitting on a bench. She is only the second woman I have seen this morning, through the bumpy roads and the cloud of morning walkers. She's dressed in candy pink pajamas and a black and white striped t-shirt. It's athleisure that belongs to two worlds—the urban, bright velour tracksuit world, and the more practical jungle-visitor world. We have almost walked past her, when she calls out, loudly: '*Ei, suno*. What are you doing here?' There is some hostility in her eyes.

We turn towards her. 'We are here to see the birds,' Sohail says.

'Birds! What birds?' There is disbelief on her face. She expects we are secretly making fun of her or her forest.

'Woodpeckers, hornbills, barbets,' I offer. 'Trees,' I add.

'Why, don't you have these trees where you come from?'

Sohail and I look at each other and smile. Almost together, we begin to say: 'We are from another part of Delhi. And no, we don't have these trees there.'

The lady looks flabbergasted.

'These trees? These old trees?' she asks, brows arching. Her hostility has been replaced by incredulity.

She has many more questions. How long did it take us to reach Mitraon? Where did we buy our cameras from? How much do they cost? Can her son, who sort of likes wildlife, sort of, also buy a camera? How do we make money, walking around forests? Are we destitute or are we quite rich with all this wandering? *Kitne paise kama lete ho?* (How much do you end up earning?)

We answer her gunshot questions and move on. I am laughing. She liked you, I tell Sohail. Yeah, I liked her too, he replies. We like everyone who can care a little for a tree that's been standing longer than they have.

We turn a corner and reach an area with no people. A woodpecker's call cuts through the air like a buzz saw: krrrrr krrr krr krr. The feeling of being near the river of yore is still in our bones. I am looking for the colour of the woodpecker in between the trees, the electric combination of red and gold. Sohail walks a little way forward and stands in front of an impossible tangle. His neck has craned all the way up. The tree looks like it has been meshed with green cables, or is growing with boughs made of living, snarled barbed wires. Sohail's gaze is a caress on the snarl. He is lost in sepia memories. 'That's the jaal, with its friend, the kanthari,' he says, pointing. I see the broad jaal tree, and then discern a spiky shrub next to it. The shrub has a narrow stem and a crown of snarls. It looks like the Goth friend of a classical music aficionado. Jaal and *Capparis* shrubs are natives of the Aravallis. *Capparis* include the kanthari (*Capparis sepiaria,* also called the wild caper bush) and the kareel (the *Capparis decidua* shrub, also known as kair). The kareel is all spikes[8]—a defence against heat and aridity or perhaps being out-competed on thin soils. When it grows, it looks like a head that tosses its mane often, a wild horse running in the wind. It produces orange flowers the colour of molten lava. The blossoms are orchid-like, a reminder that the most beautiful things can accompany nests of spikes. The kanthari grows like a liana with small leaves, a bush on stilts, and it has spidery white flowers. Both kareel and kanthari often lean on or stand next to the jaal as they grow. As we look at the jaal and the kanthari, it's hard to tell them apart. It's like they are hyphenated, not separate: they are the jaal-kanthari, joined in a heart like VS loves SK. But the century old jaal-kanthari friendship is not well known or celebrated.

Sohail's whole body has snapped to attention as he follows the lines of the tree friends. He is only looking, not speaking. He is awkward in conference rooms but is in his element in the outdoors. He responds to stimulus in the most natural way. He will lie down for half an hour to get an eye-level picture of a butterfly, documenting things others might miss. I have seen him watch butterflies take nutrients from wet mud, secreting the extra liquid. That day, the butterfly carried on its ritual—taking what it needed, discarding the rest. And Sohail captured it again and again, the passing of time suspended, a mixtape on repeat, a ritualized form of attention.

Right now, he is looking at the jaal-kanthari embrace, and then looking some more. It's almost like the stillness of trees present a movement in themselves. 'You identify trees by looking at them for a long time,' he says at last, 'not by memorizing their features from a book.' He had told me this in a forest in the Central India highlands too. Trees look distinct from each other, but they can also look very similar. When it is flush with new red leaves, I have mistaken the mahua for the kusum in Central India. Both have new leaves that are the red of a Cotton stainer bug or a watermelon—fresh, fleshy, invigorating. Sohail feels looking at a tree deeply imprints it in your mind—you can discern the type of tree with an intuition, rather than a mechanical examination. For instance, the shape of a shisham is different from that of a ziziphus, even if the leaves look similar at first glance. The shisham *feels* more sprawling and has a more crooked trunk. But trees can be individuals too, and not every tree follows notes of how it is supposed to look. That is where intuition comes in handy; it is a bedfellow of experience. At first glance, the jaal-kanthari look the same, small-leaved entity, but intuition can tell you they are two wizened trunks aiming for the same sun.

We walk through the tangles of friendship. And all of a sudden we are in a grove of trees which only has jaal. They are in each corner we look in: twelve-o-clock, three-o-clock, eleven-o-clock. Each jaal has a *Capparis* next to it, either a kanthari or a kareel.

'Look at this kareel! Just look at it!' Sohail cries, pointing. It is unusually tall—as mighty as a young neem.

'It would have taken a hundred years for this to grow this tall!' he says. I too am experiencing the deep intuition one feels before the snap of recognition. I too have a sepia postcard of memory. It is the deep-rooted but buoying recognition of finding something that came before you, something older and wilder, like finding a loved, grown-up cousin at a movie theatre. I realize then I have seen kareel and kanthari plants many times before. I have seen them being cleared from parks and roadsides, burnt and replaced with flowering shrubs with fewer spiny aspects. Horticulture can be brutal: pruning, razing, eliminating, fitting squares into circles, looking for only flowers, not thorns, for sameness, not scramble. Manicured gardens look to erase the needs of time, privileging the fast-growing over the slow and patient. Standing in a centuries-old forest, I wonder if we can appreciate where we are and how we must spread the seeds of the old.

Around us comes a whirring sound. A bird flies towards a hole on a jaal trunk. We haven't got a good look, but it is the size of a finch. We wait for it to emerge. It comes out and flies off, and we get a good look: a brown bird with a wet-yellow daub on its throat. This is the Yellow-throated sparrow, the bird that spurred noted ornithologist Salim Ali to study birds seriously. He had found this sparrow and was puzzled by the yellow on the male's slender throat. He realized the bird wasn't like other sparrows. He decided to investigate further. And so, a few millimetres of yellow took Ali to his lifelong passion for ornithology.

The Yellow-throated sparrow returns, and this time he has nesting material in its beak. A little home is forming inside the tree—a heritage home in a city full of the rash of new concrete. This is heritage which grows slowly, waiting still for rivers of yore. Endless in what it has seen and the years it is yet to see, if it is allowed to live.

At least there aren't too many kikar here, I tell Sohail. He nods. We aren't talking much. The place feels hushed. Psychologist Stephen Kaplan writes about the restorative attention that being in nature brings—a relaxed, effortless attention,[9] in contrast to the overstimulation urban living brings. Moving through the trees like dryads, we feel relaxed; the jaal hushes us in a good way. We like being dwarfed by their size and age.

As we watch, a Spotted owlet flits soundlessly through the trees. It is a sleepy blur, its wings propelling like a windmill's blades, its face complaining that it's just too bright today. The heat rises slowly, the colours become sharper around us. I think we feel, together, that we want to be rooted here. Sohail picks up leaves from the ground and fists some soil. I look upwards. I want a net of jaal all over, an impenetrable net that the axe or the competing invasive cannot penetrate. A koel throws his beautiful song from the trees, and I tell myself he is agreeing with my thoughts. A Grey hornbill flutters to a peepal tree branch. He is against the light, and has the aspect of a soft-grey stain: like the faint lines from a children's colouring book waiting to be coloured in. I want to colour things with the dark green of jaal, though I won't live long enough to see a jaal shrub become a tree. We have beatific smiles on our faces. There is a fierce, acute happiness in our bones. I have owl-blurs in my eyes and jaal-kanthari snarls in my breathing; I barely want to remove myself. But the April heat is eddying up and we have more forest to see.

Through the grove, we walk towards a place that is fenced. The fence is new, much newer than the rest of the forest. And that is when the penny drops, breaking through the hush.

Inside the fenced area, all we see is vilayati kikar. Suspiciously, there is no jaal. There is also no kareel or kanthari. It's like watching a hideous turning inside-out of how the forest should be: in the right universe, it would be the kikar that would be missing.

We realize what is going on here, because we have seen a mirror image of it in the Central Ridge forest in Delhi. In Delhi, you can't cut trees in forest areas. But there is also a mandate to remove invasive species. Oddly, what the authorities have been doing in different forests is trying to subdue the invasive: a cutting off instead of a cutting down. In the Central Ridge, they have attempted to choke the foreign kikar by training woody climbers or lianas up the trees. To do this, they also clear the area around the tree base—effectively destroying old and precious undergrowth like the *Capparis*. After walking around in a real forest, seeing this experiment is akin to entering a bright green plastic universe full of fake trees.[10] It's like looking at rows of the imitation chips we saw at the dhaba—instantly gratifying junk food that slowly turns you stupid. As we look inside the shiny fenced plot, we don't know if the jaal has been cut, but we can be sure the *Capparis* has been removed. This is the only part of the forest where we can see the ground clearly. It looks naked and wrong. The very opposite of the grassy spears of the soil we saw when we first entered the forest. I long for blades of grass and spikes of *Capparis* to cover the nakedness, to see a blade slicing through this plan.

We can't be clearing the floor for a larger-scale invasion by alien species. It is literally missing the trees for the wood, and cutting off the nose to spite the face.[11] I remember what another restoration friend told me: city horticulture often means removing what is there to plant something afresh, to prove *something* has been done. Done, and underlined. Done for. Budgets grow when you cut and you plant, when you cart and chop away native resilience—as if history is only for books and not for real life. It is also a fierce form of the anthropogene: the idea that only the seedling planted by the human hand has any standing. That the new sapling is a tree, and the tree growing wild before it was never a tree.

The vice of vilayati kikar is tightening. How tragic that it is around the slow-growing, patient jaal. The jaal is one of the best trees we have seen. We agree on this without even discussing it. It is both our history and a biodiverse future; it has both complexity and an austere simplicity. How can modern practices disregard these values? We pant, agitated. How many summers and storms has the jaal been witness to? How does it hold on to the soil with its feet-claws, in droughts and floods both? It deserves respect, though what I feel for it is closer to reverence. Respect is also owed to the thorny, spindly *Capparis* plants that never register as anything other than 'jungli'. *Jungli* translates to wild—used most often as a derogatory term, referring to something that looks untidy, malnourished or tumbling; a thing that scrambles for life with a bone-deep hunger. This is the wild that is beyond our control and the discipline of garden shears—the one that disrespects hedgerow borders, that colours outside of boxes. The kareel and the kanthari look like snarls, but they need the comb of insight to unravel their true meaning. They match the poor soils they germinate in; they are parsimonious and grow just as much as they need to. No broad leaves, no juicy canopies, but a seeming desiccation which has purpose. They possess a determined gaze on building strength, not decoration: they can look at the sun, and not blink; they offer a full, open-hearted embrace of the heat of the region, of the raging summer winds that scour soils and souls, of the heatwaves that linger at 48 degrees Celsius, that kill people and hopes.

We walk further. We will be at the entrance soon, we have traced a circle though the forest. The birds are drawing a circle too: the Black-rumped woodpecker follows another, its passage low, musical and circular.

Near the entrance, we spot dark-brown tree stumps. They are huge and shaped in various ways. One looks like an octopus waving its tentacles around in the warm air. Another is so big and distended that it looks like the tree got caught in a river and the water bloated its wood. But they have something in common. They all have a neat cut at the top—the straight line of a professional cutting tool. A surgical line that also cleaves the heart of the onlooker.

'No, they're doing it!' I cry. 'They're cutting ... they're cutting the jaal trees,' Sohail finishes. A chain-link of the sequence of events forms. It is so easy to fell a tree that took three hundred years to grow, for beautification or for no real purpose. It is so neat to consider an invasive an equal with a precious native. It is so convenient to dismiss the unruly shrub because it looks unattractive. All these assumptions are acts of violence. It is a planned violence, blind because it is biased.

We don't know when the jaals were cut down, and if more will be felled. We found a forgotten forest, and it seems we are going to lose it. The pendulum of hope now swings towards despair.

Our hearts clench and unclench, irate, impotent fists. We will speak to the forest department. We also need to speak to everyone else. We need to tell them it took over three hundred years for a tree to grow and spread its arms. That the lesser-known parts of Delhi, with their tough love and tree embraces, don't need to stay concealed. That it is still possible to walk in a part of the city which is mostly untouched for centuries, and that walk will be accompanied by owl-blurs, tree-monuments and woodpecker songs. That we must look at and feel the trees that grow on the floodplains of forgotten rivers; that history can live with its cheek pressed to the present, that we will be richer, infinitely, if we borrow the patience and friendship of the jaal-kanthari.

NEHA'S FIELD NOTES

The jaal is also called bada peelu. A related tree is the *Salvadora Persica* or meswak, used as a woody toothbrush. Jaal fruits can be eaten. You can see jaal trees in parts of the Thar desert, in rural Haryana, and in the Qutub Minar complex. I found a jaal grove in a village called Badopal in Haryana, about four hours from Delhi. Finding the jaal was easy—it was where the cattle went to escape the 50 degree Celsius heat of summer. Invariably, cows would settle in the jaal's thick purple shadow, sitting for hours till the day cooled. The roots of the jaal were undulating, like they were pulling up the land around them, terraforming it.

Forgotten Words

Fireflies

We are standing near Delhi's (erstwhile) exciting market, Hauz Khas Village (HKV). The place used to have an indie streak till a few years ago. There were charming shops with vintage treasures lying between more cookie-cutter designs. Eating places had owners, not franchisees, in their kitchens, throwing tadkas in hot oil and mashing leaves for chutneys themselves. Cafes had coarse handloom curtains with imperfect splotchy prints which valued the handmade, not the mass-manufactured. It felt like a place which was one of a kind. One that attracted the fashionable and the misfits. It felt like a place of commerce and resistance both. And then, the big restaurant chains entered, replacing handmade splotchiness with monochromatic sameness. Now you enter HKV and reedy men accost you, shouting, '1+1 drinks madam! Ladies' night madam!' You don't have the space to choose, so you choose to walk away. Trashy music blares from everywhere—there is only Bollywood now, no boho.

On a monsoonal evening, we are going to Hauz Khas, but not to the HKV market. We are going to the HK park. Many people know this as 'Deer Park', because there is an enclosure with deer in it. Birthday parties have been held here and children have fed the deer through the chain-mesh, marvelling at another youngling, wide-eyed and coltish but hooved.

Dusk is falling slowly when we enter the park. Next to the gate, there is a pilkhan tree, one of Delhi's eighteen designated 'heritage trees'. Insects whine around the pilkhan, and birds move on its boughs: there are gnats and Green pigeons. Soon, the bats will come. There are many relationships here, none of which are connected to the market economy or industrial time.

As dusk deepens, purpling the sky, we walk towards the Hauz Khas lake. Hauz means waterbody, and this lake is what gives the area its name. Bats are just beginning to flap across the sky, some ethereal, others clumsy. With their slow wing-flaps, they look like puppets whose strings are being pulled by something in the sky. But flying foxes are their own puppet master. The bats detach from trees growing on an island in the water, looking like they are peeling off. They flap hard, their muscles straining, a sense of urgency as they climb higher in the sky, building into a tight nub. Then, like petals of a flower unravelling, they come away from each other, dissipating into individuals from one form. Some flap away at once, while others still scrape the sky with effort as they climb higher. I blink my eyes and look again, forgetting what I know about mammalian flight. And it appears that the wheeling, climbing bats are not just flying but straining, creating something with effort. They are sky-making. We observe the last of the purple sky before it turns to ink because the bats are shaping the sky for us. We wouldn't be looking at the sky if it weren't for the bats.

Because we have come here for the fireflies. As children you may have read the stories that starred them. In childhood tales, an enterprising child would catch a fistful of fireflies and put them in a glass jar, and they would glow, constantly and steadily, like a sentient lightbulb that knew just how much light you needed. I sense my childhood was full of firefly smudges—a distant bioluminescence on the horizon or on a line of bushes,[1] gone before I could make sense of it, gone before I could fully picture it. I seem to remember days after rains, when fireflies would blink at the world, or wink at me. I feel the garden of my childhood was awash with fireflies. Memory is an odd thing though. I don't know if these memories are mine, from the nineties and late eighties, or my mother's, from the sixties and seventies. When exactly was there an abundance of fireflies in the city, and when did they all but disappear?[2]

'The interior landscape responds to the character and subtlety of an exterior landscape; the shape of the individual mind is affected by land as it is by genes,' writes

Barry Lopez in *Vintage Lopez*. We were once shaped, inside and outside, by fireflies. What shape have we sloughed off now that we don't spot fireflies?

Perhaps memories will emerge with clarity once we see them again. We are here to see, and perhaps to remember. Verhaen Khanna, founder of the New Delhi Nature Society, is leading us. He will take us to his secret spots, lit with fairy lights that can fly.

Near the Hauz Khas lake, the air is water. We can taste the moisture on our tongues. It fogs glasses and deposits itself on beards. With beads of moisture embracing it, a pilkhan at the edge of the lake in Delhi looks like a shaggy, mossy oak standing in the Himalayas.

We are wiping the sweat off our faces and waiting for something magical and nostalgic to happen. And it is under the pilkhan that we see the first glow. It's tentative, a flash, gone even as we focus our eyes. As it grows darker, slowly, a couple more fireflies begin showing their lights. And then, there are more. Unlike in childhood stories, the light is not bright enough to read by. But it's definitely bright enough to marvel at. More begin blinking, looking like party glitter under the trees. We inch closer. One of the fireflies is sitting on a leaf, another is under a leaf. The chlorophyll of the leaf provides a canvas. When the firefly lights up, it illuminates itself but also the leaf, giving out a golden-leaf-green light. I can see the insects closer now. With their neat wings that resemble coattails and a brown body, they are a beetle rather than a fly.[3] They love moisture, clinging to soggy grass under the boughs and around the trunk. Once they mate, they lay eggs in damp soil. We bend, transfixed. One of us is looking up. When the fireflies move, the light seems like it has a tail, like a long exposure photo of the Milky Way. Or they resemble firecrackers of the best kind—no smoke, no clatter, just spectacle. We are sweating now, and surrendering to the sight. The insects dart around, but they stop at a hard edge. It is the edge of human intervention; the place where the grass and soil become concrete. We notice that wherever there are tiles and concrete, or the grass is manicured and cut short, there are no fireflies. Longer grasses catch more moisture and attract more insects; that is where the fireflies linger.

And there is yet another boundary fireflies will not cross, that of artificial light. Fireflies like their own lights. Males and females flash them to find a mate. The males flash for longer, and the female will respond, usually with shorter flashes. He will follow her light. They do this in velvety darkness. In places where there is too much light, fireflies will not advertise their presence.

We cross a stream and go back to Deer Park. Below us, water splashes, and the insects spill their lights from the stream bed. Verhaen says there are two towering semal trees here they favour often; for some time of the year, the semals become illuminated Christmas trees.

Verhaen walks in the complete darkness, an animal used to his forest. As a child and as an adult, women have been told to fear darkness. Darkness means danger. When you walk home at night, you walk in pools of light. Light feels like water: life-giving, life-saving, washing over you and quenching your anxiety. You spring from one spill of light to the other, joining it like a tributary falls into a river. If your cab driver drops you too far from the gate, you ask him to drive you beyond a dark stretch even though he will grumble about a longer U-turn and his wasted time. When you have to walk through the dark, you actually sprint, neck prickling with terror.

Now we have more light, and more lighthouses. We have CCTVs in public areas, while earlier there were just streetlights.

But that night, we use the fireflies to guide us. And they take us to the darkest, blackest parts of the park. We watch the art around us: fireflies drawing arcs and sparkles through the dark, ephemeral yet so powerful. 'I bring kids here,' Verhaen whispers to us. 'And they are struck by something they have no frame of reference for. They are like, this is so beautiful. It has its own light.' He pauses. Then they say: 'Can we take one home?'

Taking a firefly home seems so wrong, like making a canary lose her song. 'I tell them, the firefly won't flash his light in your house. What will he eat? He will die of loneliness, never to light up again.' We are both listening to Verhaen's story without being able to see him. 'Mostly, the kids understand,' he finishes.

We heave a sigh of relief for the fireflies that are briefly understood by young ones. We watch a firefly seemingly chasing something only he senses. In Thailand, I have visited mangroves with synchronous firefly displays, a phenomena in which fireflies light up all at once. This attracts flocks of tourists who wait in the dark to take in the sight. But we have no intention of recreating eco-tourism activities for this small population of Hauz Khas fireflies. Soon, we feel we must leave this dark, wet place and give the insects their privacy. We stumble towards the entrance, feeling our way forward. I turn my head to see lights winking for a last time that monsoon. A memory returns—so sharp it can cut away the years: my childhood garden awash with fireflies.

We come up to a bend and turn, and we are blinded. An outdoor gym, run by the city's development authority, is floodlit with light. The moisture in the air makes the light pool—the impact is fuzzy, not sharp. Still, it is irascibly bright. 'Why do we need this light here?' is my first question. 'Can't we leave the lights off for the monsoonal time when the fireflies are active?' is my second one. There are no fireflies near the gym.

Ed Yong, in his book *An Immense World*, writes of what he calls 'threatened sensescapes': 'We have filled the night with light, the silence with noise, and the soil and water with unfamiliar molecules. We have distracted animals from what they actually need to sense, drowned out the cues they depend upon, and lured them, like moths to the flame, into sensory traps.' Delhi now has many well-lit outdoor gyms, a new trend in city parks. Some gyms have lights turned on late into the night. But if there is one thing the last two hours have taught me, it is that some semi-wild areas need darkness too.

As we take our final steps, a rose appears in my mind. A rose is like a spiral—it goes round and round when you draw it. You hold your pen and follow the shape of the spiral. And you may feel like you have been brought back to the same spot—did you go round in circles? But you're not the same after you have interacted with a rose. Seeing the fireflies feels the same way. We have gone around in a circle in the dark. If you're a woman, and sometimes also when you're a man, you have learnt to be afraid of the darkness for as long as you have lived. But you're not the same after seeing fireflies in the dark; after going around in illuminated circles with them. You have learnt now that sometimes the darkness glitters with the malice of light pollution. But it can also glitter with the jewels of fireflies.

We need to let the grass grow, long and moist and without chemicals. We don't need hard, human-made edges everywhere. It is not so bad to have some softness, and to surrender to the dark sometimes. Little things are waiting there: waiting to be left alone, waiting for us to de-urbanize.

NEHA'S FIELD NOTES

Many older people I interviewed have told me their gardens in Delhi would be full of fireflies after the rains. Typically, these are people born in the 1960s—the parents of my friends.

The 'shifting baseline' syndrome refers to a phenomenon in which the past is forgotten and the present, depleted scenario is understood as normal. Those who have grown up without fireflies feel the normal baseline is our present world, depleted, and with fewer insects. This means that generations today may not even know what they are missing.

Forgotten Sounds

Coppersmith Barbet

A sweet, high sound rises in the air. If a child made a drawing of her favourite kind of car, green and red and with odd knobs and a candy-coloured horn, and then she pressed the horn to demonstrate she was happy, this is how the car would sound. There is the sweetness of childhood in the sound, and its stubbornness too. For one, the charming, confounding sound does not stop. At all. It carries on and on, and then on and on. It is something like a siren, only that it's not asking me to get out of the way on a crowded road which has no way to give. No, it is a siren for its own self.

And because I wait for it every day, it leaves a pleasant echo in my head when I hear it, knocking against me even as I go to work, far away from a tree with a particular bird on it. The sound the bird makes, from the top of an old peepal tree as tall as a three-storey building, is a persistent tuk, tuk, tuk, tuk. Someone was reminded of the sound made when a smith hammered a sheet of metal, and that's how the bird was named. To me, the sound is a metronome, a pendulum in a grand old clock, reminding me of what time it is. When the Coppersmith barbet calls, it is the time to look outside, and to pay attention. It is a call that tells you that high summer is coming. It is the time to listen to a bird and not the internet.

Like the Collared dove, the Coppersmith's call is a sound from childhood. The time of our childhoods was overall a quieter one, because we were able to hear the outdoors. Windows were kept open. There were fewer air conditioners sealing our houses shut. An entire sense-scape streamed in. You could hear and smell your neighbour's cooking (we perked up at the salty, umami smell of Maggi instant noodles) and someone's singing or swearing (the latter being infinitely more interesting). Vegetable sellers operated solely on low (and often nonsensical) calls their customers identified immediately—some said '*sabzi lelo*' (buy vegetables), others simply said '*ei, ei*', making a call that meant nothing in literal terms, but was musical for those who were waiting for it. Now these calls have moved to WhatsApp; that's where vegetable sellers text you. Electricity ran through our lives like a dammed river—coming in fits and starts, flooding the power supply with surges and fluctuations on some days, and draining away into distribution sinkholes like water vanishing into a pit on others. When there were power cuts, we used to say: 'The light is gone.' And when 'light went', doors and windows would be thrown open, and we would clamber up to terraces to sleep under the stars. When we lit candles in bedrooms to study, little black insects flitted to the flame. It was not a static world, but one awash with creatures. The sound of the Coppersmith barbet was one of the sounds from that world. Where did it come from? Was it a bird or a frog? That is something I never knew. Instead, like the laughter of frogs in the rain, and the meowing *aeoo aeoo* of the peafowl that ricocheted at dusk from the eucalyptus tree, I accepted the soundscape as it was.

The thing about birds that stay mostly on tall trees is that you have to be on the same level as the tree to truly notice them. Cities give you this opportunity, as they offer balconies on tall buildings. The first floor is good for seeing birds that utilize the lower boughs—such as mynas, crows and babblers. A second-floor balcony is super for shy birds like the Yellow-footed green pigeon, and the Coppersmith barbet—the latter will often sit at the very top of a tree to 'sing' its song.

Just before the pandemic, early mornings on my terrace—once the place for hot, dark nights on folding cots—became an amphitheatre for a dawn chorus as light slowly filled the sky. Every day, I would hear sounds that suffused me completely. Common mynas would chirp in a way that could only sound like gossip. The tateri tateri call of the Red-wattled lapwing entered the mix. There were Jungle babblers, and occasionally, the call of a Brown rock chat. And then like a school bell being rung for everyone's attention: the bold and insistent tuk tuk, tuk tuk. I hadn't yet viewed the Coppersmith; I didn't want to go to it. The way the sound had broken down walls to enter my mindscape, I wanted the bird to come to me.

The Coppersmith doesn't even open its beak while calling. Instead, the sound emerges from a closed bill. Only the throat moves; it is a brilliant scarlet inflating and deflating, like a truck driver gleefully pumping his favourite pressure horn. The sound comes from a deep, rumbling, hidden place inside the bird: a sound of pure effort and intention. The barbet calls most prominently when summer crashes like a wave across the sky and land, and when everything else is in the area is silent. The Coppersmith seems like a little rock against that hot wave: hard to move, indefatigable.

Peter Wohlleben writes in his book, *The Heartbeat of Trees,* on listening for cranes calling, his favoured music: 'Because the calls of the cranes are among my most favourite sounds, I hear them even when, for most other people, they get lost in ambient noise. I register crane calls … despite triple glazing, insulated walls, and the nightly hum of the television.'

And so, during the Covid pandemic, I waited to hear and see the Coppersmith.

On a hot April day, like most of the middle-class working population, I was occupied with a Zoom call. The midday heat was just beginning to set in. I worked during these hot hours, my eyes tuned to tabs lined up on my screen like palimpsests, occasionally looking out of the windows to unfocus my eyes from the glare of the screen. Like others, I felt tiny and inconsequential. Rat-like and in burrows, amounting to nothing but destruction, a chewing up of all that surrounded us. The ceiling fan whirred. A kitchen appliance groaned, the water motor whined. These were all sounds of ennui, of machines that made life easier but were not alive, sounds achingly and appallingly boring, sounds that I felt could drive me to madness. It took time before the sound of the Coppersmith could knock down the walls around me—of living domestic sounds, set in onion rings: a layer for the room I was in, another layer for the rest of the house—which had the purr of a beard trimmer, the rasp of my dog scratching himself, a dry cough which could mean exhaustion or could mean Covid. In the pandemic, my ears were tuned to this tight set of concentric circles; this was my world within the confines of the home/office.

And then the siren-sound came, knocking on the fastened door, shredding the onion rings, flooding in now, drumming against my forehead, entering my consciousness fully. Using musical repetition, a battle drum in the blood. *Look at me, look at me. Pay attention to the real world, real world.* Tuk tuk. Tuk tuk.

I got up, rushing to the door. I flung it open. Outside, the sky was the colourless expanse of midday, the time when the bright blue leaches off and the cynicism of heat begins setting in. The time when all the birds are quiet, resting in sheltered, leafy alcoves. Except one. The drumroll of the Coppersmith was loud enough for me to focus my eyes in a single direction.

A siris tree grew in front of my house, the trunk thick and forked, branches covered in small, feathery leaves. I adjusted my eyes to see the tree better, the small leaves shimmering, splicing the bright light. At the very top of the tree, something was moving, left-to-right, left-to-right. Its head bobbed rhythmically, sideways. It was hypnotic. It shimmered with its own magic. I felt my eyes surrender the way my ears already had. It was there. At long last, I was seeing the Coppersmith barbet during the toughest time of our collective lives. Its back was leaf green, matching the leaves perfectly, camouflaged. Yet its effort at making itself heard was evident. Its whole body rocked, the thick beak sliced the air, its throat trembled, the bough shook, the leaves danced.

From the road, the sound of a car horn cut the air. Yet, the Coppersmith's sound—now that I was really listening—filled the air, and filled the sky. It had cut through my domestic soundscape with style. My eyes stung from the cut. Or maybe I was just moist-eyed.

That week, I had been speaking to my friend on the phone and we had both been mumbling. We were living through the days half-heartedly. For a bird like the Coppersmith though, it seemed like there were no half measures. There was a blazing purity in its effort. It possessed no moderation, no artifice. It was a bird burning up every last ounce of focus to create its full-throated set of sounds. And that is why it was visible to me: because the effort showed in the movement of the bird. A realization struck me like a gong, rising in meaning as the calls became clearer to my screen-tired mind. There was life outside quarantines and screens, I knew this. But here was evidence, full-throated.

You don't need to be big to fill the whole room, the whole sky.

NEHA'S FIELD NOTES

Once I found the Coppersmith on the highest spot on the siris tree, it was easy to find it again. We often have favoured spots in our homes, corresponding with preference and what we like to do at various points of the day—dining rooms with morning sun, evening rooms, card rooms, with an overstuffed chair in the last one. Birds can be like that too—they have spots which are favourites. For the little Coppersmith, the top of the siris was a podium. I saw it many times at the same spot, learning that the species preferred higher parts of lushly leaved tree canopies.

In January 2022, I got lucky. On winter mornings, as sunlight fell on the siris, I saw more than one Coppersmith barbet. Their bodies merged with the leaves, but their heads gleamed scarlet. I counted them—it was something like counting red berries. There were an astonishing twelve barbets on the tree! I saw them again on other days, counting between six and twelve. They tended to turn their heads at the same sounds, looking like copies of each other.

We only see this behaviour in winter. The rest of the year, barbets explore trees alone or with their mates.

On another day, I saw two Coppersmiths, and a Black drongo came to join them. They perched together peaceably, one a frugivore, the other a hunter. A house crow arrived to mob the drongo. It left. I sighed: crows so often drive away interesting birds. A third Coppersmith barbet came then, and then another, and the crow left, disinterested. A beat later the drongo returned, a bee in its beak. The drongo hadn't picked a fight, but it also didn't leave.

Over several years in March, I have seen Coppersmiths with their beaks stuffed with fruit—two to three figs stuffed in their mouth. These are likely nuptial gifts to woo females. When their chick begins fledging, the barbet chick has an overall green appearance, missing the red on the head and throat.

In March 2022, I was watching the siris for the Coppersmith when a different bird, orange with a long tail, sallied to the branch. It had a black head and its tail was like ribbon. It was the bird from the garden of my childhood, the Indian paradise flycatcher.

And in early April 2021, just before our Covid infection, a Coppersmith sat on the siris. It had its back to me. The shadow of siris leaves fell on the bird, a delicate lattice tracery. I wrote in my field notes that day: 'The Coppersmith looks like the leaf itself, a leaf with veins turning sunlight to food, doing the best work—helping the world just by existing.'

Forgotten Trees

Semal

'What is your name, sir?' The doctor asked a bewildered man, sitting up in a hospital bed with tousled, bedhead hair.

The man tried to recall his name, his memory stumbling, confusion scudding uncharacteristically across his eyes. A nurse laughed, the sound high and cruel.

Her laugh echoed in my ears. Tears welled in my eyes at her callousness. 'You are a nurse,' I spat out, the very first words I had said to the crew gathered around the hospital bed. My hands balled into fists at my side. 'You can't laugh at a patient.' She turned and looked at me, her hair and nails neat and immaculate, her face back into a mask. 'Sorry, ma'am,' she said, in a manner that suggested she viewed apologies as the path of least resistance, and sorry was a word she said many times to patients and their families without meaning it. 'Apologize to him,' I said, 'Apologize to my father.'

We had brought my father to the Delhi Heart and Lung hospital, located in Panchkuian Marg, one of the radial roads leading to Connaught Place, the great heart of Delhi. The area bustled with market facades and bristled with the pride of old, art-deco buildings—it dived from the genteel neighbourhoods of Karol Bagh to shiny, commercial places so fast you could get whiplash. There was always a complicated way to get to the hospital. You skirted through traffic, through unforgiving roads that were belching with people, wares and vehicles. Shop boards and lights always seemed to be turned on here—even banana sellers had bulbs above their wares. It was the kind of place that could mesmerize and blind you in equal measure. And then suddenly, visible through the heat and pressure of the roads, stood the solemn visage of the hospital, like a gigantic, unmovable column thrown up by the volcano of pressurized lives around it.

My father had complained of chest discomfort and we had brought him here, and the doctor had told us in no uncertain terms that he could not leave. He had a clot in the confluence of two arteries that required immediate angioplasty. We stared at the image of the clot. It reminded me of water hyacinth, that fast-growing invasive weed that chokes wetlands and causes hypoxia—divesting the water, and the creatures in it, of oxygen. Hyacinth spreads at speed, reaching critical mass before one can exhale.

Following the detection of the clot, an angioplasty was conducted. Everything happened very fast: indemnity forms signed with my mother's teacher's pen, my father's stretcher whooshing past, the doctor telling me loudly, but not too loudly: 'Angioplasties are quite common, even second ones on a patient, it will be fine, he will be fine.' The operation took place swiftly. My father was since rediscovering his grip on reality, but not, it seemed, fast enough for the nurses.

It was a time of great trepidation. I was painfully aware of my own heart, fluttering in my chest like the whirr of sunbird wings, or doing slow, physically painful wheezes, a bird caught in a net. He had been sick before, he had been 'stented' before. But this was the first time he was sick when I was so … adult, and capable. Being older felt bruising. I had signed indemnity forms and kept my sole credit card on standby for emergencies. I had tried to prepare myself for any manner of outcomes. I had tried, but I felt I was failing. Our room faced the commotion of the road, and this echoed my own. The window in the wall was circular, like the porthole of a ship. My father had been ordered not to move too much, and by extension, neither could we. The outside world was like an ever-moving sea with its own creatures, with us passengers in a barge that was solemnly grounded. We felt hemmed in, the walls too cramped. The nurse's laugh still rang in my ears. It was, by far, the cruelest thing that I had heard, said to someone I cared about so much. It had lodged itself like a spike in my flesh and I felt it would poison me with bitterness.

I looked out of the porthole. The sun was setting, and it bathed everything in a generous, pink-orange light. Something was in the sky, wheeling, and then keening towards a large tree, as if the tree was calling the bird in. The tree had bare branches spread wide, like a school song at morning assembly sung in all parts of a big room. The branches were bare. There were no leaves, but large, beautiful red flowers hung off the boughs like sky lanterns, like wishes that one could light a flame under. Just then, the Black kite careened towards the tree trunk, where branches forked from the main stem. I realized then that it had built a nest there.[1] The tree held up the nest like a heart, and that heart would be a secret when the leaves regrew. As the kite settled in its nest, I drew my breath. My cheeks clenched. I just desperately wanted the kite to reach its nest every day and raise its brood. I wanted the bird to live and for its family to thrive. I wanted my wish to soar above the city, lantern-like, and project itself into the future.

I watched the bird all day, in between wheeling my father to and from tests. X-rays and scans littered our room. I kept thinking about the tree and the bird. The nest-heart in the semal tree was the best kind of heart—not blocking nor blocked. It was the kind of patient, eternal heart I wanted my father, the patient, to have. It was steadier than mine as I looked out in anxiety. The warm sunset light in the evenings seemed to touch everything with beauty, but I knew the tree would be beautiful even without that gilded benediction. That is how the semal entered my life—on days of desperation, on days of whispered prayers in corridors that rang with a cruel laugh.

As I left for work on one of the days, a semal flower plopped onto my white car. There were several more on the ground in the parking lot. The blossoms were richly red and intense, and their size and weight gave them a heft, a presence which reminded me of treasure hunts in the garden of my childhood. The flowers were bright, irresistible, undeniable. Even while holding a prescription in one hand, I picked up a flower in another. As I looked closer, the bloom turned into an invitation—to look at it, to breathe deeply, to steady my heartbeat even at a time of fragility, and then to look once more. It filled that dusty parking lot with colour, and me with a calmness I could morph into audacity. The spike in my chest felt like it was dissolving. It was going to be fine, or at least we were going to be stronger and kinder to each other. As my father recovered slowly, the tree continued to flower; and like those desperate people looking for a sign from the universe, I took the sign and ran with it.

The doctors did their work on my father, but it was the semal that saved my soul each time it drooped against the porthole and plopped into the anonymity of the parking lot.

The Delhi Heart and Lung hospital was the beginning of a trigger for memories. I had seen the red flowers that gave me so much solace before. I had seen them many, many times. Like the best kind of childhood memories, reality and fantasy merged together delightfully and could not be teased apart. Were the flowers in a place where no tree stood now? Had I leaned against the same tree at school? Did I squelch a blossom under my foot and wince at how wet it felt, like an animal with a face, not just a flower with filaments? Was one of my favourite memories of college a blazing red-flowered semal I had incorrectly identified?

But there was one memory that was as distinct as the others were hazy. A young me, eleven years old, sitting wretchedly in maths class. I had been told maths was a language, but to me it seemed more like a set of secrets I could not decipher. I would always ask what ‘a’ and ‘b’ in formulae stood for and never found an answer that creatively satisfied me. The idea of only one correct answer was also too rigid to bear. I sat in a classroom on the busy Pusa Road which adjoins the Jhandewalan area in Central Delhi. On the other side though lay a silent junction—that of the Ridge forest, slowly getting eaten up by ashrams, but still standing—and transpiring its goodness on the rest of us. In that fateful maths class, perspiring on an afternoon that felt more summer than spring, a bit of magic drifted into my life. Literally. There aren’t many times one can use the words ‘magic floated into my life’, but there it was. That magic was a little, white puff of cotton, and it propelled itself with some determination towards me. I had seen winged seeds before—some were shaped like helicopter blades, others with a soft white dandelion-style puff (called *buddhiya ke baal* or old woman's hair).[2] I had always snatched them up and stuffed them in my pocket, treasures to gaze at later. I did the same with this cotton ball. I grabbed with both hands and with some desperation. My teacher's back wasn't even turned, but I knew this magic had to be mine. A moment later, I slipped my hand into my pocket and felt for the treasure: the 'cotton' was astonishingly silky. When home, I examined it closely. At the heart of the cotton ball lay a tiny black seed, one that could one day turn into a gigantic tree. The seed was a rough sort of shape, like it had been hand-rolled and wished into existence. It was blackish, roundish, eldritch.[3] I asked my mother which tree it was from. Well, the palash is flowering, she said, so maybe it came from there. She wasn't wrong, in that the palash flowers in early summer, around the time the semal produces cotton pods. But the semal pods take some time to emerge from the flower, and so the semal's flowering is much earlier—in February–March rather than April.

For a long time then, I held on to two truths. One, that a flower had saved me when I was facing the worst things a child faces—the black pit of boredom, and isolation from a language everyone else was speaking. Two, for years I thought that the semal was the palash. But memories don't need scientific names. *The name of this tree is my tree*. My memories were vivid, multi-sensory, like the way you can sense and smell ink on fingers even before bringing your hand to your face.

And now as an adult, the semal had saved me again in the Delhi Heart and Lung hospital. A third truth struck me now. How important it is to pursue the things that touch our lives with meaning. How life-building it can be to unlock capillaries of memory and fondness; how crucial to build new memories on these foundations; to build a life that falls gently through stressful days, like flower-shade from a tree. How important to find community, so others can recognize the same petals and passion, and perhaps begin to share their private names, their Citris and perhaps-palash with you.

The semal was important enough to be traced, through memories, anthers, filaments, heartbeats and maps.

Forgotten Forests

The Central Ridge

'Each place is itself only, and nowhere repeated.'
—*Embrace Fearlessly the Burning World,*
Barry Lopez

I have questions about the semal tree, and this takes me to Pradip Krishen, genius naturalist who draws portraits of places through trees. We have just taken a walk around his garden in South Delhi, and he has been staring at miniscule plants in the damp places the sun doesn't reach. Most of these tiny plants are splayed out, running in a prostrate fashion on the ground—taking advantage of the niche they have: that of the dark, low places. My own thoughts are closer to nimbus and sky, clinging to the tall tops of the semal. 'So the semal is my favourite tree,' I tell him without apology, 'what do you feel about it?' My query seems angled for securing his good opinion.

Pradip takes a deep breath and looks at me sideways. It seems he has been asked this question a lot. His sigh is a rustle through tree leaves. 'Well, it has a good-looking flower,' he says. Beauty isn't the only thing that's important of course, he seems to say. 'It's also a tree that everything likes to feed on.' The luscious, fleshy flowers are slurped at by bats and birds for their nectar, and the buds are cooked into sabzi by people (the result tastes a bit like ladies' finger). 'But what I want to know,' Pradip says, 'is why does the semal grow so tall?'

This is a classic Pradip question. He treats questions like antiques—something you pursue, cherish, run your fingers through with reverence, and think about for years. You should always have one close at hand to reflect on, and another to piece together slowly.

His questions are mostly about the ecological nature of the city—what can grow, what does grow, what must go, and why things grow the way they do. 'The semal is a tree of the Bhabhar tract,' he says. 'This isn't a landscape that has a lot of tall trees. Why is the semal motivated to grow so tall then?'

I don't have any answers. My wait for the semal each year is the wait for birds and beasts running through the tree's leaves and boughs, giddy with the anticipation of a treat that is satisfying but won't last more than a month. It's the feast after the winter fast. The semal is about relationships with every being that visits it, not just about itself. It has a generosity of spirit that strengthens my own. It also lives unabashedly, with the soul of a Gauguin painting or an ikat handloom saree—splotching everything with colour, a little messy, a little out of bounds, almost too much to take in at once, always vivid. Its red flowers carpet the ground, car bonnets and verandas in spring, and its proud spine and branches hold Black kite nests like a precious beating heart in winter.

Yet, Pradip's question gets me thinking. From my favourite tree, I want to move to his favourites, to tunnel into his vision for a fortnight or so.

For forty-five years, Pradip has walked a portion of the Central Ridge in Delhi.[1] This is a green belt that girdles places in Central Delhi that are considered posh, mysterious, or both. It has the President's horses in it and faces old hotels like the Taj Palace. It has jackals, security, and people who come to feed animals, and it has Pradip, the committed naturalist and investigator writing down a page on each visit he makes. 'I have walked the Ridge for so many decades,' he says pertly, 'that I'd expect to see more snakes than I have.' Unlike many other forests of India, this isn't one that abounds with gaurs, tigers, elephants or martens. This is the forest for smaller things.

Small creatures live in the leaf litter and vegetation, some webbing up the space between trees, others shooting up from detritus, watching people and hotels with a kind of damp nonchalance.

The very first time I walked with Pradip, it was in the Central Ridge. It was September of 2022, and the light seemed golden in that precious, post-pandemic time. I was looking at the trees for birds. He was looking down. He pointed at something we couldn't make out at first. It was a mushroom that looked like a penis. This was the Common stinkhorn, and with its white body and mottled head, it looked eerily like it was part of a decaying, dead body. And yet it stood proudly, erect in the auburn leaf litter, hungry for life.

A little ahead, Pradip murmured to himself and pointed out small vines twining through things. There were small flowers here and there. One was blue. One was white. I didn't know any of their names yet, but one day I would, I told myself. A bird call ricocheted from the canopy above, and a loud flapping sound filled the air. It was a Grey hornbill, flying with urgency, its mate following closely. The sound of the hornbill revealed just how quiet it was. We weren't so far from the road, yet the noise of the city had regressed. Perhaps it was the silence without the impatience of horns, but the time here felt different: it was slower, more deliberate. The smell of mycelium, decomposing leaf litter and beetles dug into my nose. It was a smell I knew intimately, and with the sense of the slowing of time came the realization that this was the feel of the garden of my childhood: the soil and my animal and human friends, dirt under nails, time pooling into circles as we came to the same realization each time, after each bit of play—life was outdoors, life was in the mud, amidst the grasses and bugs, and we liked each other's company. There had been no screens that could be ruined by rain or mud, there had been no expensive clothes which would snag. The most important thing was us and nature and the creatures. The same feeling gripped me on that Central Ridge walk: our relationship to nature, our presence there, was more important than photographs, gear or designations.

With each breath, thrill shot up my spine. The ground was undulating now, but we had reached that point in woodland walks where you become both easily sure-footed and uncaring of niceties, where you are unbothered even if you step on animal scat. *This is Delhi too*: the thought knocked around the side of my head like a hornbill being chased by another, wild birds flying into the horizon, unfettered by electric wires and window-bars.

Pradip wanted to show us a part of the Ridge which is its deepest, and lowest. He walked ahead, a sharp pair of secateurs in hand. He went confidently into the thicket, clipping away branches that lashed at his face; walking like he would amble anywhere else, like he was going into a meeting. And we all walked up and then down, climbing down steep inclines and roughly hewn steps.

Something tugged at the corner of my eye. I turned around to see a ronjh tree. This is a tree of dry places, with small, feathery leaves. It was lit up with tiny, buttercup-yellow pompom flowers, taller than other trees in that particular spot, and it looked old, but not elderly. It seemed to be sighing in the fullness of some majestic, indescribable emotion. The silence of the forest relayed that sigh, and it touched my shoulders and face, making me shiver. It was as if someone had put my clothes out in a lightning storm, and the linen returned smelling of something wilder and bigger than me. That ronjh was a sniff of the outdoors, a feeling of vastness, and a sense of the entire earth being contained in a single tree. It must have stood under many lightning storms, but it nevertheless seemed happy, not victimized, by its travails. It had a pride and a wildness that I could only aspire for. Perhaps, if we were lucky, there could be a small portion of that wildness in us as well. Perhaps it already existed.

Ahead of us, an aak bush grew in a sprawl, its arms everywhere, holding up its velvety quarter-plate leaves. A single Amata moth went in and out of the aak's violet, doll-eye button flowers.[2] If you break off the leaves and stems, the plant 'cries' milky tears. Unlike many other moths, the Amata is diurnal, active in the day. As Pradip had said, the Ridge teems with surprises that belie their small size.

As we walked, our feet made little clouds go up. These were whitish moths—called Cream wave moths, from the genus *Scopula*. They looked like animated, handwoven lace springing up and down, delighted in the life they had to frolic in. Higher up, near the ronjh, currents of dragonflies drifted through the air, as if dancing to music they alone could hear. Each step and each look by us had consequence, I realized, and so we had to place our feet—and our attention—with intention. I wanted to see everything. I wanted to walk with a careful lightness, a fairy-like soft touch that bent grass without breaking moth-wing. I wanted to be *of* the forest, not just going to it. I knew this forest would change me. I could already feel it happening. Was my blood getting galvanized the way cold-blooded moths alchemize in the sun?

We approached an amphitheatre of trees. Underneath the trees, a dry streambed coiled on the ground. It lay like a grizzled snake with old memories, the scaly stones on its bends smoothened with time and water. These rocks seemed just as historic as those from the weirs of the Tughlaq dynasty which were nearby. Again I felt that time flowed differently in this forest. It had seen, and continued to see, the ephemeral in the small seedlings, the mushrooms and the monsoon annuals. And it had seen the ancient because it forms part of the Aravallis, considered the world's oldest fold mountains. And it continues to see the comings and goings of polity and empire: the Tughlaqs, the AAP supporters, and those that consider politics to be someone else's problem.

It has seen jackals scurrying, dragonflies dancing, perhaps tigers skulking.

The forest was a secret place, a sacred place.

I took in the trees next to the stream bed. They were kaim or Krishna kadam, *Mitragyna parvifolia*, merry trees that produce ball-shaped flowers. In some of the rockier areas, dhau erupted forth, their roots holding the earth with deft surefootedness. This was the Ridge's deepest spot, Pradip told us. One kaim rose nearly 60 feet tall. I felt like I was in the company of giants, growing to the size that nature intended. I hoped these giants were not threatened by an asteroid, that they wouldn't face mass extinction. We stayed there for a while, soaking in this place untouched by the evils of horticulture and chemicals.

In other parts of the Ridge, the canopy is blotched by *Neltuma juliflora*. Pradip wants these trees gone but bemoans the way they are removed. The earth is like a tapestry for him. He watches the weave and how it is different at each site—a little denser here, looser there. He senses that there are threads of meaning, and longing, in the earth. In the Central Ridge, Pradip says, the jungle is how it was 'supposed to be'—preserved in a somewhat natural space, free of weedicide and with a laughing insect diversity. Ironically, the authorities' efforts to remove invasive species has gouged holes in the tapestry. In 2022, Pradip pointed out places where machines had been brought in to uproot trees by dragging through the soil, removing not just trees, but undergrowth, shrubs and vines. Looking at the cleared, oddly sanitized spaces—

no stinkhorn mushrooms, leaf litter, or bugs under leaf litter there—was perhaps the way marine biologists feel when they see a trawler raking through the ocean floor: a single-minded, robotic intent that wipes out everything in its path. We need to remove juliflora, Pradip says, but it has to be done by hands that sift and tug, not by earth movers that rip and churn. The tapestry of the earth needs repair, not ripping.

It is 2025 now and we are still thinking of soil. Much has happened in the intervening years. Pradip led teams to restore two sites in the desert—Kishan Bagh near Jaipur, and Rao Jodha Desert Rock Park in Jodhpur.[3] Most, if not all, liken the desert with death and suffering. Yet Pradip found that the desert soil held several lessons, some of which can be applied to other places. He learned of the things that knit the tapestry of the soil—roots, rain, life, bio-crusts. He learned of life that suddenly flourishes, learning to laugh as the benediction of rains arrive. He learned of plants that go back millions of years and know how to survive the harshness of the desert. These are the plants that stand up to the thin soil and the searing winds that scour the earth, that flourish in adversity. In a sense, the soils of the Aravalli in Delhi have a similar spirit. They too exist in an area deprived of moisture, they too have to survive cold nights and scorching days, they too have to face loos, the desert winds that wail through spiny treetops.

When Pradip began his projects, he was asked to plant fruit trees and luxurious flowers. Erecting such an enterprise could only mean one thing—watering the plants when they were growing up, when they were grown, and potentially, when they were dying too. Finding water in the desert is a mirage in more ways than one. Not only was it an unsustainable dream, it would also go against the principles of valuing native plants and the spirit of resistance they display.

Instead, he said gently to the CEO of the trust at one of the sites, that he would plant things of the desert.

We are in the Aravallis now, and the lessons from and of the desert are amongst the rocks here. In Mangar, Pradip found plants growing on thick layers of what looked like smashed rock particles. These, he learned, were biological soil crusts or 'bio-crusts'.

His eyes light up when he talks about what essentially looks like whiskers on rocks—a five-o-clock stubble that is nine-o-clock in some places. 'It takes hundreds of years for bio-crusts to form. Sometimes more,' he says. Bio-crusts are active communities of the littlest things that form over rocks—lichen, cyanobacteria, mosses and more. Bio-crusts could be just a few centimetres thick but are mighty in their intention. They are a way to crumble the toughness of rocks, to harden a seed's resolve to grow, to freeze time so a young plant can have a chance to live rather than perish.

Appreciating bio-crust comes down to the smallest unit of understanding, sensing how a very small-scale ecosystem can sustain something much larger than itself. In the desert, Pradip found hectares of grasses, waving wildly in the wind, their aspect jubilant, able to grow on bio-crusts. Some were oropetium grasses, which look dead in the dry season, but come gloriously 'back' to life when it rains. Some were liverworts, a non-vascular plant like moss.

If you really look at the landscape, the desert feels eternal, timeless in a way wild spaces are. The horizon meets the sky, and sandstorms cover your mouth and eyes and face like a pair of hands, in a way that feels absolute—perhaps stifling, perhaps fond. Only great stubbornness—or great resilience—can thrive here. In the flora, there's an aspect of wilfulness: a sense that the plants here bely conventional understanding. A tree with a complicated bark looks like it is suffering—and yet, the jaal tree, so grooved it looks like you can mine ingots from it—flourishes. Small tephrosia flowers grow through cracks in rocks, and you would think they are deprived of rich mulch, but they grow where they are meant to be—in difficult places. A tree sprouts in dust, and looks staid till it opens orange, tubular flowers that look bewitchingly tropical. This is the roheda, which also acts like a windbreak, catching howling desert loos in its arms with the ease of a goalkeeper.[4]

When you pay attention to the very small things—cracks in rocks, life growing in wily ways, you begin to learn not just the feel of a place, but also the signature those things leave. In the Central Ridge in Delhi, Pradip has noticed the trails left by various things, again and again, with the intensity of fieldcraft and the ritualistic force of fierce personal joy. He found many termite mounds in the forest. And he observed the soil around them, and always, always found hoof marks, or scrape marks, or dung, along with evidence that the mounds had been kicked in. Possibly by cows. He saw Indian jackals often or found their tracks. Jackals are dog-like animals with black-rimmed, soulful eyes. They hunt and scavenge for food and are one of the few larger mammals that are still in their historic range in the Delhi Ridge.[5]

Naturally shy, they often watch you from cover. On the last day of 2024, I was in Kolkata's Tolly Club. Something brown and shaggy, loping low to the ground, streaked through the path adjoining the golf course. A strong, sour smell hung in the air. I looked through a gap in the bushes, and my gaze locked on a pointed, fox-like face. Its eyes were rimmed with black, and they looked at me bashfully, hoping I wouldn't call it like a dog, and ideally, I would just disappear. It was a jackal. It wanted to make sure I wouldn't follow.

Pradip has had a similar experience. Jackals are so shy, they will run away and then watch you from a distance, he recounts. He calls them 'peeping jacks'. He first heard them in his home in Central Delhi. A street which is today full of embassies had jackals once. They would start calling at dusk, and each time an animal bayed, another would follow, one pair's call chasing the other. It would be a chain-link of 'woo-woos', and Pradip, his wife Arundhati

op: Count the red heads: ten Coppersmiths perch peaceably together on a cold
nuary morning in Delhi.

ottom: The sun rises, gilding a tumble of grasses in Aravalli Biodiversity Park,
asant Kunj.

Top: Ballerinas in white and pink on blue: Greater flamingos in the Yamuna river at Okhla.

Middle: A peacock parks his casual beauty against the fireworks of a flowering semal.

Bottom: Scarred soldier: a Blue tiger wears her torn wings with fortitude.

Top: A Brown-headed barbet looks out amongst a star-burst of neem blossoms.

Middle: Grey hornbills share semal blossoms and a quiet moment in the Humayun's Tomb complex.

Bottom: An Indian Scops owl becomes one with a banyan tree.

Top: A robberfly waits to ambush prey in Aravali Biodiversity Park, Gurugram.

Bottom: A Greater flamingo forages in the Sahibi river at sunset.

and his kids would tune in to the nightly symphony, loving the feeling of the non-humans starting their day as theirs ended. It reminded them that a different Delhi was always pushing through the one that was apparent. A parallel Delhi, an ecological Delhi.

If you watch closely, animals display personality—individualism, fear and ease, and sometimes, rebellion. As he walked with his dogs, the jackals would always dart away. 'In the Ridge, jackals have become beggars,' Pradip says. 'People come inside the forest to feed the macaques and feral cows. Jackals take the collateral stuff—mangoes, chapatis and bananas. I have seen jackals hundreds of times in the Ridge, including this one time I came across a den, squeaking with pups. Usually, when I have encountered them, they cross the road—then throw a look at me—and calmly walk away. They seem to know that there is a boundary me and my dogs will not cross. That, after a certain distance, they will not be followed.'

Yet, one jackal was different. 'We were walking as usual,' Pradip remembers. 'My dogs were with me. We spotted a jackal ahead of us. Instead of darting away, she took a stand. She stood where she was. When a dog went closer, she bayed loudly. The sound was completely different from the ones jackals normally make.' It was loud, sharp, and a little shocking. She wouldn't budge, she wouldn't run, she made her voice heard. What could the jackal be doing? 'Perhaps she was a mother protecting her cubs.' She wasn't yet another 'peeping jack'. She was different; she left a different a kind of signature.

In India, our lives twine often with wild lives. Human and animal paths cross, or collide, or merge together. The jackal crosses the road, the hornbill flies overhead, the spider jumps away, the mongoose visits our garden. If one pays attention, there is a wealth of the more-than-human to see beyond our own immediate concerns. And if we are careful, our paths will merge into a new-found wealth of appreciation for the non-human.

I usually look for animals, and Pradip looks for plants. I find it hard to photograph objects that don't move—such as plants—but I also know the idea of plants not moving is a misnomer. Plants rustle as they stand, twine together, spin seeds, forge meaning and relationships through their roots and mycelium. They move under soil and over trunks and towards the light. They move sinuously sometimes—vines that spiral up like pythons—or slowly, like the jaal or dhau that grow as little as a wrinkle's progress on a face. In walking the same forest each day for over forty years, Pradip found both movement and pattern. Some of this was delightful: it was heart-shaped.

Under the trees of the Central Ridge, there were many climbers. Sometimes they seemed to rise, rather than creep—they had grown taller than Pradip. He has folder upon folder of their photographs, and with his intense study came his inevitable questioning. Did the leaves look a little similar? And why were they mostly shaped like hearts at their base? Was there a pattern to be discerned here? Perhaps it's because the heart shape gives strength to a large-sized leaf, at the point where it adheres to the leafstalk. This reinforced design helps soak up precious dregs of sunlight that break through a canopy. When a plant grows under a tree, catching sunlight at the base is like getting the first raindrop in the vibrant air of a cold desert, the last tug of whiskey at the bottom of the glass. It also feels like something that doesn't happen every day. 'Imagine the leaf to be like a solar panel. It has to optimize its surface area to snare the light,' he says. The heart-shaped leaves have a capability that is instantly visible if only one pays attention. The sides of the leaf spring out like wings. In form, it is like looking at a butterfly, that creature of impeccable design and stunning beauty; and then you remember that butterflies look whimsical, but they also migrate across cities and countries. It is then, looking at beauty with power: a sting ray doing its perfect, silent ballet in the seas. It is, in fact, looking at a plant with a strong leaf and a pliable stem breaking through glass ceilings. That heart-shaped leaf has an extra vein around the top to strengthen its endeavours, its climb. I think of the heart-shaped paan-patta, the betel plant, which has ruffled so many hearts with its taste, and lined so many dates at the corner *paan-wala*, the paan-vendor.

When we look at the plants Pradip mentions, they all look like hearts of different shapes and sizes. It feels like a microcosm of life and longing. Many decades of walking have revealed these patterns—this symmetry of hearts that look identical on the left and the right side, with the survivor's spirit of the underdog. There's *Cissampelos*, a bright green cartoonish heart with tiny clustered flowers. There is *Diplocyclos,* with a leaf that looks something between a maple leaf and a heart. There is the lilac-flowered *Ipomoea arachnosperma,* a creeper with hairy heart-shaped leaves and flowers that one wants to steal. There is *Trichosanthes cucumerina*, a kind of snake-gourd. There is another vegetable, jungli karela (wild bitter gourd), with its bright yellow flowers. Then there's a creeper called wattakaka in Malayalam and *Dregea volubilis* in Latin, with green-coloured flowers. The Central Ridge is an old arena, and one would think a lot is known about it. Yet, there is much more to glean here. A heart is a cherished metaphor to remember the Central Ridge with. I think again: *This is Delhi too*.

In so many ways, our lives are tethered to soil. Our food comes from it. Soil gives us our staples like potatoes, and is also a springboard for things more whimsical, like those on our breakfast tables—chia seeds, sunflower seeds, flax seeds. Soil grows flowers, those tokens that accompany us through life—our companions at births, hospitals and deaths. It is also mutable: a commonplace annoyance when it thins to dust, a rich nourishment for the world when it is allowed to ripen with mulch.

Soil has stories embedded in it, waiting to flower, waiting to be recognized, and told again. These stories are richer and more polyphonic when the soil is chemical-free.

While collecting seeds, Pradip found a batch of bistendu seeds in the Central Ridge. The bistendu (or bishtendu), *Diospyros cordifolia*, is an Aravalli plant with bright fruit that look like mini oranges. These aren't oranges though, and the leaves have a poison used by communities to stun fish (this might also explain the name, 'bish' or 'vish' which means poison). Despite its reputation, the bistendu's ripe fruit is relished by birds like Brown-headed barbets. Pradip collects bistendu seeds to grow in other places. Once, he found the seeds in civet poo. Civets are small mammals that look like weasels, often considered 'cat-like' carnivores. They live largely unnoticed amongst us because they are nocturnal.[6] Some of the world's best coffee comes from seeds that have gone through the guts of civets. Pradip found the same is true for bistendu seeds—they germinated much more easily once they had been in a civet's mouth and tummy.

From the soil, layers of stories thus grow—soil upholds trees and the creepers that caper over these giants; it holds in its open palm the histories of seeds that have passed through the belly of a mischievous, nimble predator; it bears the remains of a tree trunk that turned into a termite mound, which later became a powdery, soil-like tumble when kicked at by a curious cow.

While studying the text of the soil, Pradip observed the places where plants succeeded in growing. These were climate survivors that survived on almost nothing (such as the ones on bio-crust), or those that survived in conditions other plants would find tough (like the dhau or dhok, which grows naturally on slopes where rainwater does not tarry). He also noticed plants that seemed to be coming out of cracks. These were the dark, inky places between rocks, places that didn't seem to have any soil, what appeared to be 'minus' places. There's beauty to be had in the things that fall between the cracks. In southern India, the 'missing check' denotes a particular pattern in a saree or a fabric where missing dents create a textured, undulating, and ultimately breathable fabric. The missing check is also a visual delight. In Rao Jodha Park in Jodhpur, Pradip found plants that have learned to embrace the missing, the minus places. These were the chasmophytes, specialists that grow out of crevices and cracks.

I think back on the plants I have seen on rocks and hard places. Mosses, velvety and luminous, grow on walls and rock, vertically or horizontally. Portulaca, a succulent with bright flower heads that open when the sun is out, grow on millimetres of dust on the terrace. Yet, they also grow in soil and in pots. What Pradip was talking about were things that grow specifically in cracks. 'The longer and thinner the cracks, the better it is for the chasmophyte plant. Only the smallest particles of soil make it inside the crack. The plant thus uses clay-like particles of soil,' he explains, his voice reverent.

And what plants they are! One of Pradip's favourites is the gorgeous *Blepharis scindica*. It has vivid indigo flowers. The coloured petals look like the back of a plush throne; its hue contains both the immediacy of red and blue in it. I imagine an insect on this flower-throne: completely at home on the springy texture, surrounded by fabulous beauty. Amongst the rocks in Rajasthan are also the *Seddera latifolia* with its silky stems and a range that covers sub-Saharan Africa, the horn of Africa and western India. A plant that springs up like a jack in the box after the monsoon rains is the nearly indestructible and always cheerful *Tephrosia uniflora* with its hot pink flowers. And it isn't just tiny things that grow in the minus places. It's also trees. The kumat tree, *Acacia senegal*, is perhaps one of the most prominent trees of the Thar. It produces edible gum, and the leaves are browsed by wild and domestic animals. The tree is a thorny acacia which is very much at home in places considered lacking—for water, for soil, for a firm foothold. Yet, the kumat thrives in this seeming matrix of neglect. It can also grow *on* rock and is thus classified as lithophytic.

These plants show us a minus place can also be a plus. Resilience comes in many shapes and sizes, and they wipe away notions of parks where you need to tend to plants day and night, with sticks for scaffolding, pipes for irrigation and dining tables of manure, creating scarecrows on behalf of plants that may nevertheless die from the cold, the heat or aphid attacks. The right plants—the native ones—don't need handholding. They need establishment, and they need place. Once established, they make their own way in the world, through soil, rocks and winds. Henceforth, they may not even need watering.

Will there come a day when we recognize a *Blepharis* and not just the buttercup, the kumat and not just the plumeria? Perhaps we can start by creating a dictionary of native words. And a vocabulary of appreciation for the unconventional: for its tough roots, hard spines and the will of needles. As resilient as a kumat thorn. As colourful as a blooming *Blepharis* in the desert. As cooling as the jaal tree. As invigorating as kair in the desert.

While working with the natural lay and signature of the land, Pradip suggests examining natural soils—with the thinness or richness they might have—and introducing plant communities that work for that area. Like his restoration in Rajasthan shows, places in Delhi—with their crevices, rocky spurs and woods—can harbour restored plant communities which are like both light and shade—ephemeral annuals that come in a flash after the rains, and desert-land trees that may outlive us. 'We don't need to bring a lot of water and fiddle with the land. We can just find plants that adapt to its crevices,' he says.

At Rao Jodha Park, he learnt that removing *Neltuma juliflora* is a delicate task, rather than a masculine, mechanical one. Unlike Delhi's authorities who trawl the ground with JCBs, scraping the ground and throwing the baby out with the bathwater, Pradip and his team make sure they can get rid of *Neltuma* without radically disturbing the landform. At Rao Jodha, the land was special. Achingly so. No two portions looked the same. There was serene sandstone with ripples on it, remnants of the great Tethys Sea. There were dimples of volcanic rhyolite. The stoicness of stone nevertheless bore tender marks of experience and becoming. To remove invasives from the area, rock specialists—not just soil specialists—were required. The team invited local miners to the park. They came armed with small hammers and chisels. A man called Dhan Singh sat on the rocks, tapping them with his hammer. He would hit the ground three times—tap-tap-tap—and then turn his face away to listen to the earth. By listening, he would know when he had to go into the rock to take out *Neltuma* roots.

'Dhan Singh told me to come back in two hours,' Pradip says. And so, Pradip went for a walk. When he returned, Dhan had taken out long, ribbon-like roots of the *Neltuma*. It was decided then and there that a team would be established for the chiselling. The team wore white floppy cricket hats and tapped away for seven years in order to clear 70 hectares of land. 'We would follow after them, planting wherever they had cleared the area of *Neltuma*. We didn't use heavy earth-moving machinery. That would have damaged the soil. We would have lost decades of soil richness. We followed a routine that would take time, but yielded results,' Pradip says. And so, the team wove the tapestry of the soil again. And they lived and planned around tree-time. It takes time to remove an invasive, it takes even longer if you want to preserve the decades and millennia in a good bio-crust while you remove the alien. Life begins anew, in the correct way. On this tree-time and soil-time come flashes of monsoon annuals and chasmophyte plants: a dance between the new and the old, a twining of the vascular and the non vascular.

There is an immense plant variety waiting for our acknowledgement and involvement: heart-shaped leaves under towering trees in Delhi, desert grasses living on volcanic soil under a sky full of stars in Rajasthan. I have always found wildlife extraordinary for the things it endures every day. I now know plants are superstars for similar reasons too. There has grown in me a lot more appreciation for the plants I walk next to, and under, and through. The native must be encouraged; and there are better ways to clear invasives and start with a clean slate. There are other places to learn from.

And this is why I ask: what is the other place in Delhi that Pradip loves?

He answers in a heartbeat. Apart from the Central Ridge, there is another part of Delhi-NCR which he values, one that resembles what a natural forest for Delhi's climate would look like.

This is an emerald forest, a secret that can be accessed through the bustle of the Faridabad–Gurgaon road, next to a towering garbage mountain. Behind these evidences of urban life, lies Mangar Bani. The forest is a sacred grove for a local baba. Because of this, there is a bar on the cutting of trees. When you enter Mangar Bani, it is easy to forget that Delhi is an area of dry deciduous forests. Other forests in the city, with the exception of the Central Ridge and one part of the Sanjay Van, look dry, spindly and dusty. Mangar instead grows lushly, in layers, outwards and upwards, moist and complex, a frothy cake you want to sink into and swallow.

I have always gone to Mangar for the birds, as you will read about in other parts of this book. Pradip goes there for the plants. In Mangar, there are splendid white-blossomed *Vallaris* creepers, growing under trees of great age. Papdi seeds, packed like candy in their pods, shimmer as the wind passes through branches of the tree. Barbets call, woodpeckers drum, and there is a nightjar in the woods. There are birds everywhere, and leopards visit often. I go to Mangar every year to see the summer migrants—Indian pittas, Indian paradise flycatchers, Common cuckoos. In the rains, the place leaps to life even more than normal. Red velvet mites run amok, in giant circles. A Common hawk cuckoo, a bird that mimics a Shikra, comes to the ground to snap up termites. The ground is soggy and dark in parts, red and sandy in others. A peacock calls raucously. Close to the hawk cuckoo, a bird arrows into a four-inch hole in the ground. This is a green bee-eater, a bird that sallies—catching prey in the air in a flourish, then returning to its perch like nothing has happened. The bee-eater sallies, and then goes to another branch, preparing to take its prey inside the hole. The entire dance is over in a few seconds, and I know now there is a nest in that damp hole, with a chick waiting earnestly for its parent to return. Ants march on the ground outside this home, forming soldier lines that disappear into the undergrowth. There are little puddles on the forest floor that reflect the moisture-laden sky through gaps in the trees. Frogs call from the lips of the puddles, telling everyone about the bounty of water. It seems everything is outside—making the most of the short spells when the rain ceases to fall. That ceasing does not cause stasis, but catalyses movement, like the rain uttered the words of a spell and woke everyone up, and by the time the shower ended, ant and bird and frog and bug alike were ready to come forth. Mangar is alive in a way one hardly sees in Delhi-NCR.

But Mangar was once unknown, and Pradip helped find it, and translate it. He first heard of Mangar in a history lecture in Delhi's South Campus. The speaker was talking about a Stone Age site that had been found at Mangar; she also mentioned a sacred forest there. Thus, the forests survive as a relic of what Aravalli forests once were—embroidered by chasmophytes, corseted by giant trees, laced through with creepers and belted with streams.

Birders flock to Mangar, and rock-climbing enthusiasts do too. Yet Pradip's reason for cherishing Mangar isn't just its diversity, but also its *sameness*. Much of Mangar is dhau forest. This slope-loving tree looks purplish from a distance—blue clouds on grey slopes, dreaming desert dreams. The slopes near Sariska tiger reserve are full of them. But apart from their ability to grow on tilted ground, dhau has another superpower.

'I knew dhau grew well on quartzite slopes. But what I found in Mangar is that dhau is actually a clonal forest. The tree effectively replicates itself. Dhau reproduces by growing another trunk through stolons, a kind of horizontal stem. These are natural monocultures,' Pradip says. The expanse of dhau in Mangar is a good example of native forest; it is also a good example of how far a single tree can go if given the space to grow.

When I visit Mangar, my friend and co-walker Sunil Harsana shows me dhau that's been razed down by ravenous livestock. Instead of dying, the plant splays out, growing horizontally in a bush-like way. It wears battle scars, but it is still smiling; what remains is a net that surrounds and protects the meristem, the main stem. As the sun rises above the slopes of Mangar when I walk with Sunil, he points out another thing. He is smiling, golden hour gilding his face, white adusa blossoms turning into champagne behind him. 'See this,' he points at a spindly plant with feathery leaves. It is the enemy—the dreaded vilayati kikar.[7] 'And now see this,' he shows me the short but robust looking dhau next to the vilayati kikar. The dhau has been levelled but it looks more animated than the vilayati kikar, like it will outlive the latter. 'I believe the dhau is fighting the vilayati kikar. And I believe the dhau will win,' Sunil says. In many other parts of the Ridge, the vilayati kikar has dominated. In some parts near Mangar, it has crept in. But as long as there's dhau, Sunil believes the forest has a fighting chance.

Pradip has special words to describe Mangar's dhau forest. 'Dhau is a clonal forest. A natural monoculture by a habitat specialist that was meant to flourish on Aravalli quartzite.' I want this sentence on a t-shirt.

I add one more line to my idioms, etched in a heart-shape in my mind: As resilient as a kumat thorn. As colourful as a blooming *Blepharis* in the desert. As hard to beat as a dhau in the Aravallis.

These are words and spells I hope to spread: as their names get repeated, perhaps they will germinate. Perhaps love will grow for these epic plants, these climate survivors.

January 2025 is ending.

In the middle of January, a few days after meeting Pradip in his hobbit-like home, I have a sharp pain in my stomach. I know in my blood that something is wrong. Instead of going to work that morning, I go for an ultrasound. As I lie on the ultrasound table, with a radiologist pouring gel over my stomach, I fight back nausea and a mounting sense of dread. I tell myself stories to pass through the soar of discomfort: The goop on my stomach is kumat gum. I am a kumat tree. The radiologist clears his throat and announces he has found a 16-mm stone in my gall bladder. Even as the news penetrates my brain fog, I say to myself: kumat grows on stones. So does the kullu. I will conquer this stone. A second later, the radiologist finds another gall stone, a smaller one this time. He tells me in no uncertain terms that my gall bladder will have to be removed, and this has to be done swiftly. It reminds me of what the doctor said at the Delhi Heart and Lung hospital for my father—you cannot leave without a procedure, without foreign hands rearranging one's body. For my surgery, a camera will go in from a wide incision in my navel, and through three other cuts in my abdomen, the stones will be crushed, the gall bladder shrunk, and then pulled out.

At around the same time, my father collapses. He has to be carried and taken to hospital. In the hospital, he is incomprehensible, speaking only in Bangla, unable to understand where he is, or that the nurses can't understand him. I can't go to him, and I hope the nurses will be kind; I remember the mocking nurse from the Delhi Heart and Lung hospital, and how the semal outside girded me into a brittle form of peace. The doctors have now found a skip in my father's heartbeat, and he is fitted with a temporary pacemaker while I prepare for my own surgery. It is decided that he will be operated upon for a permanent pacemaker in North Delhi on the same day that I will have my surgery in South Delhi.

The day arrives. It is a Saturday. After a drought of no water, no food, I am taken for surgery under the hospital's artificial lights. I feel my own pain but it seems indistinguishable from the worry for my parent. When I come to after general anaesthesia, with no memory of surgery or incisions, I run my hand over my stomach, frantically, finding a set of bandages there. 'My liver has been stolen,' is the first thought that comes to mind, rushing in like the sea in high tide, invading every corner of my mind, possibly echoing millions of girls who think something bad has occurred if they don't remember what has happened. A nurse comes over a little while later, telling me my surgery is over and my gall bladder has been removed. I will be in hospital for another day. I am taken by stretcher to a suite with an ugly painting, a lampshade I can't sit up next to, and a grey sofa. It is depressing. No natural light comes in. I feel bereaved at losing a part of me I had never seen or thought about, but want to hold on to, now that I have lost it. The place where my gall bladder was is now a minus place. I think of my mother and father who also had their gall bladders removed before me, and in the grey grim light of that room, reflect on how gall stones are like an epidemic in modern India. Then I worry about my father, lying on another bed with nurses around him, speaking a language they can't mutually follow.

Will my minus place grow a chasmophyte, a greater will to live, no matter the storms I encounter? 'I'm going to take the gall stones and make a pendant out of them,' I tell myself in that ugly room. 'I will have the gall to go through life without a gall bladder,' I quip. But these are just platitudes. What I really want is to do everything again: to walk, to leave the hospital, be outdoors under trees, to have my family healthy, and together again. To grow through stones. To be vascular in a city that steadily increases blood pressure and heart disease; to really live here, though to live here for long is to have a shorter life span. I remember a semal growing on and through the roof of a building in INA market, that place which is an ode to Malayali food and knick-knacks. The market is dirty, with suspicious rivulets of liquid crisscrossing it. There are fields of garbage and currents of scents that basically reek of old, raw fish. Through all this, the semal is resplendent on one of the roofs; a tree, not a sapling. The tree is a statement. I remember it, while wishing for a hospital window with a tree-view. For wishing for a Delhi Heart and Lung hospital room style porthole.

A little later my room is changed by the hospital staff. The new room is much smaller. It has a lower, perforated ceiling, parts of which look more punctured than perforated. But on the left, there is a window. And outside the window, there is a glorious semal. It shimmers as it presents itself to my vision, a spectacle and a triumph. Its leaves grow in an arrangement of five to six leaflets radiating from a central point, and they are merry, like they have been stuck on by a child. A wind ruffles the leaves, brown, yellow, green. Because it is January, the leaves are yellowed, preparing to fall, preparing for the festivities of flowering. In my post-surgery fever, it seems like the tree is giggling. As I look again, I travel through time. My mind goes back to the semal covered in scarlet flowers outside the Delhi Heart and Lung hospital when I attended to my hospitalized father almost ten years ago. That tree was swathed in lipstick-red petals; this one is a patchwork of yellow-green leaves. He was sixty-five then, I am forty now, but our feelings are the same—we want to be free, to be in the flower-shade of trees, in nature instead of in the jail of the hospital. All of freedom feels like being able to stand under an Indian tree, unassisted. As I watch, a solemn Black kite circles above the semal and settles in the middle of the tree's crown. I can make out the kite's yellow beak, the strong angle of its neck, the way it grips the branch in its loose but confident way. There was a similar kite outside my father's room in 2015. So much has changed, but some things are the same. We attract illnesses and soldier through them, but kites still come to the semal, as if compelled. Semals are the bays that the crashing waves of a kite's flight dock in; semals are the bays that have protected us from the high tide of negative thoughts. In life, we manage to laugh because we understand cyclicality: we know relationships like that of father–daughter keep coming back to each other despite words left unspoken; we know trees will flower again with the clockwork beauty and certainty of annual flowering even in polluted cities; we know medicines and love cure illnesses, that pain does not always mean suffering if there is love.

Lying on the hospital bed, with my minus place throbbing, I think that life's outline is a heart-shaped leaf.

Life goes up, it comes down, but it needs a little stoicism as an extra vein to reinforce it.

I will go back to Pradip and tell him my new semal story. Undoubtedly, he will listen with patience and tell me his favourite tree is still the dhau with its cloning properties and the anjan with butterfly leaves that twirl on their branches.

And I will promise him to look at the soil more closely, and think about the time trees need to grow, and return to favourite places with growing trees again and again. To my body, I will promise to give time—the gift of tree-time, lined with soil-time.

PART 2

A City of Its People

'Whoever you are, no matter how lonely,
the world offers itself to your imagination,
calls to you like the wild geese,
harsh and exciting—over and
over announcing your place
in the family of things...'
Wild Geese, Mary Oliver

The Found City

Vallari's Delhi

Vallari Sheel is a rare individual in the din of Delhi: she is a quiet person, studying things that can't speak. In completing a PhD on Delhi's trees, and in examining them in avenues, in parks, in monuments and in places she has begun to call home, she has found her voice, and perhaps, her power.

I joined Twitter (now X) in 2013. On most days, it felt like I had stepped into a gutter.

Most conversations went this way. I'd put out a tweet or post with what I considered was my valid opinion, and people would begin to attack me.

For instance, my original post was: 'It's the age of Artificial Intelligence and I realize we still haven't learned to kill mosquitoes.'

The responses would rumble in, whining like the subject of the tweet.

'It's mosquitos' (a mansplainer would tell me).

'You call yourself a conservationist. Still you want to kill.' (An angry uncle puts forth his opinion, like he's throwing coins to the poor, expecting an instant rush of gratitude from me.)

'Empty your room. Keep your room free of furniture. U shd be able to have just bed and 4 walls. Take a towel & smash at mosquito with high speed. Then use a plastic broom and hit flying mosquito ... bang everything to eject flying mosquito.' (A follower fails to see the rhetoric in my tweet and gives a staggeringly literal, typically unrealistic solution.)

'When I was posted in North East. Lot of mosquito bit me. Nothing happened to me.' (Another mansplainer recounts his thirty-year-old experience; his words are bordered with schadenfreude.)

'India is not just mosquito, disease. We have done a lot to reduce disease.' (A false equivalence response from a chest-thumping patriot.)

'Didi machhar se darti hai' (young male with a misleading profile photo laughs at me; he alternates between laughing at women and desiring them).

'Am I not mosquito enough to out-mosquito you? This is from a DH Lawrence poem we studied in school.'

(A circumspect response, thoughtful, not overbearing; finally, my favourite kind of response flies into the whine of the conversation.)

And so, for every seven or eight terrible responses, there is this one post which gleams. Shining with authenticity. Fun. Like a real conversation, unfettered by the bravado of an online persona. This final response is what I was on X for: it was the trickle of river water in the gutter.

One such follower was Dr Madhusudan Katti, an academic based in the USA. He had done his PhD on birds, tiny creatures known as warblers. Warblers come in varying shades of grey-brown, and though they are plentiful, they possess a healthy disdain for the camera. They also look remarkably alike. And yet, they are wondrous creatures, because they migrate to India in the winters, propelling their tiny bodies (weighing a few grams) in a way that belies their size, and with a kind of super-bird determination. And so, the prospect of photographing and identifying warblers is both an important and a daunting one. It is what has inspired birdwatchers to call small, unidentifiable birds as LBJs—Little Brown Jobs. Madhu and I would often chat about LBJs in mango trees, and how their quick, furtive movements would make the leaves shake—as if the tree was gripped with laughter. One day, I had asked the birdwatchers on X for help in identifying a warbler I had managed to take a photograph of. It was a little bird on a shahtoot tree in February. The tree was mostly bare, with little nubs of leaves beginning to appear. The warbler visited the shahtoot daily, easily visible in the bare branches.

I thought it was a Green warbler, but X thought it was the Greenish warbler (these birds are so similar looking, even their names are an echo of one another). The moot point also was the tree, that little tree that hosted a migratory bird every day, and for years in a row.

In between everyone giving their opinion, Madhu told me I should meet his student. Her name was Vallari, and she was studying the trees of Delhi. I tucked away the name like I remembered the sight of a seam of clean river water.

Summer rose. On a hot day in Delhi, I was stepping off stage after delivering a talk. People waited to meet me, to share their views and make a joke. The space right next to a stage after an event is not an ordered one. Somehow, everyone wants to make their point first. Some people speak quickly, while others speak in a complicated way full of backstories, and mild shoving is not unheard of. The after stage has an afterglow which is almost as dynamic as the stage itself. I understand the rush to be heard. It's not often that we meet people who care specifically about what we think about (the night sky leaking with light pollution, the differences between the Green and the Greenish warbler, unexpectedly finding a Purple sunbird nest in one's garden). Especially on days which are harsh outdoors, the stage and its aftermath is a refuge and an amplification. The only problem is that the noise drives off the quieter people. So often, people wait their turn at the back and then walk off, overwhelmed. I always bemoan the loss of those conversations. At the end of my talk that day, I noticed someone waiting for me.

She stood at a distance from us, like she was enforcing a six-foot quarantine. She had a small smile on her face, like she was bursting to tell me something, and the effort was creating a thought bubble over her head. She was wearing a red and white top with an ajrakh pattern. I hoped she wouldn't walk off. I'd look up repeatedly to check if she was still there, feeling stung that she had to wait that long. But she waited, right till the end. I walked up to her.

'Hi, I'm Neha,' I said.

'I know,' she laughed. 'I'm Vallari. I think—maybe—my advisor, Dr Katti, told you about me.'

'Yes! He did. So you're one of the few people who comes up in an online conversation and then appears in real life!' I exclaimed. (This was 2018. Offline and online did not meet as often as they do now.)

'I loved your talk. We should go on a tree walk someday. And I would love to interview you, you know, if you have time obviously, for my PhD,' she said.

'What's your study on?' I asked.

She told me it was on what the trees of Delhi mean to humans and non-humans. The ecological and social aspects of urban trees, the way people shape treescapes, and also how trees shape us.

'What a lovely topic! The semal is my favourite tree,' I told her.

'Mine too!' she exclaimed.

And instantly, I realized we were friends, like we had picked out the same colour, semal red, on tip-tappy-tap-what-colour-do-you-want as children, and were now meeting as adults, recognizing the menace and mania of doing fieldwork in the brutal city of Delhi. I knew then that both our notebooks were suffused with semal red observations, the tree tugging at us not just academically but also in a deeply personal way that had become mutual, that our field journals would be a mirror of each other.

I realized too: there is life in the online gutter.

And so, we started our friendship with the semal, in the spring-summer of 2018. The semal had become more than a tree. It felt like an entire universe. The semal has an ornithophilous flower, bird-loving, bright and full of nectar, and designed in a way that ensures it is easily pollinated by birds.[1] But other creatures come too.

I watched everyday as squirrels walked up and down the branches. I studied the tree in the mornings from 6.30 to 8.30 a.m. every March. The spring air was soft and sweet, and I wanted to bottle and drink it. The unexpected happened daily. A Rose-ringed parakeet couple had an argument on the branches. The male pecked at the female's face, and she drew her head and shoulders back, a look of avian disdain on her face. He hopped closer to her: a little hop, a big entreaty. She moved away, putting physical distance between them. He hopped closer again. The tiny moments I parsed through binoculars become indelibly tattooed into me. We make grand stages for these little rituals in our own lives. We write poems about the forks in the road, the paths less travelled. We have entire music and entertainment industries erected to finding (and keeping) love. But the birds and animals on the semal are writing their own poems too. There is no reason why theirs should be any less important than ours. I wanted to hear these songs, I wanted animal notes inscribed into me. I wanted to find what the city doesn't give up easily—an unfettered, uncalculating, animal joy, with no strings attached.

Fortress of Flowers

We go looking for semal red before the Covid lockdown happens, before we have even an inkling of the fact that the world will careen to a complete halt.

We have made a plan of exploring the streets of Delhi for our favourite tree. Vallari has an old Alto car, with an unexpected clock sitting on the dashboard. I have an old Figo that once went into a large neem tree, breaking bones on my face and chest and damaging my left eye. We don't like driving, but our faithful, broken-but-pieced-together mechanical steeds seem fitting for our quest. If this was a movie, we would be threading flowers into our broomsticks. But in real life, we have both done fieldwork in Delhi, with patchwork steeds to carry us, and it's always been bittersweet—with difficulties in transport, with our private joy at the birds and trees ruined by very public teasing. While it hasn't been easy—we also know we are not looking for easy. I think the more accurate articulation of the experience is that it has never been smooth; our body has been constantly calibrating to prepare for an awful thing that will happen and collapse the pack of bird/tree cards we have set up since morning. It's that wait for the inevitable awful that poisons the very adventure, staining it with a deep turmeric yellow that doesn't wash off for days after.

Together, we want to change this narrative and wash off our hands. Maybe it will be better together. Maybe it will be fun together. We get a thick felt pen, and I draw a terrible map of Delhi, with less terrible drawings of semal trees in it. The trees are flagposts for us. We are recounting a map of the places where we have seen the semal: growing on the triangles of land next to a traffic light at the beginning of Aruna Asaf Ali Marg; spotted at the site of a protest in Sarojini Nagar, ironically against the cutting of trees near Dilli Haat; growing like a torch next to the grade separators at ITO and AIIMS, so they remained on eye-level as we passed; one in the iconic Teen Murti building; and trees that line roads we can picture but can no longer place.

We drive to the places we remember. We feel we cannot miss a single tree. We start with South Delhi. We go to Defence Colony, Chanakyapuri, to little parks in Sarojini Nagar, and avenue roads near the government flats in RK Puram. In North Delhi, we go to Alipur and Wazirabad. In Haryana, we go to Aravalli and Mangar and Bhondsi, promising to return to see the flowering of the palash trees we spot. We trace the Delhi Ridge, running a finger down the green spots on the map of Delhi. The largest patch of the Ridge is at the very bottom of the state. It looks like droplets condensing at the bottom of a window.

Year after year, we wait for semal flowering. In the interim, we read, and we observe. We catalogue butterflies in a plant nursery and find that nurseries are a great place to find birds and insects. We walk through neighbourhood parks to find an odd remnant of a native tree that horticulture has spared. We find entire groves of semal, and single roadside trees that feel like an institution. Years pass and our notes pile up. Vallari and I are fast friends now, bonded with the sap of trees. She stops for every plant while I look for birds. I didn't even know it, but I used to overlook plants, and spending time with her is curing my plant blindness. She is so sweet and generous, she feels like a once-in-a-year blossom, and I wonder how she has survived Delhi.

It is March of 2022, and the Covid lockdown has ended. We have decided to make our way into older places, which we hope will have older trees.

We are to go to the oldest place of all, at least in name. The Old Fort in Delhi, the Purana Qila, a Mughal structure that is almost five hundred years old. The Old Fort is an interesting backdrop to many other events in the city. It has a small waterbody next to it, and the water is dirty, yet people delight in it, in the casual way citizens inhabit pollution as if schooled by the metropolis to do so. Next to the Old Fort is Delhi's zoo, presenting a strange confectionery—an ancient building full of somnolence next to a zoo full of pacing creatures.

Once, while walking in Sunder Nursery (which is behind the Delhi zoo), I heard growling. It was the sort of hair-raising, deep-throated snarl-growl I had heard from tigers in sub-Himalayan, river-girded forests. The sound had resonated through woods of depth and mystery, adding another layer of the unknowable, creating a place as majestic as it was frightening. Here in Delhi, could it have been a big cat in the zoo grumbling about his evening meal? The zoo was a pinning together of things to make a scrapbook—a foreign snake, an Indian monkey, a Black jaguar native to Central America, a baby giraffe from Africa, all kept in enclosures in varying conditions. Things collected and acquired, to suit all tastes and nationalities, things collected because they could be. *This is Delhi too.*

And now we are headed to the Old Fort to see what kind of Delhi resides there. Perhaps there will be good, old trees.

It is early morning. There is a big lock on the gate of the parking area for the fort. We think we can park inside the zoo but find that it's closed to visitors for the day. We decide to wait, chatting in the car till someone comes. A man appears. He is grumpy. He looks at us and begrudgingly opens the padlock. The parking lot is a big, empty expanse. This is a sight only early mornings reveal—hundreds of square yards of neatly swept parking lots, clean only at this time of the day, shaded by trees, like mouths waiting for car-morsels. We park in the centre, some distance from the gate but not at the far end that could be dangerous, and get out of the car. It is when we are almost at the gate that the man comes running up to us. 'Park over there,' he says, gesturing towards the far end. He is not looking at us while speaking. 'The whole lot is completely empty, and we have parked well. A hundred more cars could fit in here. Why should we move?' I ask him. 'So others can have space,' he says, his face twisting with a sudden, suppressed anger. We are used to this—a flash of sudden irritation from a man, coming without warning, making us feel threatened. We are used to this, but it never becomes comfortable. In a second, we become the outliers, suspects, the bad people, nay, the bad women, the witches that need a public trial with everyone listening in. It has happened so many times it seems inseparable from the main stem of our experience of driving in Delhi. There has so often been a parking attendant telling us to shift our car a few inches, having waited for the vehicle to be parked, locked, and rear windows rolled up. A man who is not a parking attendant has appeared suddenly, saying the parking is so wrong he just can't allow it. I have been told to go back to my car, open it, re-park it, move a couple of inches to the left, and make space for cars that are not even there. Parking attendants have sniggered at me, dissolving into laughter after they made me change my car's position by the ordained few inches. A few inches of them humiliating me, a few inches of other cars driven by men around me being parked anyhow.

It has taken me time to realize this is a few inches too much. That the advice is gendered, for me, and other women drivers. When I first started driving fifteen years ago, I listened to how male drivers were categorized through their clothes or cars—as 'red Cielo', 'silver Corolla', 'laal jacket sir', while I was always, like other women, just the 'ladies driver'. Women had no other distinguishing features. We were ladies drivers with no idea how to drive the cars we bought with our own money. We were ladies drivers who got by on the grace of other male drivers.

I have taught myself now that as long as we park well, we don't need extra advice. And as long as we can walk away, we should. We aren't going to move the car by a few inches or a few yards, I tell the guard. He is so angry now his hands are trembling, and he doesn't meet my gaze. He is still pointing at a spot that is not in the middle, but on the far end. There is nothing wrong with parking here, I tell him. He looks at me finally, and our eyes lock. He mutters below his breath. He knows what he is asking for is unreasonable, and yet he must not relent. We stand like that for a beat. At the end of this battle of wills, he just walks away, his feet pounding the ground. He is outnumbered, and we have created the formation we often do: me standing in front of Vallari, defending her right to park sanely. She stands behind me, watching.

The moment passes. We unclench our mental fists. We leave the parking lot and climb the gentle slope towards the fort. At the security check, we step through the metal detectors and slip our bags through a conductor belt in which the bags will be X-rayed. The buttery morning light is waning. We must get to the trees on time. The birds are calling, and the sunrays are still making the charming slanting formation they do in the morning—beams of gold, not a mesh of heat. Though not for long. I hear a Brown-headed barbet go kroo kroo krroo, and I pick up my bag and start walking. Vallari is behind me.

'Stop. Stop madam,' comes a voice from behind us. 'What is this?' a guard says angrily, pointing at Vallari's bag, and specifically at her binoculars.

This is the second time that morning that we are facing sudden male rage.

'Binoculars,' I say, droll as a robot—a stiff, formal response to an odd, intrusive question.

'Why do you have binoculars?' he asks. From another side of the room comes another authoritarian male voice: 'You can't have binoculars with you.' There is assertion and finality in the voice of the other man who has spoken up: we just *cannot* have binoculars. It is singularly impossible. I bristle at the entitlement. I want to say something rude in response.

'We have binoculars because we want to see birds, and trees,' I say instead.

'What—for what?' He is now suppressing mocking laughter.

'Binoculars to see birds, and trees.'

'But why do you want to see birds and trees?'

'Because we like them,' I say.

'Because we teach about them,' Vallari comes in, hoping to collect the seemingly endless goodwill reserved for educators in India.

There are four guards in the room, and they all look stunned. Disbelief pierces the conversation. They can't size up what they are facing: women here without men, carrying something associated with terrorists, in a city obsessed not with actual security, but the pretence of it. You have to be frisked even before you can get into a theatre to watch a movie in Delhi. And depending on who checks you, a mall attendant may ask you to swallow some of the cough syrup you are carrying to demonstrate it's not something else; at other times you might get waved through even if metal detectors cry out as you walk past. I have a nagging feeling they are saying no because they don't know what else to do.

But for a birdwatcher, binoculars are special. They take you closer to a bird: whiskers, feathers, wattled facial skin, in a way that a camera can't. They hearken back to older times of birdwatching when cameras were too expensive, and most people used binoculars and took copious notes for records, thus knowing infinitely more than just bird identification. Through binoculars, the black sheen of a male Oriental magpie-robin gleams with a velvety effervescence, you see that a male Grey hornbill actually has long, sweeping eyelashes, that the common Red-whiskered bulbul sports red cheeks that look like they are reflecting semal flowers. Common birds shine like rarities, and in the right light you see feathers transforming: into lush fur, into smooth petals, into chiselled precious stones. Binoculars show you what your eyes can't, and they transform what you see. Like a river current, they physically carry you closer to the object of your attention. They also have the advantage physical books have over digital devices—they don't need batteries or electricity. They simply need your gaze placed through them, fitted in slots adjusted for the specific width between your eyes.

They are intimate in the best way: they become you, you become them.

And so to say we can't take our binoculars is to say that we must leave our vision behind. It means we would miss out on the micro-behaviours that make birdwatching special. Based on the calls I was hearing, I knew my binoculars would show me the pause before a hornbill regurgitated his throat to feed his mate, and a barbet twitching its head to escape filaments of wood as it drilled a perfectly round hole to nest in. Leaving our binoculars was leaving our purpose behind. We weren't going to leave ours.

'Where does it say that we can't take binoculars?' I ask. There are three men and one woman standing around us.

'We have a list,' one of them answers ominously. 'A list of banned items.'

'That list should be up here so visitors can know,' I tell him. 'What does a secret list achieve?'

'But we want to know why binoculars aren't allowed,' Vallari says, soft to my brittle responses.

'Because you can see far from them ... and because they are not allowed.'

'I can see further with the zoom lens in my camera,' I tell them, showing them my camera, zooming the lens in and out.

'And what would I look far at? The zoo animals? Or the lake and its boats?' I ask.

The morning is slipping past us, silvery sand through a tightly clenched fist. We have already lost both golden light and time in the parking lot, and now we stand at the lip of the fort, unable to get in. Though it seems a ridiculous request, we say we will leave our binoculars behind only if we can see the rules. But there is no list they can show us.

We keep arguing. Time keeps passing. Finally, the guards relent. We don't want any trouble, the female guard tell us. But I don't want trouble either, I say, with a kind of annoyance that feels deeply familiar—the annoyance of being told to sit in a punishment corner because I didn't conform. Why should I want trouble? I came here for the birds, I mutter to myself. Our combined anger is a miasma that clings to the walls of the security room, a room that deals with confiscated packets of chips and cans of beer, not binoculars.

We walk out, reminded of all the times we have been asked to not be odd, not be unusual, and to take comfort in convention. I don't want to feel chastened. I don't want to be admonished for some vague convention I didn't even know I was flouting—the equivalent of 'Why are you wearing a white skirt when you know you might get your period', 'Why are you laughing when you are in a serious place?'

Why are Vallari and I so different? Why can't our backpacks only have lipstick like so many other girls? Why can't we look at ourselves through our selfie cameras, and not at birds through binoculars? Why can't we be normal?

'I was holding in my anger,' Vallari turns to me and says. 'I didn't want to make it worse.'

At Hauz Khas DDA Park in South Delhi, Vallari has been stopped many times from taking pictures of birds with her camera. She was also stopped from taking pictures in Talkatora Garden near Central Delhi, because, the guard said, they didn't want their prize-winning gardens to be copied. There are others who create content in public places—a bower of flame vine in an arch in Lodhi Gardens and the passageway next to PVR Priya in Vasant Vihar, both in South Delhi, are now well-known because they are the backdrops for hundreds of videos. But somehow, it's inconceivable that a single woman would want to capture a bird which has nothing to contribute to the selfie-makeup-photoshoot economy. It also calls into question how we treat our common areas. It is an intensely human wish to be photographed in a beautiful place. But are common areas only for staged photoshoots, and not for observation of the more natural? Should nature be commodified and made the subject of fees in public parks if the subject of attention is birds and trees?

We realize it's easier to intimidate a single woman and ask her to put a camera away, than to halt an entire crew. We have had to learn how to snap out of these unnerving incidents, then summon our curiosity and amble into the place we want to go to as if nothing had happened. I want to walk into Old Fort with the keen sense of poetic justice a misfit wants: a desire to prove themselves. Make something of the misfit's misery. To make art that speaks to others like it speaks to the artist.

We haven't even started, and we are so exhausted. It is a familiar feeling.

'Maybe,' Vallari says, 'maybe we will find lots of trees ... and birds,' she adds, knowing I prefer the latter even as she looks for the former. I am always the one fighting for her, and she's always the one comforting me. In a sense then, she is the one who fights more.

We enter the Old Fort from the Bara Darwaza, a sweeping sandstone entrance. It has all the grandeur of a really old place, displaying its obvious age, but somehow still preserved—a rose that's blown out, its petals opened to the maximum extent, just before it falls apart. I feel again the displacement one senses when one sees something truly old, like an old tree with wrinkles on its trunks—the feeling that one is suddenly in a different age, that a doorway has opened into the past, pulling you into a place you don't fully understand. A place that feels glacially distant even on a hot day, a place to be hushed in. A place where *you* aren't important, but the setting is. Emperor Akbar walked here. The arguments of those times would have sounded different, but were likely about the same things Delhi discusses now—the heat, the mosquitos, how to hold on to power, how to make alliances that outwit time, how best to spend a moment of repose, what to eat for better digestion.

Inside, we find ourselves in an unexpected park. The place is so old it is like a palace of ruins. Many of the buildings here have been worn down to beautiful, careless rubble. The Old Fort today seems more a natural space than a built space. But there are trees. Many of them. Neem and ficus surround us. We rush towards them, exclaiming at the natural grass growing in their shade. The light is sieved through their foliage. In that hushed place, we hear a blunt, tap-tap sound. Woodpeckers? I ask silently. I think my question is to the unexpected grove rather than to myself. We move through the trees, thrilled to be here at last, the events of the morning draining away from us, dispelled by the sweet smell of grass. We follow the tap-tap sound. The source of the sound is a Brown-headed barbet. Its eyes glint in the green sunlight, and its beak pecks at a perfectly round hole in the wood of a neem tree. Once the hole is ready, the barbet will raise a family in there. It has whiskers on the base of its beak, perhaps for protection from the flying filaments of wood it is tapping out.

The bird is on a tree, and we remember we are here for our tree. We sweep the area for semal, and we find none. We do find other flowers though. A medium-sized tree grows close by, with glossy leaves reminiscent of olive trees. A scent envelops us as we go closer. That scent becomes a signpost: it's like there's a Persian rug under our feet, asking us to tread a particular floral path on it, but with due respect. We walk closer and the source of the fragrance are clusters of pearlescent white flowers, some hanging close to our faces. This is a murraya tree, also called kamini, and its flower petals are unusual, like the ends are stitched back, the flower frozen in a charming half-open, half-closed state. Their scent is that of a spicy lime. This could be what low-hanging fruit best alludes to: flowers that nod near your face, flowers you can bury your face in, that you can enjoy without plucking. How old is the rootstock here? We know that hundreds of years ago, the Mughals enjoyed their gardens and planted trees to perfume their steps. They understood that beauty too was a kind of power. Did they plant murraya trees? Is this tree a remnant of Mughal gardens?

In the places where the grass has spidered into wild clumps, ink-bright splotches of perfect, tiny flowers peek through. These are shankhapushpi.[2] We are taking in the mosaic in front of us—white flowers, ink blue flowers, patches of porcelain blue sky through the green-gold sunlight. And just then, between a distant gap in the trees, we see a flash of red. Red flowers on the ground, so bright they could be singing their own song. Semal? We rush in that direction, crossing more shankhapushpi flowers, wanting to tumble in the grass. We find a resplendent semal tree, tall, covered in dense colour. It stands quietly in between the neem trees. It's like looking at a bridal dress draped for the benefit of just the birds—a red dupatta on the ground, a billowing red skirt on the body. As we look at the branches, we spot movement high above our heads behind the tree. On the walls of the fort, two boys are walking. And behind the wall, more of what we came for—a line of lush reds and oranges. Semal trees also grow behind the Old Fort wall. Our hearts leap. We know what we must do.

This isn't a monument with fixed selfie points, or 'must-visit' places. Most of it is in ruins, and so it has become something else. It is an in-between place. A place to amble in, a place to dream in, to remember in, to forget in. There are people here just sitting on the grass under the trees, a few more looking at a portion of a tumbled wall. I get the sense that people come here more to spend time with each other—and with the old stone and trees of the place—than anything else. Somehow this seems more meaningful than taking a picture and rushing off to the next tourist attraction. We go closer to the wall the boys are walking on. We realize it is a rampart. There is a way to climb up, and the top is broad and lined with stones. We want to go closer: after all, the walls and ramparts are the very purpose of a fort. They keep things in, and they kept the enemy out. Behind the impressive rampart, the semal trees grow, in a patch of land between the fort and a busy road. Beyond the road, there are the gates of Bharat Mandapam, the erstwhile Pragati Maidan, a sprawling exhibition and conference complex.

We climb up the rampart. Thanks to its height, the semal flowers are now at face-level with us. It's like the murrayas, only better. This is a unique experience, one that is often not possible with the semal which grows as tall as a four-storey house. Right now, we have a ringside view. On the red and orange blossoms, birds frolic. A Pied myna, in its black and white tux, drinks nectar from an orange flower. Brown-headed barbets dart from one flower to the other, as if they are in a hotel, going from room to restaurant. Rose-ringed parakeets and Common mynas descend on the flowers, the former doing acrobatics of hanging upside down, while the latter fix a mean eye on any other bird that dares come too close.

It is a bird's-eye view, and it is also an unusual one. The birds are completely relaxed on the trees. Perhaps because there is a sheer drop between the rampart and the trees, they know they won't be disturbed. They are behaving like nesting Baya weavers do at the edge of Delhi. Those birds pick thorny trees near wetlands to build entire apartment complexes—each male will make many nests. The wetlands protect them from intruders, and they seem relaxed and happily focused on nest-building rather than their security. Here on the rampart, I realize that the birds wouldn't have the same ease if they were closer to the main road. On the road, cars whizz past in a molten stream. Beyond that is the sooty ITO, consistently one of the most polluted places in Delhi. Looking at the main road, with the warm fort rocks next to us, it seems as if the semal is creating a moat. Instead of crocodiles in the moat like older times, there are flowers. The moat itself is a safe place for the birds, but it also keeps the bad things out from the fort. It is a buffer for noise and dust pollution and encroachment. And what a photogenic buffer it is. It filters against the polluting enemy and it keeps in what is a sight for sore eyes—Indian trees flowering and passing their benedictions to the rest of the world. In this old place, we have found a tale for the times: trees always have been, and always will be, our fortresses.

'I'm so glad we came here,' Vallari says. 'I'd never have come up here without you.' I don't answer. I wouldn't be here without her, either.

Sewage and Semal

The next old monument we go to for our semal search is Humayun's Tomb. This is a beautiful structure not far from the Old Fort, and is less dilapidated. It stands opposite the Sundar Nursery and is always overflowing with tourists. It is less a place for drifting daydreams and more a place of heavy activity. If your dreams can survive the interruptions of tourists and traffic, then you can dream here. Vallari has been observing semal trees inside the complex for her research here for many years. She smiles as she tells me about it, and I think this is the Delhi she wants. One with monuments that are tenderly protected by trees: trees that are seen as useful, as heritage, as the forts that buttress our lives. And so, we decide to visit Humayun's Tomb.

When I usually enter monument complexes in India, I am always interested in the side structures. The main monument is well covered, appearing in glossies and selfies, but the overlooked side monuments have interesting details and their very own character. As we enter the complex of Humayun's Tomb, we go towards the right. It is early morning. The light is melted butter. A gentle glow nourishes the area, and dust particles dance in sunbeams. The place is private, oasis-like. It seems like it has heard a hundred stories and kept them well-preserved, locked in symmetrical old walls: A story for each slab of stone. The story here isn't just of the age of the monument, or the people who walked here centuries ago. It is also the stories of its wild denizens speaking their own words. Plucking a stone would be like plucking an entire story, perhaps singing its truth in a language I may not have the wisdom to understand yet.

We walk through the glowing morning, towards a semal tree that's beyond a tall, heady arch. At the feet of the tree, the grass glows, fizzing like it is made of bubbles. The light also makes the red flowers a fleshier colour, nearly translucent. The flowers look like they are part of a body, the sun shining through ears, glinting off plump cheeks.

Vallari's intern is with us too. We find a spot where we can watch the tree without disturbing the birds. No people are visible here. We love it. 'We caught the semal just in time you know,' Vallari whispers to me. 'It's at its peak flowering. Soon, it won't have so many flowers.' I realize again she talks about trees the way people talk about other people. Those who grow plants attribute agency to them. But Vallari seems to attribute something more. She attributes a kind of sentience we usually award to people.

'The trees get confused when it rains at odd times,' she says. I like plants as much as the next person, but speaking to Vallari demands more than just liking them. It demands calibrating one's brain to imagine the unconventional—that trees have schedules akin to dreamers and philosophers; that things like odd rainfall can upset them deeply. The growth of a tree is not a simple mechanistic, algorithmic process of input and output. It is a growing and stunting which is deeply intertwined with the cards they are dealt with. 'Trees feel confused as the weather patterns change. And they are individuals. One tree will flower first, another one will flower later,' she carries on. She is suggesting trees have a kind of autonomy: that while they suffer, they also push back.

In an interview, Zoë Schlanger, the author of *Light Eaters*, a book on plant intelligence, reflects on what she has learned about plants. She speaks of plants not just as individuals, but as social beings, attributing spontaneity to them: 'They [plants] do strike me as very competent, going about their lives with a certain sureness. What I didn't realize going into this was just how many decisions a plant is making at all times, how much vitality goes into their every phase, and how spontaneous and social they actually are. It brings a certain enchantment to my life now.'[3]

I watch the Humayun semal now, enchanted. I tug at the sense my mind is making of it. Something feels different about the tree. It is tall and impressive. But is it just the height that is so moving? I look again at the arms which are spread wide—and the crown of the tree in the sky feels mirrored on the ground, with its thick Persian rug of flowers. I walk this carpet in slow, deliberate paces. It takes me fifteen paces to cross the circumference. And I realize then it isn't just the height of the tree, but also its shape that is so important. The tree is growing in the shape it wants—a vaguely A-shaped sprawl, a rather plump 'A', tending more towards an 'O'. It hasn't been trimmed and tidied into some ridiculous alphabet it doesn't want to grow in. (Trees and hedges are often trimmed to look like an 'I', and that means finding the human gardener in the tree, and not the tree in the garden.)

We look at the semal like it is the only tree in Delhi, drinking in the sight and the luxury of space around it. This creature is free: it doesn't stand pinched next to a road or apologetically hemmed into a colony park. It grows as a part of the scenery in a forgotten part of a protected archaeological complex. It has no leaves, only flowers, as if it has decided leaves are too commonplace and only the silken luxury of petals will do. There are nectaring birds all over the tree, also drinking in its presence. We are lucky to gaze at a kind of heritage that stops time—the kind built by man that has trapped time and stories in its solid construction, and the living kind that uses its branches to create time and opportunities for wildlife. This tree too is a fort: It scaffolds lives, and it serves as a keystone for the birds.

Common mynas frolic in its branches, singing and ebullient. They seem fitting residents of Delhi, taking over property from others—the tree's real estate is nest holes, fought over by parakeets, mynas and hornbills. How many nest holes in private places are available for birds to nest in, in a city? I wonder if there is something of a housing crisis here. At my right, Vallari is whispering notes into her phone. Her intern writes things down furiously. There are little wet patches in the grass, gleaming like anthracite. Though the birds are singing, the place feels like it is silent and growing. A peace steals over us. It feels like a bucolic ideal.

A woodpecker calls from one side. Above our heads, a grey-brown blur sails on to the semal branches. It has a greyish body, and a faint cap on its head. If one looks through binoculars, one can tell it has a luscious set of lashes. It has a long, capable beak, and a casque on top. A Grey hornbill. And if there is one, another must follow—they are usually in pairs. Sure enough, a second hornbill arrives, flapping loudly and settling down next to the first. They share a branch like it's a loveseat. The sky is blue, the flowers are red, and it is a perfect backdrop for the Grey hornbills. The blueness is a rare sight—the skies here are usually brown, or grey, or sepia yellow. I am suffused with wonder: I want to freeze this moment and carry it with me in a snow globe.

Movement on the tree takes me out of my reverie. One of the hornbills hops towards a cluster of semal flowers. The hop is sideways and perfectly timed. The bird leaps and then lands perfectly, a ballerina with a beak. For a large bird, it is both agile and exact. I am watching a move that has clearly been performed a thousand times before. From the loveseat, the hornbill now hops to another bough, inching closer to the blossoms. It cocks its head to one side, seeming to listen to the semal. Ever so carefully, it moves its huge beak around the base of the flower it has selected. It tears off the ovary, a small bud-like portion which will later become the seed pod. It tosses it in the air, neatly catching it, now a spin bowler practising his spin before the final throw. Once caught, it rolls the little morsel, holding it gently between its mandibles. That's it, the bird's going to eat now, I grin to myself. It is very satisfying to watch wild birds eat. Sometimes you may have planted the thing they are going to eat, and sometimes you have done nothing at all. Yet, watching a bird find food is knowing that it will survive a little while longer, find the energy to raise a family, and have success in being a wild bird.

But the bird doesn't swallow. Instead, it hops over to its mate on the left, offering the morsel. I am struck by a realization. Two facts make themselves clear. First, the bird gathering the food is a male. Male hornbills will feed females to habituate them with their nesting periods in which the female is sealed into a tree hole with their chick. For weeks, that sealed-in hole, with a little postbox-opening through which the male feeds the female, is the locus of the hornbill family. We are watching a tender mating ritual: if she hasn't yet made her mind up about the male, she will likely do so now. The flower-food will seal their companionship—it isn't just sharing a plate of freshly steamed momos, it is passing it on, it is in fact, feeding her first.

I see the tree now from Vallari's eyes. It's not just a tree. It's also a destination, a refuge, a place to find food, a place for mating gifts. Its branches have fused with the birds, their inter-relationships pulsing and vibrant. It is the tree pushing back against the noise of the city, it is the tree awarding power to the birds. The tree is the platform from which the birds stage their lives. 'This is just amazing,' I whisper. The male hornbill is now finding and selecting more morsels to feed the female. The scene is achingly tender. I feel if I speak loudly, the spell will shatter. So I whisper to myself: *This is Delhi too*. Vallari and I both have our arms up, filming the scenes with cameras. We stand like that for a long time, so long that the light begins to change, from the sweet warmth of early morning to the sultriness of mid-morning. My shoulders have begun to ache, and because I pay attention to the pain, I also notice a smell beginning to bother me. It's sour, rancid, old, the smell of urine. My toes are cold, sodden, and even the sunlight can't gild the dirty wet look my perforated shoes now have. A doubt falls across my face. 'So, Vallari,' I murmur, 'what is this awful smell?'

She doesn't turn her face away from the tree. 'Oh, that,' she says, 'that's sewage water. It's lightly treated. That's why we are wearing closed shoes.' What! my mind screams at me. I want to shake her a little: why didn't she tell me I am standing in a puddle of piss? I could have picked another spot. And I might have walked over to the same one eventually, but that would have been my choice. 'You didn't tell me,' I bite out instead. Before she can respond, I have my answer. She is so engrossed in trees, everything else recedes into the background. 'We were here for two mornings in open-toed sandals. I never realized we were standing in sewage puddles. But then my car smelt a lot, and so did my feet, and I realized what had happened,' she explains, finally looking at me.

'So what did you do?'

'I went home and washed my feet, my sandals and my car mats. And the next time I wore shoes. I told my intern too. That's our Humayun's Tomb gear now. I forgot to tell you, sorry.'

She has turned her head away and is looking at the semal again. She isn't exactly absent-minded, it's just that her attention is always on trees. I can't help but smile. I am standing in some form of waste. My friend doesn't mind. The trees don't either. Neither bat an eyelid. It's just another part of life, like nutrient processing. Plants like dead things, decaying things, smelly things like mustard cake, bonemeal and old leaf litter. Stinking millipedes, like the ones from the garden of my childhood, efficiently break down detritus. Roses famously love being fed blood and chicken bones in their soil. I remember how I think of gutters when on social media. Now I really am close to sewage. To see the semal, to see myself in this strange city, to find meaning that might be incomprehensible to others, I sometimes have to go through gutters. I might as well get used to it.

The year rushes on. Summer squashes us all in an embrace which chokes. It is April 2025, and dust storms blow through the city. In the Himalayan mountains, it is cold and raining. Delhi doesn't have its own weather—it is influenced by summer desert winds from the Thar desert, and rain, hail and snow in the Himalayas. The capital gets the crumbs off the table—the afterthought of a cold downpour, the tail of a hot summer wind. Even then, these are powerful weather changes that suddenly rake through the city, changing the sky and the smell on the wind. In April 2025, there are mild showers and dust dervishes everywhere. And when we head out, the sky is a popsicle-yellow colour.

We go to Safdarjung's Tomb, not far from Humayun's Tomb. Again, instead of walking up to the main monument, we take a right. In a corner of the complex stands an old palash tree.[4] The trunk has grown almost horizontally, nearly parallel to the ground. It looks like it was touched by a god, flattened at its core, and decided henceforth to grow prostrate. We look again. There are two main trunks that cleave further as they rise. The trunks are old, mottled and weather-beaten, and somehow, they look right for that old place. Perhaps we are looking at two trees that grew apart from each other? Instead of being locked in an eternal rivalry, perhaps the trees decided to share the little space they had, and turned their bodies far apart so they could minimize competition. From another angle, the turning away appears to be a conjoining. It is like watching family members staying apart so they can, in a sense, stay together.

Looking at the old trees is an attempt to read the history of the place. Which family members came before me to enjoy the view? Who planted these palash trees in a city that still has only a handful of these? How long did it take for this slow-growing native to grow horizontally and then reach for the sky? Who had the foresight to think decades into the future? Because that is the very business of seeds: it is bringing the future into the present.

The sun is about to set in the yellow sky. The star itself is a candy-orange disk, huge, flaming, alive. It is the exact colour of the palash blossom on the trees. Palash petals, orange and burning, are so vivid that the UK-based Royal Horticultural Society gave them their own adjective: 'Indian-orange'. The light slants, and in a blink, it is now golden hour. Everyone is taking pictures of the sun over the tomb. We are taking pictures of the golden hour on the palash tree. We know the birds will come soon, as the heat abates. The first to arrive are a pair of green Rose-ringed Parakeets. The male has a ring, black in parts, pink in parts, around his neck. The female has an unmarked neck. Both have bright, semal-red beaks. They squawk as they hop on branches, after landing in a whoosh. Golden light washes over them; their beaks now a gentle orange, and the flowers touched into a mellow gold rather than flaming fire. The female parakeet settles in. She cranes her head forward and tears into the flowers, ripping the petals to shreds. The male sits above her, cocking his head, looking around him with a serious aspect. They look like the perfect Delhi couple—she doing something she relishes, he holding space for her, fixing his eye on potential threats.

It is believed that parakeets do not pollinate the palash. The flower itself is a complex, fierce structure. It has wings on two sides, a standard petal, a keel (that contains pollen and nectar), and a cup-like calyx. The keel appears like an Indian-orange claw, with ornamentations to the side. Parakeets have beaks which are curved. In order to open the keel, perhaps what is needed is a long dagger, rather than the plier-like curve of the parakeet's beak. Observed true pollinators of the palash are three-striped palm squirrels and sunbirds, both of which take the time to open up the flower gently; but there could be exceptions here too.[5] The parakeet is all passionate, tearing motion; they are birds that land in a flurry and are always in a hurry. But while they may or may not be pollinating palash blossoms, the claw-like petal nevertheless reminds people of the beak of a parakeet. Thus, the other moniker for the tree is the parrot tree. In the way that local names can be more colourful, more bursting with information than formal names are, I let the name softly settle over me while blinking at the flowers.

As I pay attention, I feel more names rise in my understanding. The female is done with a few of the flowers, and she jump-flies to another branch above her. She is electrified with urgency. It is clear that she has many flowers to rip and many cups of nectar to drink from. Looking at the birds in the last light of the day, I can imagine 'parakeet' to be not just a name, but a type of being, a verb rather than a noun. To 'parakeet' through life would mean to face life with a defiant squawk and eliminate threats through the sheer force of frolic. The female jumps again, now perched at the edge of the branch. The branch sways. A flower falls, joining others that are carpeting the ground. I look down. The ground is a mélange of orange blending together. There's burnt orange from dried palash flowers, a fresh, juicy orange from the blooms that fell this hour, a desiccated brown from the ones which have lain in the sun for a few days. The colours are a whirl of time travel: yesterday, today and the week that was in one place. I take a step forward. The dried flowers crunch under my feet. It's like I am stepping on Indian-orange chips.

Then I remember that the palash loves heat. Instead of mourning the fried flowers, I should rejoice in them. The tree is exactly where should be. Colouring a historic building with fire in all its forms—leaping flames, single candles flickering in the wind, banked embers. The flower litter on the ground seems true to the monument, because when the tomb was made, there would have been more native Aravalli trees around it. Perhaps not far from the same site, another palash stood. Preserving native trees, those indigenous, stubborn beings that can withstand furies that come from deserts, frost and the force of parakeets, is also preserving historic authenticity. In their own way, native trees parakeet their way through life too, with flashes of tenacity that morph into elegance a little later in life.

The sun slips a little lower and rolls behind the tomb's dome. There's a hornbill in a tree behind the palash, and he is nudging at what look like small clusters of fruit.

I look through my camera. I can hardly believe it. The hornbill is pecking an iconic tree that grows in the jungles of Central India, the mahua. Here, it is a lone tree, and it is laden with flowers. By now, the bird has snapped up one of the flowers. It disappears down its beak. It takes a second one, the sphere-like flower looking ridiculously small in its big bill. It tosses its prize into the air, but slips. It lunges at the flower again, its head a slashing movement, but the flower falls out of its beak's grasp and tumbles to the ground.

The mahua is an Indian forest tree. Nearly everything in the jungle loves its sweet flowers. Elephants get intoxicated on fermented mahua blooms. Birds and bears love eating the blossoms. So do people, as chutneys and liquor. I have seen mahua trees standing tall in the forest, the leaves oblong and clustered, striking in their simple beauty. The mahua tree is tall and grand, but its flowers are its real bounty. In Madhya Pradesh, I have relished dried mahua flowers, as browned as the dried palash. I have drunk mahua liquor, unable to see its true colour in the night. But I've never eaten the flower fresh from the tree, foraged by my own hands.

I look up at the tree again. As always, one Indian tree has led me to another, a bread crumb trail full of rewards. There are three Yellow-footed green pigeons on the mahua now, and they are gobbling down the bounty. One pigeon opens its beak wide to stuff the flower in, frenzied, anyhow. It hardly fits, but the bird swallows. I can almost hear it gulp. Instantly, it moves to another flower, then another. I make up my mind. 'Let's gather some mahua,' I tell Vallari.

We walk to the tree and look at the ground, rich with the cream flowers. I angle my body and pick up just one blossom from a particular spot. 'I bet this is the one dropped by the hornbill,' I grin. We look at the forage and see it is circular, with something coming out of it. This appendage is a pistil—because my forage is flower, not fruit. I pull at it, and the pistil comes out smoothly, satisfyingly. The snack is ready, I decide. I pop the mahua in my mouth and begin to chew, imagining myself to be a deer, or a little girl competing with Shakuntala to crush, eat, swallow first. The flower is chewy. I try to comprehend its taste. Perhaps it's a little nutty, perhaps a little vanilla. It's sweet, almost shockingly so. For adults who don't eat sugar, it is a hearkening to childhood, to sugar and butter rolled into rotis, to fingers made sticky with birthday cake ganache, friendship in balconies in summer. It tastes of sunshine. And because it takes a second to hit my taste buds, it tastes of patience. I realize then that I am tasting honey made solid. I grin beatifically with a sugar high, feeling like a lumbering bear who got her prize.

Vallari tells me she knows of other mahua trees and we should go and observe them. We go near Lodhi Gardens, to a street full of mahuas. I hear a loud squawk, then another, impatient knocks on doors: rat a tat tat. I know I will observe more parakeeting. The bird reveals itself to be the Alexandrine parakeet, bigger and rarer than the Rose-ringed parakeet. He is on the mahua tree, his head looking overlarge, eyes shining with mischief. He grips a mahua flower in his beak, and then in his foot. Unlike the green pigeon, he doesn't immediately swallow. Instead, he takes gentle bites, with all the delicacy of an aristocrat using a flat fish knife.

The light is almost gone by now, the golden hour getting smudged into greys.

Something flaps up to the mahua in front of us. The wings move slowly, deliberately, liquid in their motion. For a second, it's like watching stingrays doing a ballet in the ocean. Then I notice what looks like a claw at the peak of each wing. The flying creatures are not birds. They are bats, flying foxes.[6] The 'claws' are thumbs, and its fingers vein its wings. The bat lands on the tree, and I imagine a thumping as its heavy body makes arboreal contact. It hangs smoothly, suspended upside down. I look closer: it is a male. He moves towards a clump of mahua flowers, an upside-down walk on a tree-highway. Then his puppy-like face goes forward, bagging a flower. He swallows. He must like what he ate, because he immediately goes towards more. He appears to know this is a once-a-year bounty. As I watch, he pauses and seems to think. A car shoots away on the road under the tree. The bat extends a wing out, and then neatly pulls it back towards its body. He repeats this in smooth motions. He is hot, and so he is fanning himself, and the action is nonchalant, a moving accordion pleat. It's incredibly endearing, like a puppy panting or a bird shaking water out of its face. It seems so far removed from the monstrous lore around bats that rose during the Covid pandemic. We don't know what really caused the coronavirus, but one kind of bat was blamed. And thus, all kinds of bats were blamed too. In many places in India, trees which functioned as old bat roosts were burned. In residential colonies, people made hunting packs to prod, burn or kill bats whenever there were rumours of bat activity. Bats were chased out of their hiding places, and they fluttered into the sky, the sunlight and shouts a rude shock. It was like everyone's rage had turned towards a subspecies that weren't even responsible for Covid. They were burning not bats, but the proverbial witch, the 'idea' of a bad thing, the totem of grief and shifted blame.

I look around at the other trees, and there are many bats. Some have paused their snacking to fan themselves. The trees look alive, full of bats and parakeets, some hopping, some fanning, some just hanging out. There are no bears or elephants in this jungle, but this is very much still a mahua party.

We look and grin, content to be party guests that stand against the wall. This is a safer part of Delhi, and no one has heckled us yet for standing at the side of the road and gazing upwards. More cars whizz past. All the trees have flowers, and by now, all the trees also have bats. The bodies of the flying foxes gleam a rich, furry auburn. The snouts are darker, like the wings. The faces are furry and the wings leathery, and it seems astonishing that they belong to the same animal. Still, the flying foxes look like their names: like foxes, or like puppies. It is immensely satisfying to watch them sample the honey-flavoured mahua again and again, to see so many bats without bloodthirsty calls from people to burn or chase them, to find that the sun slipping down is just the beginning of a new chapter for Delhi's denizens.

In this busy city, no one has noticed the animals. The sky has darkened. The bats continue their foraging and fanning. I can continue dreaming of bats. I don't have their wings or their liquid grace, but somehow, evolution brought us here: We both like tasting the honey and patience of the mahua.

NEHA'S FIELD NOTES

There is a sudden thunderstorm on 2 May 2025. By some estimates, hundreds of trees have fallen in the city. In a five-kilometre radius, I count eight fallen trees. We always forget storms after they are over, like an umbrella left in a cab once the sun is out.

On 17 May 2025, another storm chases us, felling more trees and all expectations of a calm summer. Climate change is truly upon us. Now we know: it's not just birds and bugs that trees sustain. Where do the bats go when trees fall?

The Found City

Pankaj's Delhi

Colonel Pankaj Sharma fought in the Kargil war. He came to Delhi to recover, but the city only felt his when he started recognizing its birds, some of which come from the Himalayas he patrolled in.

The year was 1988.

A young man, packed with muscle and determination, walked beyond the Chang La pass. He was swept by frigid winds, and surrounded by what looked like remote desolation, but his excitement was like a field knife in his pocket. Alert and shining. The area around him resembled a lunar surface—chequered with dry undulations, secretive, an austere and forbidding beauty. The young man was in the Army and he delighted in exploring areas beyond civilian reach. He was always accompanied with his spirit of exploration, and an endless need to stretch his legs, and so he was never alone. He also carried memories of his camera, which he had used since Class 8. The camera was a primitive affair—a 200 mm prime lens. His eyes swept the vistas in front of him, taking in the mountains, thinking of his camera and what he could do with it in this untouched, brutal place, its silent rocks and blazing sun. And as he looked, he spotted two birds. Till that point, birds were classified as colours and sizes in his mind. The options were: white, brown, black, small or big. These two birds stepped neatly out of those boxes of classification with their long, long legs, and perfect confidence. They were tall and white, with a red forehead, black neck and a back ending in a tapering, feathery mop. They looked like no other bird he had seen before, and they had a pride in their bearing. A fierce feeling of belonging to that wild set of mountains.

Who were these birds? Pankaj Sharma had no idea, but he needed to know. He asked acquaintances and they told him the birds were those of legend. Siberian cranes. Siberians, or Sibes as they were often called, were rare birds that visited India for just a few months in the year. They came from far, from cold countries in the North, lands of ice and wonder. With their snowy necks and red faces, they were memorable to look at. And they were always few in number—like rare Himalayan blue poppies to the more prescient wild daises. The birds would come to India from Iran, winging over a flyway that had so much hunting pressure that it felt like a black hole. They were proud, territorial birds, and their annual arrival gave them a near mythical status amongst those who knew birds. By the 2000s, cranes were extinct in India; but for a few decades, seeing a wintering crane in India could mean chancing upon the Siberian crane. Pankaj didn't know for sure what he had seen but was going to find out.

The birds pranced near a lake, which was almost fully frozen over. He spotted two pairs. They would cavort next to each other like in a dance, and they also seemed to enjoy the place with a deep seriousness. Pankaj felt they were calling him. That night, he wrote a letter to his brother. He wanted his camera sent to him, as soon as possible. In the end, it was not the breathtaking landscape, but the mysterious birds that took him back to his beloved, heavy camera. After a long wait, the device arrived. He triumphantly took pictures of the birds, knowing he was creating some kind of art, slow-moving, the sort that took time. He knew he would need to wait some time before he could see the birds on film. He'd need to take leave, travel to a city and develop the photo reel. He stopped in Delhi for a day just to develop the photos.

When the photos were ready, the birds could be studied more closely. In the end, they turned out to be Black-necked cranes, not Siberian cranes. But even getting a bird name wrong is the beginning of something. *The name of this bird is 'my bird'*. It is the start of a hungering curiosity, so sharp it cuts through the clutter of life. It is the start of wanting to look for an ancient bird which has stories, even rumours, shimmering around it. And it is the start of noticing specifics—the bold behaviour of a high-altitude species, strutting where most other birds of the world seemed to cower. Pankaj never forgot those big birds, which had so neatly broken the boxes of 'white, brown, black, small or big'.

A few days later, he was told he would be a liaison officer for a motley bunch of people. In the group were two wildlife photographers who also wrote children's books. Their names were Rajesh and Naresh Bedi. They had a German visitor with them, and they intended to explore the area for wild birds and animals. Pankaj was happy to be able to explore some more. 'But what will you see there? There are no animals to see!' he told the Bedis. Nevertheless, he could now take out a huge vehicle, a field car that looked like a classic Jeep, a burly four-by-four which would give wings to his dreams to explore not just widely but deeply. The Bedis didn't say much, only asking him to trust them. And within a few days, Pankaj saw more birds than he had ever seen in his life. Between the peaks and that lingering feeling of barrenness was a fecund land just waiting for the right pairs of eyes. They spotted Horned larks, Alpine swifts, Snow pigeons, Snowcocks, and hundreds of Chukar and Tibetan partridges. Until now, Pankaj had thought the Snowcock was just a sort of mountain pigeon. Now, he had a name for it, and a realization—there were birds even in the most remote, naked-looking places. And they were not all the same. There were also mountain mammals, running through a life of freedom and space, naturally found in restricted, high-altitude areas. These were kiangs, ibex and musk deer.

'The Bedis showed me these creatures which the normal eyes don't see,' Pankaj remembers. Now his eyes had opened. He decided then: each time he explored the fantastic, isolated places the Army posted him in, he would look for birds. It seemed amazing that the sensitive, strained border areas could also have another facet to them—as habitat for wild birds, the very epitome of sovereignty and abandon. He began volunteering for patrols so he could cover vast distances. In 1990, he patrolled from Shimla to Leh and explored Hanle and adjoining places.

On a long-range patrol in Spiti in Himachal Pradesh, the troops crossed the mountains beginning from the Chumathang hot water spring. In the stony soil, they had pitched 'pub tents'. These are tiny tents for two men each, and rise about two feet high. The men ate from heated ready-to-eat rations. One morning, Pankaj crawled out of his tent to look around him. Near the leftovers, just forty metres away, something crouched silently. She had a bushy tail, and a still posture of absolute, muscled power. She was a snow leopard, the ghost of the mountains. Near her, a small cub crouched. That day, Pankaj didn't have his camera. The bag he carried was already 28 kilograms, and the camera would have weighed a few kilos more.

But he had learned to look by now, and the image was unforgettable: a mother with her young pressed against the ground, her power coiled and awe-inspiring. It was almost like the leopard family had chosen to show itself. Their jagged wild beauty, their large eyes, and their coats like rocks, pressed upon him, marking him. 'I saw them because they were near us, and in the open,' he says. 'If they weren't so close, I wouldn't even have recognized them.'

In the 1990s, tensions between India and Pakistan rose. In 1999, the Kargil war between the two countries began. For the Indian middle class that had seen peace for a long time, this was the first real brush with the horrors of battle. Many Army people were asked to serve. Pankaj was called too. In the battle that followed, several of his friends died. Till today, in between his bird posts, he posts memories of soldiers who have passed away. 'Lest we forget' say all the posts—a song against the brutal extinction of memory. Don't let the soldier die in vain. Or, if one understands the deeper message—don't forget the things of value. Cherish life. Don't let the bird go extinct.

The war left its toll on his generation of fighters. Places marked by battle scarcely get remembered as anything but violent places. Kargil would always be the place of battle, and the place where his friends fell. Where two bullets lodged into his own body.

It was 2000. This was a time of recovery after the war. Pankaj was now posted in Delhi. He stayed in the Delhi cantonment, in a lovely house next to the Manekshaw

Centre, ensconced in an open and quiet defence enclave warded by tall trees. As he watered his plants every morning, he would notice an orange and black bird, its head perky and with stripes on its body. Every day, the bird would move through his lawn. It had eyes that blazed with interest at the world around it, and a motion that was an electric bolt through the grass. As he watered the lawn, worms would emerge from the soil, wriggling with mad desperation and exposure. And the hoopoes would be there, waiting to stab the worms with their beaks. As they plunged their heads down, the crests on their heads would open, bright as exclamation marks. Pankaj would look around and see a fence of exclamation points—three to four hoopoes hunting each day, their opening crests giving away their kills. It was a daily rhythm between man and bird, one each party understood well. It was like the birds had followed him, from the bare windswept mountains to a lush, domestic lawn.

Twenty-two years have passed. It is winter of the year 2022. Pankaj and I walk through the wetlands of Chandu-Budhera,[1] on paddy fields next to a highway. We are looking for migratory birds. In a way, the actual setting doesn't matter. We are fast friends and we go to a lot of places together—inside a national park, to a wetland no one has named yet, to the slopes of Aravalli hills which are still unexplored. I have picked up some of his military jargon. Chandu, the place where we are standing in, is an interesting complex—there is a water treatment plant here, with large enclosures of water. There are fields that sow paddy and gram, and these merge seamlessly with the larger tapestry of the tanks. A few minutes of bird flight takes one to Sultanpur National Park, a sanctuary with both wetlands and wooded areas. To the birds, it must seem like a soggy wonderland.

When I first went to Chandu with Pankaj in winter, we watched a bunch of black birds with silver beaks swimming electrified from one end of the wetland to the other. They flapped their wings and moved their legs, fast, very fast. Both motions together confused the eye. It wasn't the speed employed for feeding, I realized. It was the speed that comes from fear. The scared birds were coots. Above them, turning in a lazy, assured circle, was a bird of prey. It wasn't a very large bird—smaller than an eagle. But its head remained trained on the fowl below, its gaze cool and unforgiving. I saw it complete a circle, and then bend to circle again, wider this time. As I watched I saw that it had dipped lower on its second circle, the birds below still splashing in pure terror. 'That's an Eastern marsh harrier doing a reconnaissance survey,' Pankaj said calmly. For a second, the coots were earthworms and the harrier was a hoopoe—both with the ageless strength of the bird that hunts, haunting its prey even if the strike isn't successful. The haunting hangs over the wetland even after the harrier flies off, an unforgettable memory for the rest of the year. The Eastern marsh harrier migrates to India from colder places in winter. It is thrilling that it chooses the outskirts of Delhi each year,[2] slicing through our apathy and pollution, to feast on our fowl.

We watched the harrier harrying its prey, becoming a verb from a noun. A Ruddy crake called loudly from the reeds below. It was in a patch of sunshine in the foreground of the coots, and light was burnishing it into a rich burnt-orange colour. The crake remained completely still, even as the harrier drew circles in the sky, faster and faster. I felt the circles grow tighter, becoming a gyre. The raptor dived. The coots screamed. The crake flinched. There was a splash of water—or many splashes of water—as scores of fowl attempted to angle away from their current position and change their destiny. The harrier had harried—and it rose in the sky again. Its talons were empty. The coots had found safety in their numbers. They moved as a mass together, confusing the eye, looking like an underwater grey-black shoal of lightning-quick fish, or a gelatinous mass with no beginning and end. This time, the harrier had missed. The coots had lived to see another day, their bodies not yet lethargic, buoyed by the fear of being harried. In a way the reconnaissance survey, as Pankaj called it, was successful. The prey was there for the taking for a predator that was skilled enough.

And there were more migratory birds to see in this place of life and death. We went in a set of circles—perhaps mimicking the harrier, roving in the area and forging deeper into the fields. Mist hung over the green-brown fields, looking a little like clouds. There was a pair of Sarus cranes ahead of us. But Pankaj's eyes were trained much further. In the distance, partly obscured by a mist, were the large, graceful figures of more cranes. There were ten of them. Were they Sarus? Or could they be the smallest of all cranes—the Demoiselle cranes, who barely stopped in Delhi? The birds had a dirty grey body and a graceful, tapering end. At once I was reminded of Black-necked cranes, stately and sacred, which I had recently seen in Phobjika valley in Bhutan. But Black-necked cranes—both from my Bhutanese memory and Pankaj's Himalayan one—are prancing and confident. These cranes seemed to quiver with nervousness, their necks sinuous, their eyes angled towards us, watching every step we took.

The fog was everywhere around us, the sun long gone. We had all dropped like stones to our knees, watching quietly. Pankaj's voice broke the silence. 'We will leapfrog,' he said.

'What?' I asked, not understanding.

These are shy cranes, he explained. 'We will go forward slowly, leapfrogging, covering one portion at one time. Then, we rest. Then we move forward again in formation. Slowly.'

I understood. He was using his military learnings to cause the least disturbance to the avian visitors. We leapfrogged ahead. The ground was so cold we could feel it through our thick hiking shoes.

As we crept forward, the details became clearer. The birds were dirty white. Their heads were touched with jewel-red. They were about four feet tall, and they stepped on the chilled ground with no discomfort. For a second, they could have been the Black-necked cranes of snowy places. But these appeared more flighty, their bodies shot through both with wariness and beauty. It was like they would become water and run through the furrows of the field if we disturbed them. 'Common cranes,' Pankaj whispered.

The world stilled. This was amazing. Unlike what their name suggests, Common cranes are not commonly seen in many parts of India. They sometimes visit Delhi on their migration ostensibly from Russia and Siberia towards the Western parts of India. Like Black-necked cranes, these are mostly cranes of colder climes. And unlike the Sarus, which are resident birds of India, and have learned to tolerate people, Common cranes will not easily allow you to go close.

Not far from us, a Greater short-toed lark—a small bird that is roughly the size of a crane's face—flitted over the field. Like the crane, this too is a migratory bird, and this individual had decided to stop on our particular patch of mud. Larks can look something like a house sparrow, but have an alert, upright posture. As I watched, the bird nabbed an insect. Ahead of it, a White wagtail alighted on a thorny acacia bush. And a Siberian stonechat called from a nearby bush of spiky, silver-flowered *Celosia argentea*.

When I looked down, I saw the ground was grooved by little tracks—the footprints of birds. Our muddy trenches, cold but imprinted, became a place—a place of meaning for both the migratory birds and for us.

I breathed in deeply, wanting to inhale the mud, the richness of its visitors. 'There are more birds here. We should wait,' Pankaj said. He has a bird-sense that has aided him for over two decades. We waited.

We looked further into the fields with their brown-yellow grass, some with a fine sheen of frosty dew. A couple of young Nilgai bulls stepped into view. Like the Common cranes, they were sure-footed, never slipping, their hooves grey, with white bands above them, falling like chatter over the earth. This part of the fields were partially submerged, water suffusing undulations and flowing in streams. Something moved in a little stream. It was alone. It had long legs and a crest that swept behind its head in a sweeping calligraphy flourish. I looked through my binoculars. The bird's body had a patch which was a giddy, indescribable colour—iridescent, with metallic hues of green, gold and wine, an exposed camera film. It was reminiscent of peacock tails, Purple sunbird necks and Glossy ibises. This was the Peewit, a bird that breeds in Europe. The Peewit or Northern lapwing isn't commonly seen in Delhi and its surroundings. I had a little cry packed inside me—I wanted to shout for joy but made do with a silent squeak. Seeing a rare bird in the wild is wonderful. And it can also be an exercise in restraint. Your excitement prickles you, and it becomes tiny thorns that push down into your soft points, your vulnerabilities. You are uncomfortable, and scared of messing it up. Surely when you move you will be clumsy and startle the bird. You want to do so much all at once, but you must calibrate your movements and limit your excitement. You want to take a photo, but the light is fitful. A cloud suddenly covers the sun. You want to see what the bird is carrying in its mouth, but a branch comes in the way. You look some more, and another bird crosses your line of vision, like it's competing in a race and the finish line is to obstruct your view.

Your heart races, and your hands shake, and so the shots are blurry. By the time you are done practising mind-over-matter, the object of your affection may have disappeared, not to be seen again that day. Like many others, I've had rainfall breaking over my head the moment I actually found a Rufous woodpecker after following its tapping in a forest in Assam, have had leeches bite into me the moment I locked my camera on an impossibly swift Himalayan treecreeper in Uttarakhand. I've left bloody trails in the forest, and got no observation or photo to show for it. So while I watched my first Delhi Peewit in the mud, I tried (in vain) to still my heart's beating. Pankaj's voice broke my thoughts. 'This is the Northern lapwing. We can go a little closer, it won't fly away.' I looked at him—he had the sense that we would find unusual birds, if only we went a little further, if only we did the labour of exploration. If only we surrendered fully.

I decided to surrender. I went forward, and dropped to my knees so I could stabilize myself and watch. As we looked, the Peewit ran over the stream of water. It was very fast, fire catching over kindling. It seemed like a young bird. But it also felt very old. Its coming to Delhi-NCR was reminiscent of old passageways that birds have taken for migration over centuries. The fields felt richer with this tread of international visitors, and I wondered how long this would be viewed as a form of wealth. I wouldn't be surprised to see the Peewit in the UK, where it bred, and where I had lived and studied. But I was surprised, and overjoyed, to see it in the outskirts of Delhi, so far from its natal home, and so far from one's expectations. I wanted to say the bird was courageous and a warrior, but the Peewit was just living its life, with a casual elegance that asked for no labels.

The cold swept over me again and I felt madly, intensely alive. I realized then, in that muddy place: the map of Delhi was being drawn by birds, some of them locals, and some immigrants from far shores.

In 2005, not far from where we were in 2022, Pankaj had gone for his usual solo explorations which he described as 'small scale operations'. He had newly come back to Delhi, and he was headed to Basai, a wetland close to Chandu and Sultanpur. As he turned down a dirt track from the main road, he could hear a lot of sounds. 'I couldn't understand what these sounds were,' he says. He walked on towards the wetland, and then stopped short, entranced. Thousands of whitish geese filled every inch of the water and the ground. They were calling and interacting with each other in the loud, boisterous way geese have. But these were no ordinary geese. Bar-headed geese migrate to India to spend their winters here. They come from Central Asia, China and Tibet, and on the way they pass the Himalayas. To cross the world's tallest mountain range, they have to not just fly high but also endure the freezing cold. To do this, they slow down their heart rate. Their blood chills over to maintain a state called hypoxia. This reduces the amount of oxygen they require to fly in thin, oxygen-scant air nearly nine kilometres above sea level.

Also coming from cold, oxygen-thin areas, Pankaj had seen what the geese had seen, and had breathed the same thin air. And it buoyed his heart to see them land safely, and raucously, in Delhi-NCR. It was like a bit of the mountains had arrived. He stepped forward. The geese didn't mind. 'I walked amongst them, I was ten metres away from them. They didn't fly. I was standing in between so many champions of long-distance flights,' he says. He began counting, and he estimates there were 10,000 Bar-headed geese at Basai that day. It was an astonishing number. But it was happening.

He visited Basai more often after that, waiting for hours on end to see different kinds of birds. The area had stretches of shallow water and bushels of reeds. Parked near the reeds, he would wait for birds to show themselves. There were Streaked weavers and Black-breasted weavers, and Tricoloured and Red munias. One day in 2005, a long wait revealed a new bird. It was the Smoky warbler, about half a foot from the ground.

It is 2022. Then 2023. And then 2024. Basai is unrecognizable. The road is a busy highway now, whizzing with fast-moving cars. The horizon is full of high-rises—twenty-five storeys high. One would think wetlands, holding tens of thousands of birds, should be treated as natural spaces, inviolate and precious. Instead, a construction waste and demolition plant came up right next to Basai. Though the plant turns waste to wealth, it also does so on a wetland whose inherent value is jeopardized by hills of rubble. Now, there are hardly any Bar-headed geese to be seen in Basai. Smaller birds call from the reeds. We go through Chandu and the Sultanpur flats with a sobering thought. How long can these special places stay the way they are, as close as they are to the national capital?

The flats, the buildings, are rising, and the real flats—the stretches of unhindered ground where birds can run free—are getting carpeted with concrete. But before the slow creeping of a certain kind of development that erases all traces of history, there is Pankaj's own memory.

He has mental postcards of places in NCR which are new words for many others. In 2015, he found birds in the dusty village of Munda Khera in Haryana. He visited during an odd time of the year, during the November rains. A gentle shower pattered. The village had several small ponds to receive the rains. Belying the size of the ponds were the large numbers of visiting birds—pelicans, reef egrets and herons. He found twenty-five to thirty Grey pelicans there. A particular banyan tree was flush with waterfowl—it housed nakta, Knob-billed ducks, and Lesser whistling ducks.

On another day of exploration, he went to Haryana's Khawaspur village with a friend. The sky was a sapphire blue. In it, two birds of prey were sallying. These were razor-sharp, arrow-fast Red-necked falcons, beautiful birds of prey with wicked speed. And on the ground, were innocuous-looking mounds of mud. Something moved, sprinkling dirt like flour. Spotted owlets sat on the mounds, blinking at him. These owlets have large, round yellow eyes. When they look straight at you, with eyes set in the way a human's are placed—in the front of faces rather than sides—it is like you are being interrogated. Seven yellow pairs of eyes looked at him, sweeping him with their gaze. They were at eye-level with him, unusual for a shy owlet. Usually, one sees owlets high up—in the boles of trees, in a hole in the wall, on a perch that is camouflaged.

So this is what makes Pankaj's memories—a bargad tree, indistinguishable from its ducks, mounds of mud with curious owls, small, secret village pools that exist without names. It is the kind of real estate Delhi-NCR is loath to consider. This is housing for the more-than-human, recognized by glad wings which don't speak to us.

Or maybe they do.

Pankaj explores with a kind of intuition that has come from decades of listening and observation. In 2015, he went to Mangar village on a hunch.[3] He had a friend with him. They walked around in a wood with the original trees of the Aravallis—kaim, dhau, papdi, kair. They ambled, listening carefully to bird sounds. A little later they were rewarded with the sound of clear whistles. Pe-pe-pe-pe-twe-twe. It was the Black-headed cuckooshrike. This was assumed to be Delhi's first sighting of the bird. Pankaj was overjoyed. The birds were there. One just had to look, listen, and pay attention.

'The next day I felt I should go there again,' he says. And he went, by himself. He found the Asian brown flycatcher, an uncommon bird for Delhi.

It is now summer of 2024 and we are not far from Mangar. Rain is falling, and in a break between the showers, we have decided to enter the dripping forest. This is the hottest, most humid season in Delhi. But it is also a special time for birders. Leaves are saturated with moisture. Heart-shaped giloy vines climb up trees, while other vines hang down from them. The hard earth is showing a little bit of softness. Saplings sprout forward with a gladness of life, their frenzied energy chanting 'we want to live, we want to live'. Everything is growing. Behind us a rocky hill rises, an Aravalli slope covered in kikar trees. We are looking at the world through bird memories. We once saw a Short-toed snake eagle in the sky here. We saw a Paradise flycatcher, the male in cinnamon morph, flying through the trees, his long tail streamers like gentle ocean waves. We found a fantail flycatcher, looking for a nesting place. And we found an Indian pitta, in Delhi from Southern India, gathering nesting material.

It seems amazing to me that birds come from other states to nest in Delhi-NCR. Of all places—dusty, sweating, struggling Delhi, which feels more like an armpit than an embrace; that feels like it's trying to stuff its new girth into trousers from the tenth standard.

As we walk, we hear birdcalls. There is no waiting in the monsoon—birds come out as soon as the rains pause. On the left: a flurry of movement, silver-white, moon-lined; it is an Indian paradise flycatcher in a white morph. A moment later, a flourish on the right: this time, it's an Indian paradise flycatcher in cinnamon colours. There will be more, Pankaj says, I better get my tripod. He walks away in clipped strides and returns with his heavy camera and gear.

We decide to circle the area, again copying the Marsh harrier. We see birds flying through the thick, saturated foliage. They alight on trees, and we lose sight of them. But there is no hurry between us. 'We will wait,' Pankaj announces. There are three of us, and each of us walks away, strolling between trees and undergrowth, looking up. Some birders can look up and down at the same time. I am not one of them. I have just heard a Golden oriole, and my neck is craned up. An acacia thorn snags my ankle, and it begins to immediately bleed. I walk forward, and mud spatters my ankle, making it burn. I have never heard Pankaj complain about physical inconveniences. He goes through heat and cold with a soldier's stoicism. I will leave my complaints at the entrance to the forest.

We have re-assembled and are now under a babool tree. It has inch-long thorns that jut out at various angles. My bird sense is tingling. I am sure if I wait, the bird will sally out and then return. Time stops in that grove of trees. The mosquitos don't. They buzz near our heads, a discordant whine as much at home in concrete jungles as in this stretch of native woods. Pankaj calls me. I step towards him. He has set up his tripod and points something out. I can't see anything but leaves where he points.

'Wait,' he whispers. 'The paradise flycatcher will come to the nest.'

'Where's the nest?'

'Look ahead at the dry branches. Keep looking till you see it.'

'And,' he hisses, 'don't go ahead. No one will go ahead. We will not disturb the bird.' He is very talkative otherwise, but while birdwatching, he says only the bare minimum, his voice lowered.

My friend Bhrigu and I are now flanking Pankaj, looking at the tree.

And then we see it. In the lower reaches of the tree, on dry, bare branches, hangs a nest. It is shaped like a cup, a half-circle, and it is deep and symmetrical. It's so beautiful that it could be a brown snowflake, the same on both sides, intricate. Over supple twigs woven densely together, the bird has looped spider silk strands. Pieces of thick paper stick to the nest, glued by the web. The image of a bird finding and taking strands from a spider's web is like imagining a surgeon at work. The overall impression is that of great artistry; it's almost like the nest is more beautiful than the bird. Just then, there comes a russet whoosh. The flycatcher arrives, it is the male and his tail is long, and his eyes are bright. He perches on the branch next to the nest. He looks around, his eyes taking in everything.

'He needs to feel safe before he goes to his nest,' Pankaj whispers.

The bird waits. Then, he decides. He has recce-ed and ensured there are no threats. So he darts into the nest. He sits there, still as a stone, his long tail like a slope, rising and falling over one side.

Sweat runs into my eyes as I take it in, the heat, the effort of the bird, its alertness, its hopes of raising a brood. In a few minutes, the female arrives. She has a crested head like a bulbul, a white front and a cinnamon back. She hops on the branch, her head bobs, and a silent understanding passes between her and her partner. He can leave now, she is here. Her feet are very small, and the branch they have clasped seems like it could snap any second. With her movement, the nest sways, a feather shivering in a ghost breeze. The birds never leave the nest alone. He and she swap places like a dance with partners taking the same spot in effortless, well-rehearsed circles.

A couple more birdwatchers arrive, and we decide to move. We can't unsee the nest now. It seems so exposed, so easy to spot. I don't share nest photos, and I feel they should be discouraged. We are not done watching the bird's behaviour, but we pack up and leave. After a few more circles of the area, we find a pitta's nest. The nest has an amazing structure. I have seen pitta nests to be regular, roughly cup-shaped structures. This one has a roof. And a balcony. It is a ball of love. A pitta sits inside it. It looks out at us, a black mask on its eyes, its gaze unflinching. It will not leave its nest. It's probably incubating eggs. It is a wonderful moment. We are so invested in feeling special due to our relations with other people, we often forget that animals too are deeply bonded, that they too go through days and nights of parenting. And before the incubation is the long process of preparation—the migration to Delhi, the search for a mate, the gathering of materials for nesting, building the architecture of the nest, the egg-laying and guarding. All of these are aspects of complete attention that each pitta puts in. Not everyone will or should see the pitta sitting in its nest through a storm, but it does so anyway. With or without our witnessing of it. It continues braving the elements, like a soldier, and it makes something good out of the struggle, like a poet. Yet, all we tend to see is the bird, and not its efforts.

We are on our last round of the area. The mosquitos whine and whine, but I am glad. The birds will have something to feed their chicks when they arrive. We find two more nests. A fantail flycatcher's, black-and-white, with its fantastic, splayed tail perking out from its nest, and a Golden oriole's. A small area with so much life, and so much nurture. A small area with lives waiting out storms and rainfall with an unabated patience.

A few days later, listening to his bird sense, Pankaj goes to the area again, as he did after his cuckooshrike discovery.

He waits quietly, in the rain, observing the nests we had found. When he goes to the Paradise flycatcher nest, he is aghast. There is a gaping hole in it. There are no birds visiting, no swap between the male and female for egg-warming duties. Nearby, the fantail flycatcher nest is also empty. Did the rain get the better of the parents? He rushes to the Golden oriole nest. There, he sees the female feeding an egg to her chicks. Turning, he makes his way back to the flycatcher nest. This time the female flycatcher is there. The Golden oriole male arrives, and he launches himself at her. She darts out of the nest to drive him off. Almost at once, the female Golden oriole swoops in, neatly picking up a flycatcher egg and flying off to her own chicks. Pankaj watches as she lowers the egg into her chicks' mouths, cracking it just as it is in their bills.

Her actions are precise, her feeding immaculate. It is beautiful, and it is brutal. 'The birds had planned diversionary strikes with military precision,' Pankaj muses.

He doesn't think the birds were copying military moves made by human soldiers. I suspect he believes birds are just as clever as we are in their contexts; that they spin nests and stories of survival as capable for their natural worlds as we do for our own.

The problems come when the two worlds collide.

The highway near Basai has exploded in size and volume of traffic. The tens of thousands of Bar-headed geese are gone. Mounds of mud—nesting sites for Blue-cheeked and Blue-tailed bee-eaters have been excavated and moved for the construction of the Western peripheral highway that circles Delhi.

'When you are younger,' he says seriously, 'you are fighting your own battles.' He pauses. 'When I became a bit older, I started watching birds. I tell others, the moment you can settle into life a bit, look at birds. They will soothe you.'

In 2023, Pankaj made the difficult decision to go back to Kargil. The wind was bitter and the place was full of memories. And yet, there were birds. He saw Chukar partridges, many Snow pigeons, and a Himalayan buzzard. Some of his friends were now gone, but the birds remained. They soothed him.

Back in the capital, the map he has made of all the birds he has seen—on the bargad tree, the choked wetland, the mounds of mud which are not there anymore—also includes a map for the future. Mud and trees are important landmarks for explorations to come. 'The birds are there. When I can't see them, it is because they have moved. I have to find them, even when they move,' he says.

I don't believe he will ever stop looking.

The Found City

Sunil's Delhi

Sunil Harsana lives near the Delhi–Haryana border and is a warrior for Mangar Bani, a sacred grove which may be the last remaining primary forest in the region.

Climbing after Covid

There is a sea of thorny, choppy green, and a serpent cuts through that sea, in smooth, grey coils. That serpent is the Faridabad–Gurgaon highway, scaly and long-reaching in its turns, glittering with mica-like pieces on it.

The snake deposits us to the sea of trees, from which we are to climb down into the belly of a mine.

The Aravallis are considered the oldest fold mountains on earth. The spines and spurs of the mountains are there for anyone who wants to see them. In front of the Vasant Kunj malls on Nelson Mandela Road, a line of rocks watch passing cars silently. Their colour is a deep, burnished brown, the brown of shisham heartwood. Some of the other rocks are paler—the whimsical white-brown of salai tree trunks. Some are pink, the colour of jungle jalebi wood. If you go along the Delhi Ridge Road, off the Hanuman temple and Pusa Road in Central Delhi, the road bucks and rears, going up and down slopes. On the right is the Ridge forest, which itself is made of rocks, hill-slopes and trees. In North Delhi, you might amble in the Northern Ridge forest, surrounded by picnicking Delhi University students, and find yourself looking at a seam of rocks you haven't seen before. In various parts of the city, the rocks girdle us, firmer and older than our concrete. Undulations exist beneath our feet, resisting the flatness and sameness of human landscaping. The Aravallis make themselves evident in ways we may or may not notice. But the miners have noticed. Radiating from parts of Delhi and around it, mines for red sand (bajri) and quartzite have scoured the land. They have left behind cavities with unconsolidated, scree-filled slopes that can collapse under a storm. Sometimes they have dug so deep they have created pits that fill with rainwater or ground water, forming lakes of slurry. Often, they have erased mountains. Ahead of Delhi, in Alwar district, the Aravallis have been cut down for dolomite and limestone. It seems silly, even laughable, to obliterate a mountain for sand and scree, to flatten an entity's very existence. It is an ironing out of a complex geological and wildlife refuge into just another piece of land that looks nothing like its history; bearing grasping, oppressive thumbprints of exploitation without end.

Today, we will go down the scrabbly belly of such a mine, down to its wet, beating heart—to Niharika lake and the remains of the area. Near the side of the highway, Sunil Harsana is waiting for us. Sunil lives next to the sacred grove of Mangar which his village protects. He will lead this walk.

Near the road, Sunil unrolls a length of paper. It is a well-thumbed map of the Aravallis, full of coloured features. A line of wetlands, including Niharika. Dots for a ridge of hills, shaded green lines for forests. About thirty people have gathered for the walk, and Sunil raises his volume to tell them that we aren't in just any other place. We are in the Aravallis, which is pulsing with life. 'I came here a few days ago to see what path we can take to Niharika lake. This lake is not easy to get to. We will walk in mined out gaddhe, in the pits. We will climb a little and go down a little. You will see what mining did to this place,' he says.

We look towards the mine. The descent is not for the faint-hearted. But Sunil isn't faint-hearted. He walks with a limp, with the help of a stick, but he walks better than me. He speaks from a place of deep thought and half-smiles—like he's holding idea-seeds inside him, just waiting for the right loam to put forth shoots. Just waiting to dig his feet a little deeper into the soil. 'But you will also see how the place can rebound, how it can come back with nature,' he announces. We set off. It's a motley group—college students, nature lovers, middle-aged walkers, and perhaps some people who don't know whether they like nature yet. The group is large because the city is limping back from Covid, and people feel the need to be outside, to live life and have daring adventures.

Above our heads, that effective invasive, vilayati kikar (*Neltuma juliflora*), blots out the sun. This was the choppy sea visible from Google earth and on the side of the highway. It's foreign kikar, with feathery leaves. Yellow thorns cut through the leaves, giving the sea of trees its roiling, disturbed look. Soon, Sunil tells us we have to climb down.

The group titters a little. 'But can you do it, can you climb down?' a middle-aged woman asks her husband. 'Of course I can! Everyone else will follow me,' he responds, almost too quickly. The couple look like they aren't used to hikes. He is wearing a red t-shirt that strains around his middle. She is wearing footwear that's closer to flimsy sandals than rugged walking gear. But women don't often get to go on long, adventurous walks that morph into light trekking. Men wear walking shoes that are both for sports and walking. Women wear sturdy sandals, not so much for playing sports, but for the game of life—walks to fetch milk and vegetables and schoolchildren. The difference between the two is that of privilege—one is a pursuit, the other a chase.

I am lucky enough to be here on a pursuit, able to focus all my attention on this neglected part of the world.

I follow Sunil. He asks us to begin clambering down. The slope is unconsolidated, full of the orange bajri sand this place was mined for. The sand looks like crumbs from a loaf of bread that was baked for too long. Sunil hesitates for only a moment. He goes down nimbly, barely looking. He doesn't use his hands to grasp the side, only his legs. A few others follow. Some prefer running down the slope and then pausing at a ridge. Others go more slowly, without stopping. I watch the middle-aged couple descend. The lady is half-sitting, going forward in a shuffle and using her palms. The man tends to run, scramble and then brake to a stop. Her face is wrinkled in acute, worried concentration; his face has a devil-may-care look that seems more than a little put-on.

I pace slowly, mentally circling the path, running it through my mind before I actually take it. My lungs are still recovering from Covid, and my breath is coming in wheezes. I have a new ragged kind of circumspection, and it teaches me that a hike or trek must be done twice—once in the mind, and then with my legs. And when going downwards, one must remember that one also has to climb back up. This is close to what recovery days are like—a set of crests and troughs, scissoring into the other, indistinguishable sometimes. I don't run, and I don't sit down. Instead, the steps in my mind are careful, trembling. There are people behind me, so I can't be too slow. I am feeling egged on, while wanting to be ponderous. The claws of long Covid inside me flex, even as I feel the push behind me growing. This is life after the disease, when we are medically okay, unremarked but still scarred; everything seem to happen before we are ready for them. In the end, I have to move because the impatience of those behind me is physical heat.

I take the first step down. Immediately, the bajri around my feet crumbles away, appearing like smoke going down the mountain. I feel I could fall—I never fell with my pre-Covid body, but now, I am not so sure. I have lost trust in my body. I need reinforcements. Anything will do really. I need to use my hands. For that, I need to give up my pride. I splay my hands out. I hold the first thing I see. The grasp is desperate. The ground moves below my feet in sandy shifts, a mini tectonic shift. My left hand is around a woody plant. The plant has small green leaves. But we are in the Aravallis and plants here survive by being tough. Between the leaves are thorns. Two thorns enter my skin, in the meaty part of my palm, neatly puncturing my overthinking. This isn't the time to ponder the lack of trust in my body. This is the time to move, with the other parts of my body: my instinct and my gut. I clench my teeth. I place my foot forward. My bleeding hand goes into the edge of the hill. Mentally, I let go. I am no longer walking steps in my mind. The next step is thrilling, but easier. Now, there is someone right behind me. I realize we can all move like a murmuration in the sky—together, complimenting each other, without bumping into each other. Or perhaps we are a caterpillar, learning to move each leg at the same pace.

We half scramble, half walk. Sand gets into my neck, hair and cuts. I have surrendered my ego. When I need to sit down and crawl, I do. When I need to stand and tiptoe around a cliffside, I do. So do the others. It feels like a kind of freedom: making our way down a hard but spongy slope anyhow, but together.

The 'way' Sunil is cutting through isn't really a way. He has come down here many times before, but the unconsolidated hill keeps shifting. Now, he is halfway down, and his head pops up. He grins. 'Wait, wait, let me make another way,' he says, watching us. He goes forward, shuffling, looking for an easier path. It's like he is talking to the hill and the hill is talking back. 'It rained, you know,' he says, serious now. 'That's why the path changed. But there's always another way.' His grin is back. We resume crawling-walking-scrambling. How does the vegetation survive on this slope? It's like the area is under tides—with a shifting baseline, a high tide attenuated to the whims of something bigger than the mountain.

At a drop of several feet, Niharika lake winks at us. It looks like a jewel, multifaceted, even though it's still and even. The water is blue and green, shining silver in places. After all the grit and sand, it's all I can do to stop myself from jumping into the lake. The water is laughing. It has a secret: the hill is alive, and the lake knows this.

People who have reached it have stopped moving. Cameras are out. Our caterpillar is nearly at a halt. Some of the freed bajri falls on the ones ahead.

'Damn, I *just* washed my hair,' a young girl wails to her friend.

My jeans have turned orange with sand. It's the kind of deep, nature-induced stain that will never come off. It's reminiscent of a leaf or wild gooseberry you eat in the forest, which leaves your tongue tingling for days on end. It's a legacy, dressed up as an inconvenience. I love my new orange jeans.

Behind the lake I see rock formations. They are black and white and covered in the patina of age. They have a complex shape, as if a giant ice cream scooper took out their chunks. It is hard to tell if these standalone formations were mined. A solitary wagtail flits between them, a cartoon mouse delighting inside a wheel of cheese. The bird is in a great hurry, and it also looks fully content to be alone. It's the first bird I have seen on this adventure and it feels like a flag post. I feel my gut taking over, strongly and irrevocably. My overthinking gets punctured for a second instance that morning, this time by a bird feather. Now, I am weightless, free to slide down the hill. I sit down. I dig the heels of my palms into the sand. It's time to make my blue-orange jeans more orange.

There are more thorns on the way, but I manage not to get cut because I am no longer holding anything but the ground. 'Be a monkey,' Sunil says helpfully. He is keeping a watch on all of us, while his friend holds up the rear. That's typically how Sunil talks—in the simplest, most direct way possible. 'When you stand up again, put your weight on the backs of your heels, not your toes. Forget what you've learned as a person. Be a monkey.'

We reach all the way down, in terrible monkey impersonations. *Ziziphus nummularia,* the jhad ber, sprouts on the slope. This is a ber plant which bears sweet fruit, and has long, slightly curved thorns. Some are like hooks, the others are a little straighter in their gleeful wickedness. This is what I cut my hands on. Other plants grow on the slope too. A young neem has beautiful, fresh whorls of leaves. Banyans clasp the side of the hill, a lover's grasp. At the beginning of this trek, my hair was in a braid, and the needle-points of thorns have wrenched my hair out. A year ago, we couldn't go anywhere; now the needling by the thorns feels therapeutic rather than malicious. I feel again that the hill is alive, like it is participating in the walk.

We are now at the bottom of the hill in our respective orange trousers. We feel an urgent need to go to the shore of the lake and touch the water. The large group quietly disperses, parting browned grass to find a corner near the shore. Vallari and I find a rock and sit down. I want to lie down, but it feels like we are inside a tongue of lava. Around the lake, with the exception of the black and white formations, the rocks are orange—the same burnt-pumpkin orange of the bajri sand. Mining scars reveal many rock facets, making them more complex at second glance. Some rocks are smooth, some look chewed. It's looks bizarre. To a poet, it may look like hot lava solidified while it was slashed by wind. To an environmentalist it looks like what it is—the no-sense and nonsense of mining, where ancient things are trawled, blasted and snatched out anyhow: kids stealing with their greedy hands in cookie jars. In between this dramatic backdrop, the lake is a placid amethyst. We lean forward. The water reflects the rock, and suddenly it's like we are in a faraway planet of lava-forests.

A hush has fallen over the boisterous group. The break after the trekking is well-earned, and the water has calmed everyone. It is old, and cool to the touch. We aren't far from the highway, but it feels very distant. We also know, each of us, that the distance we have traversed inwards is significant.

Through my binoculars I spy movement on the orange slopes. Sand martins are hopping diagonally across them. On the other side of the hill, a male Rhesus monkey sits on a banyan tree that grows out horizontally from the rock. Red figs surround the animal. The horizontal branch is a perfect seat, even though there is a sharp drop from the tree down the slope. Sunil joins us. 'A bird came and perched there. It released its droppings on the slope. From those droppings, the banyan tree emerged. It grew tall. Now, a monkey sits on the tree and eats the figs. This used to be a mine, but now it is a complete ecosystem.'

We are all deep in thought. We have realized the belly of a mine is no more a pockmarked wasteland, but its very own place. Grasses, mostly browned, run next to the lake shore. On the top of the hill, where we came from, the green is the uniform green of vilayati kikar, but along the slopes, there are several Aravalli shrubs and trees; its their roots which hold the loose orange soil together.

We begin climbing up. It's going to be hard, because the path Sunil had taken earlier has disappeared. The group is a little tired but eager to get back home. 'I have sand between my toes,' says the girl with freshly shampooed hair. The middle-aged couple has quietened down. The not-quite walking shoes may be hurting the lady. The bajri is brittle, nothing like the feather-soft sand of the Yamuna riverside.

On one side, I see aak, *Calotropis*, growing, the reason why the black and orange of the Plain tiger and Striped tiger butterflies are still common to see. The plant grows like a bouquet, each part of it shooting out with the intoxicating energy for life wild plants have. It's good to see it here, expanding its girth and reach. The flowers are open, capable of withstanding the extremities of the place. It's almost like the vegetation is able to hide the marks of mining.

I have to keep moving, because we are now a caterpillar going up a slope, trying to move our many legs together. People hold out their hands to help others to climb. We don't know each other, but nature—and venturing out in nature—has a way of gluing people together. You can spend years with your friends and learn nothing more than their preferred order of coffee, or the kind of humour they like. When you're hiking or climbing together, you learn the most important thing—can you lean on them? Will they help when you're on a slippery slope, whether metaphoric or real? Will they laugh at you when you fall?

We reach the top. Our hands are scratched by grabbing the hill side, the bajri scored into nails and palms. I turn my head and see the monkey, still serenely sitting on his sofa-branch. The sky is an unchanging blue. A bird calls. The hill has touched us, but we have left no mark here, which is as it should be. We start walking, a broad path now spread beneath our feet.

Above us, there is the canopy of *Neltuma juliflora*. We made this difficult trek and the invasive is still there. Looking up is like seeing a firmament of antagonists. The ground is thickly covered by their tiny golden leaf-dust, and our steps send them up in flurries. Some branches have been brought down, perhaps by a tall Nilgai. As I walk, my thick hiking shoes are pierced through. I stop and pull out a sturdy, golden thorn, growing straight and then curving—a gift from the *Neltuma*. 'I hate this tree,' I tell Sunil. He turns to me, his face patient, like he has said the same things many times over. 'Yes, I know you don't like vilayati kikar. But it is the kikar that has saved the area.' His voice is steady, though I get the sense he is steadying it further to say something of gravitas. He is referring to the many court cases for saving the Aravallis. In one of its orders, the Supreme Court said the area should be preserved as forest, the fact that there were existing trees helped the case. Sunil's voice builds. 'It may not be the tree you like, but it is a tree.' He moves his hands over the area, capturing the mined pit in his palm. 'Now imagine if there were no trees here. How could we convince anyone that this place shouldn't be turned into houses or shops?'

The point Sunil is making is a practical one. What he is talking about is essentially the green lines on his map.

'Vilayati kikar have taken over everywhere. We must replace them with better plants. Look at that beautiful aak. We need more aak, more ber, more dhau. If there are more native plants, more animals will come here,' I say. He nods. He already knows all of this. I realize how close we are to the road; the fact is that the climb and the descent seemed like it took us to another planet. It would be too easy for developers to snap up this scarred place, if there was no cover of trees. The cover makes the place look less like a mine and more like the Aravallis. It almost hides the violence of its past. The vilayati kikar still needs to be replaced by native fronds, ferns and foliage. There is a long, unconsolidated road of restoration in front of us, that we all need to engage in. If the hills indeed were alive and speaking to us, it would be through tendrils of ziziphus, ligaments of banyan and the violet eyes of aak flowers.

Later, we go and sit in Sunil's garden. It is Saturday. The next day—every Sunday of the month—he holds an eco-club for the students of Mangar. There, kids learn about native plants, making bird lists, and identifying local biodiversity.

He has a wild corner in the garden, where he will allow anything to come up. In the rest of the garden, he has planted native saplings. I rifle through the plants and stop short when I see an aak plant. It is still small, but it has all the frenzied promise of a wild plant, one that shoots up like a gigantic Jack-in-the-box after the rains.

'You have an aak!' I squeal. 'You are so lucky. It doesn't grow well in pots. It has a really long root system. I had a potted one, and it didn't grow much.'

Sunil looks at me and smiles his half-smile. 'This is the problem in the world. Those who love wild plants like the aak don't have the garden space to grow it. Those who have the money for gardens would never let the wild aak grow in it.'

I think back on the present day: all of us climbing out of Covid like it was a mountain to be conquered, panting for a long time afterwards. Some of us joining hands. Calming our inner voices of despair, but also seeing hills being reduced to dust. Ancient rocks becoming a shadow of themselves—cut till sand loosens out like spilling intestines. It is time to heal ourselves and the land. What the ravaged land now requires is armour. The ability to grow its parsimonious natives, and the protection to grow them forever.

And I think we all need this armour. The city needles us, and we grow our own thorns to get by. Our skin becomes thicker, our embraces stronger. But hopefully we will not become so tough that a seed cannot wing itself in and take root in us, the way it does in Aravali Biodiversity Park[1] or Mangar.

I want to see Mangar Bani through Sunil. I wait for a few months to pass, and I meet him there.

It is early morning in the monsoons and I am waiting at a police station near Mangar village. To reach the village, one must take a steep road. I feel my little red car won't make it, and so Sunil will come to pick me up. On the other side of the road, a pair of rhesus macaque monkeys wrestle with each other. A man squats on the ground, unbothered by them, sipping tea. A few paces away, buffaloes wallow in a pool dug by the bovines, which has since filled with rainwater. Sunil arrives at last in his car, and we decide to go to the bani to see what we can find there. I know what I want to find: the Indian pitta, which comes to Delhi-NCR to nest from the southern parts of India. The Indian pitta is a lovely bird with an upright posture and nine kaleidoscopic colours on its body. Its call is a two-toned whistle—something that sounds like a sweet 'piu piu' to me. This is also a bird that has become a celebrity. Each year, photographers throng the places where pittas nest. One is Bhondsi, a reserve forest in Haryana, and the other is Mangar. Each year, there are heated debates on bird groups on how much disturbance is too much disturbance. Most bird groups do not allow nest photographs to be published. Yet, there is always a veritable crowd of photographers looking for perfect pitta shots.

Sunil and I decide the best thing to do is not to photograph the pitta, but to sit and observe it. We reach the bani. I step out, my feet sticky in wet mud. The smell of the place is that of bugs and old pages. I remember what I have learned walking with Pradip: a place is all about the soil. This is fecund soil, and it's waiting to be read. Perhaps even waiting to be written on, as new seeds germinate. We move towards the trees. The sky is overcast, the colour of a Blue rock pigeon's wing. I have a distinct feeling I am in the forest's mouth, and if I misbehave, it will sneeze and expel me. We move slowly towards the foliage. As ever, Sunil moves soundlessly. The air is warm, a ripe fruit about to split and rain its seeds down on us. I look down at the ground, and the colours of the leaf litter are dizzying. There is every shade of brown here—milk, dark, marbled chocolate, peaty, smoky, mossy. This leaf litter will soon become a bed for monsoon saplings. It is not monsoon yet. It is only May, but the heat and humidity already feels like the rainy season. I know there is a fierce sun behind the cloudbank. It could roll out of its bath of clouds any moment, and crack angrily like an egg. The tension in the air will only dissipate if it rains.

We walk squelching through this mood of the forest, listening for bird song. There is, at first, the sound of light taps. Not as forceful and obsessive as woodpeckers. More blunt. Coming from a thicker beak, the sound that resonated in the Old Fort complex. It's the sound of a barbet making a nesting hole, the pleasant thwack-thwack of avian industry. In the city, birds and animals can struggle to find the right nesting material. Sunbirds and Indian white-eyes will use spidersilk in their nests if they find it. Brahminy mynas will use what they can gather, including pieces of plastic.[2] Squirrels will steal your socks to line their ball-like nests. And birds like hornbills, parakeets and barbets use holes in trees to nest. For them, the question of finding nesting materials is not as urgent as that of finding the right tree. This barbet had happily found its tree in a sacred grove, where it could stay undisturbed.

The sluggishness in the air means most birds are hiding, hunkered down, waiting for the storm. But the barbet keeps chiselling, building something new. Just then, something buzzes past us, a brown blur. One of seven Jungle babblers, birds that usually travel in groups of seven. I feel like the forest was chewing, masticating us. 'I think we have come on the wrong day,' I tell Sunil. 'My camera and gear will get wet,' I say to myself. 'Nahi nahi, nothing will happen,' he replies. He is always unfazed by the forest, reading it like it's the easiest book. 'This isn't the time of the year when it rains too much. It will be fine.' He wants to just sit in the forest, sit till the day ends. I agree to this.

We climb a gentle hill. Here, the light is different. Sunlight has broken through some of the clouds, and it falls in solid golden shafts on the ground. The leaf litter is in alphabets, breathless with the anticipation of telling a story. There are papdi leaves and amaltas flowers on the ground. This deep in the forest, it is birds, not people, who have planted these trees. Beneath the leaves, there is decay, fruity and rich to smell, the abode of the detrivore, the little bugs that break down litter to make it into rich nourishment. That smell, overwhelming in its notes, makes me breathless. It is the scent of the garden of my childhood. How hard it is now to smell clean soil, lived in by industrious earthworms, soil littered not with garbage but spell upon spell of leaves, layers and layers of the personal histories of trees. Sometimes, the wind shakes the leaves down to create this wealth. Sometimes it is a bird, at other times a leopard, leaping between boughs. Each leaf has a different impression and a story to relate. If the leaves were to stand and join hands, they could cover the earth from one end to the other many times over. The sense right now is that they are resting, having done some of their work, waiting for the wind to pick them up again. I envy them, their fierce sense of belonging to the forest, the effortless way in which they are useful when green, when brown, when nothing but slime. They belong as wholly to the thick protection they form on the ground, as they do on trees, hiding pitta nests and the emergence of new birds.

The air rumbles. At a distance, on another hill, I hear the wind whipping the trees. The trees here are used to getting walloped by winds both monsoonal and bone-jarringly dry, during the rains or summer loo[3] periods. The forest creaks now; the first raindrop falls. It is a relief. The overripe fruit has finally split. After the first drop, the splat-splat-splat gunfire of the rain follows. Then, it settles into the softer sound of water falling on now-wet surfaces. I know all the birds we have come to see will now be tucked under the protection of leaves. But now we are part of their story. We are huddled up, just like the birds. We don't talk. We just sit in the rain, waiting for nothing. I think of us as mushrooms shooting up from the leaf-detritus, content to feel warmth and moisture for a couple of millimetres of growth, adding one more colour to this rich soil.

After two hours, the breeze is cool. The rain a mild spatter. I prepare to leave. 'But you know, the pitta is here,' Sunil says. He wants us to stay longer. I have to get back and do some work. I look at him, about to say something, when a bird hurtles past us. Its flight is the turning of a pinwheel—revealing a bright colour at certain turns. It is impossibly and secretively bright.

I sidestep a line of wet ants. This is the pitta, we both know it without having had a clear look. I smile. We move together towards its direction. On the crest of a gentle slope, we wait. Another blur through the trees, and there it is. For all our strenuous searching, it is such a small bird. It looks so tiny in front of the huge papdi, the *Holoptelea integrifolia* tree it is on. The papdi bears pods packed in little winged segments in April. When ready to fly, the pod appears like a deep-sea creature—with its silky-brown, ruched surface, looking like it's been shaped for eons by a sea. And in May, the tree is full of big green leaves. The pitta has something in its beak amongst those leaves. It is a mouthful of browned grass. Sunil and I look at each other. We are lucky—we have found the bird on the tree it has chosen to nest on. The bird perches on the branch and throws its head back, its beak full, like its taking in the sky. Then it straightens and hops to the site of the nest, laying down its load carefully. It pauses, takes stock of the placement, and then it flies off, its beautiful wing-blur like the delighted music of a child's toy. We wait, knees tucked up to our faces, hands braced on wet soil. The bird returns. This time, it is carrying damp mud. I can see the clods of earth shining, waiting to become the walls of the house a chick will grow up in. The rains have served everyone well. The pitta daubs the clay on the nest, which still doesn't have a discernible shape. Then, it is off again, returning every few minutes to shape the structure. As the minutes pass, there is a sense of a place—a nest with a bowl shape, one that needs to be hidden. Each time the bird returns, instead of landing directly on the papdi tree, it perches on another tree, watching everything around it so it doesn't give away its nest location. Now it is holding a papdi leaf, an olive green-brown colour, perfect for camouflage, one that has been picked up from the ground to be re-purposed for a new life.

We sit there, and the rain falls, and the pitta comes back again and again, alternating between carrying leaves, grass and mud. For most part, the bird could be a leaf itself, carried on the wind, green-sometimes and brown-sometimes, and then with another turn of wing it is fish-shaped, built to swim through matter, changing in the way things in nature change constantly.

But the most exciting thing is the mud. We are watching a capable pair of beaks finding soil with just the right plumpness, just the correct hardness, and taking it many feet into the air. The soil moves in this way, being the ground, and then firming the sky, becoming both the bedrock and the ceiling.

I have tried Sunil's way of watching the forest, and come away immeasurably richer.

NEHA'S FIELD NOTES

The mined-out landscape near Niharika lake is a study in contrasts. The broken crags of rocks are stark, softened by gangs of Rhesus macaque monkeys sitting in various relaxed positions. High up, they are safe in numbers. They could be on the sets of *The Lion King*, where Mufasa and Simba look down on their kingdom from Pride Rock.

Apart from the actual Mangar Bani, there is a lot to see in areas around Mangar and Nuh. On violet aak flowers, I watch a fly shining purple. This is a tachinid fly, a parasitic creature whose larvae develop inside other insects. In summer, green bee-eaters hunt from a flowering palash tree, sharp eyes like barbs for their prey. Flies settle over us, and we wish for more bee-eaters in the world.

PART 3

The Found

'The vitality of the world depends, in part, on whether we turn our ears back to the living Earth. To listen then, is a delight, a window into life's creativity, and a political and moral act.'
Sounds Wild and Broken, David George Haskell

'The great burden that now rests upon writers, artists, filmmakers, and everyone else who is involved in the telling of stories: to us falls the task of imaginatively restoring agency and voice to nonhumans.'
The Nutmeg's Curse: Parables for a Planet in Crisis, Amitav Ghosh

Found Forests

Aravalli

The Weight of a Seed

In the middle of the amphitheatre, a bush falls in a glorious tumble. The leaves are long and confident, attached to thin stems that cascade downwards, as if the majesty of the florid bush is too much, the plant bush sighing gently with its load. There are endless clusters of orange-red, tubular flowers in a tangled arrangement. The numbers are dizzying, making my eyes scramble for a hook on which I can hang my comprehension. That hook is the extraordinary, unexpected colour of the flowers. I cannot grasp the numbers of flowers, but I can comprehend their colour. They contrast with everything around them—shooting out of the wild-looking scramble with a breathless, vivid, orange force of being. The blossoms are the wild colour of leaping flames. Or the merry colour of an undersea coral, visible after a long journey and a tough dive. Or the colour of the resin that comes out of certain tall trees growing in secret, shaded places. The flowers are a surprise in form too: the buds have a closed mouth, puckered and prim, and when the mouth opens, the flower petals are serrated, with edges that look sharp. These teeth juxtapose beautifully with the lushness of orange—it is like looking at a lovely creature that can't be taken for granted. It is facing a bunch of blossoms that have none of the muted, eyes-down sedateness of cut flowers—this is a plant delighted to be alive, its blooms expression marks in the rough and tumble of the world.

The bush changes appearance as I walk closer, becoming human-like, like the blossoms are tossing their head, with orange beads in their hair, smiling. The bottom of the bush—the collarbone—is inky, a liquid blue-black, so black it could be a black hole next to a smattering of stars. That dense blackness is a place of stillness: a place of rest, a spot of relief in the hot March sun. I can imagine a small mammal creeping there for shelter, a bird stopping for a beat before its next quest for nectar.

Suddenly things move. I look again. There are birds, many birds, inside the bush. Still, watching us. And then they become blurs: there in the thicket, but barely visible—like lightning behind a cloudbank. They move rapidly but methodically all over the flowers. I spot chartreuse-yellow hued Indian white-eyes going in upward-downward motions, choppy waves through the vegetation. There are two, then three. Then they are upside down, upright, sideways—moving too fast to comprehend. There is also a Purple sunbird, iridescent-hued, seeming for a second like a highly polished Christmas bauble, his colour so shiny it's hard to look at him. But no Christmas bauble can be this lustrous. He moves in poetry, fluvial with the force of a small bird that lives off sugar. As I step closer, I see there's also another bird, brown with an eye-ring that is a fierce orange, the colour of the flowers. This bird is hanging upside down to drink nectar. It is larger than the sunbird, less breathless, its beak sturdy. This is the Yellow-eyed babbler, a bird of dry places that is not as commonly seen as it should be. It remains upside-down as I watch, its beak in the flower, unhurried. Below it, there's a brown warbler in the inky shadow of the bush, snapping up insects so tiny only the bird can see them.

The dhaula—*Woodfordia fruticosa*—is not a bush that looks you in the eye to meet your expectations. It is more sophisticated than that—it makes you stride up to it so it can subvert your expectations. You expect a poor thing growing in this hot place, but it is wilder and happier than your imagination. It gives off a confidence that seems unbelievable, given that it lives off—flourishes on—very little. I bend down, touching the soil it grows in. It is pebbled with little stones, dry as paper, like gravel. It is the singular cement-grey colour of the dirt you see on roadsides. But the dhaula has no need for manure. It isn't a pedigree that requires petting. Instead, it reminds you of a wild antecedent that knows how to survive anything.

It springs from the very centre of the amphitheatre. When I look again, I realize it is creating the centre, circumscribing the locus. It is a representation of the very soul of the Aravali Biodiversity Park in Gurugram.

The park was started, a few years ago, to rewild and restore native forests and grasslands in an area otherwise known for its dusty highways and energy-guzzling malls. The very land had stood for a defeatist view of nature—it was mined for quartzite and Badarpur sand. As many as eight stone crushers operated on it. Pits pockmarked the area. The new park was an attempt at rewilding, to blow fresh air into a new city that already had a tired soul. But how do you restore a place with degraded soil, without lathering it with immeasurable support—tons of manure, gallons of water, heaps of frenzied attention?

'When we first started with this concept, I was told to plant guavas and mangos,' recalls Vijay Dhasmana, the curator of the park. The impulse to have one park look like any other was very strong in those who advised him. Usually, foreign species are chosen in horticulture because they look neat. Like a school curriculum made of white-man fiction, it is also familiar and global in the way you find the same textbook in various parts of the world. But Gurugram's Aravali Biodiversity Park will not copy parks that have the silver oak, growing tall and demure, with white-backed leaves that look prettily silver when ruffled by the wind. They will not plant the eucalyptus, a long-lived tree that arrows upwards and parches the soil it grows in. It will not plant trees just because they have an easy-going disposition, like plumerias which flower all year round, but are not visited by pollinators in the way native trees are. These are part of the aesthetic you see in other parts of the world, bringing memories of gentrified neighbourhoods, order, safety and a flabby sort of sameness.

'I was told to lay marble for the auditorium and manure for the plants,' Vijay remembers. There was an impulse to showcase some of the affluence of the area—the way to 'develop' forests would be planting rows of familiar trees and flowers, and erecting built-up 'interactive areas' with materials reminiscent of Gurugram's malls and offices.

But this wasn't the path Vijay and his team wanted to walk. They were rewilders, not horticulturalists. They weren't going to just make a green belt; they also believed opulence wasn't just a function of expensive stone. It could also be the rare privilege of recreating history, of peeling back layers to rebuild what once existed in the region. Nurturing a biodiversity park is the very opposite of the global. It is hyper-specific. It means bringing a specific past into the present, and then the future.

And so, the team consciously and defiantly chose the laughing sprawl of native species over neat lines of foreign trees. These are complexities that arise from this particular region—its desert-like conditions, its quartzite ridges of rocks, its short monsoon, its thin, impoverished soil. In the Aravallis, the tree imagination is not simple, clean or imported. It is instead shot through with ways to survive water shortages, barbed with thorns, snarled with making much of the little they get. Many Aravalli trees have root systems which go wide for precious water. And many of the shrubs have thorns—a classic adaptation to save water. Others grow slowly, almost painfully so, staying bush-like for a long time. The palash, jaal and dhau remain small for years, seemingly bent in a complicated conversation with themselves—before they start looking like trees. The kullu grows on rocky substrate. The dhau and kaim need very little. Still, horticulturalists have traditionally favoured trees that fulfil a narrow, textbook definition that comes from a children's drawing book: growing straight, growing quickly, flowering splendidly, having green leaves all of the year, remaining obedient staff rather than uninhibited spill. But the Aravalli trees are not from foreign textbooks. They will not grow straight, nor are they evergreen, and many look more scraggly than lush. At first glance, they seem to be trees that plant themselves, not ones *you* would plant, the ones you would uproot as weeds. These are the trees you look past, growing on roadsides and through rubble, while looking for parks with imported grass.

In 2005, Vijay started studying the Aravallis. In 2013, he conducted a flora-mapping survey of Mangar in Haryana, the sacred grove near Delhi with nearly undisturbed native forest.[1] When he started rewilding the park, he knew he would first have to get it right, and then have it loved by visitors who might not have seen such trees. He started by collecting names and seeds of the pioneer trees which could survive the scorching sun, the touch of winter frost, and the degraded soil.

Years later, we are standing in the amphitheatre. It now has a different layer of meaning. This was the place where Vijay was asked to lay shining marble—a bit of the Gurugram malls in its 'green belt'. As I take in the amphitheatre in 2024, with its glorious, unpruned dhaula, I see it through his eyes. The place feels like it is run by plant lords; like the land is cracked open by the wilful feet of a tree. The dhaula is the well of the amphitheatre, its shape amorphous and so right for this place. The plant is growing in the way it wants, in the directions it is actively choosing. It seems to have an agency, a purposefulness to its spread. It isn't the greedy sprawl of an oil spill. It is instead, the way vegetation grows on a rugged mountain—slowly but inevitably, taking its time. This perhaps is the biggest difference between restored 'biodiversity parks' and all other parks—plants here escape the gardener's shears and whims, and they make their own way. They aren't cut into shapes of bears or comical Christmas trees; they aren't sequestered in metal cages, growing like bricks in the wall. It's a subversion of the usual plant imagination that seems to have taken a long time in coming.

Around the dhaula, stone slab-seats create a gentle rise. This is where you can hold hands and listen to talks about bees buzz-pollinating flowers by shaking them,[2] as real bees buzz in your ears. It's a place to listen to stories of rocks and geologies, and how plants have learned to live between ancient rocks and hard places—the dusty, narrow crevices between scorched boulders, or the sides of our roads and imaginations. I look around once more, tearing my eyes away from the orange dhaula flowers. In between the stone seats, a small tree grows. It is feathery and lovely, like a tree fern growing modestly under larger trees in a tropical forest. Its branches arch outwards, bouquet-like. They contain nubs that will become new summer leaves. They are so tightly curled in, they appear like buds. It is a salai tree, the *Boswellia serrata*. I point at it, and Vijay grins. 'This, this is the apex of our efforts here. That tree grew itself. Let me tell you how.'

Amongst the list of trees Vijay and his team had drawn up included salai, doodhi, kareel (also known as kair[3]), kullu, dhau, roheda and ronjh. These are trees and shrubs of arid or desert places, native to the region. The next step was to find these trees. This seems intuitive but is not. Surprising as it may sound, nurseries in the area often don't have saplings of indigenous trees (this is also true for other parts of India). You can find the things which are on your plates: neem, guava, moringa, curry and mango. You might find the things that are the foreign ornamentals in your neighbourhoods: gulmohar, jacaranda, plumeria. But you won't find salai or kareel. The lack of native, regional saplings is a troubling antecedent to the fact that local trees actually require propagation and conservation today.

'Salai became our struggle story,' Vijay says. 'We looked for salai, but there were few trees to be found. Most of them were in reserve forests.' When he tells me this, we are standing near a flowering salai in March. The tree is young.

I touch its lovely bark, so flaky it seems to move, and my hand comes away fragrant. The gum from the salai is frankincense, used by ancient Egyptians, Greeks and Romans.[4] In just a few days from now, the salai will fruit, which will then transform into light, papery seeds. When Vijay went to gather salai seeds from cliffsides in May, stormy winds whistled them away, lodging them between rocks or carrying them beyond his reach. This is fitting to the very nature of the salai: the trees themselves are able to withstand whippings from strong winds. Vijay then went to the Virat Nagar Reserve Forest in Haryana, but by the time the team reached, the wind had already snatched away the seeds.

Meanwhile, more seeds from other trees and plants were collected. One such seed was that of bistendu. The bistendu is an Aravalli plant whose fruit look like Chinese miniature oranges. The leaves of the plant have some toxicity—they were traditionally used to catch fish by stunning them. But the drupes are relished by Brown-headed barbets and other birds. According to other observations, civets—small, weasel-like mammals, often nocturnal—have a special relationship with the bistendu. Civet poop is often found near bistendu plants, suggesting civets eat bistendu. The Aravalli team gathered bistendu seeds and watched over them. But the bistendu refused to germinate.

It can feel quite counter-intuitive when a plant you have seen in the wild refuses to grow when you plant it. We have all seen peepal and banyan saplings grow with a decided sense of humour. Wedged somehow at the corner where your wall meets the terrace on your roof (you admire the resilience but rue the seepage that will follow), on the tiles of public toilets (an improvement of décor), on the boles of mature trees, placed there by a spatter of bird poop, the seedling likely to eventually subdue the tree it is growing on. Yet, when I pulled out peepals and banyans from my roof and put them in pots—or even in soil—they refused to root. They dropped their leaves, withered and died. It took some time for me to realize that plants, especially trees, can be very particular. They like things a certain way. Sometimes, that way is hard and rocky, not soft and luxurious as gardeners would imagine. Both the peepal and the banyan don't want an abundance of soil and water. They instead prefer poor soil or rocky substrates to grow on. They ask for a kind of benign neglect, the very opposite of the helicopter style of composting-and-pruning gardening we usually conduct.

Vijay went back to the places where the bistendu grew. He guessed the trees germinate well in nature, after the fruit are eaten by birds or animals. 'The bistendu wanted the rite of passage of passing through the gut of an animal,' Vijay marvels. It is the classic co-dependence you find in native forests, the way different elements rely on each other, producing harmony. A tree might be large, but it may require a tiny bird or animal to begin its story. This process needed to be replicated in the park. But how do you get a creature to eat the seed, and then excrete it? The team instead tried a similar process: they started soaking bistendu seeds in water. It worked. More seeds were gathered, and more experiments were conducted for germination. Hundreds and hundreds of green saplings now lined the park's nurseries, and citizens were called in to learn about seeds. They learnt that several seeds, like kala siris, hingot, ronjh, kullu and kumat, needed water treatment before germination. The water was a substitute for a wild animal or bird choosing a fruit, eating it, and depositing it in various places.[5]

And through the bistendu and kullu, Vijay realized that more needed to be learned about the preferences of trees. This information started with tracing things around the tree. 'We started trying to read the plant. What kind of soil did it grow in? Was it well-drained? What kind of biomass did the plant like? Did it have a lot of leaf litter near its roots? Or did it grow on soil that was exposed to the sun and elements? We needed to make a bed with this knowledge.' For example, the salai, they learnt, likes rocks and dry, poor soil. It grows to tolerate water scarcity, drought and even fire. After establishing, treelings didn't want luxurious tinkles of water or mulch. Somewhat like the terrace-growing peepal, the salai needed a carefully tended neglect; it liked to grow itself at its own pace. The dhaula bush grows in dry Sariska and the southern Aravallis, and it brought a similar independence to the park—each year, the scree below the bush would fill with seedlings. For sunburnt slopes, there is a tree adapted to a tilted life. The dhok or dhau thrives on ridges and slopes, having adapted to the twin challenges of searing heat and steep inclines. Its leaves look purplish, the bark silvery. Dhau often grows with palash, ber and bauhinia trees in quartzite ridges. As you go towards Sariska tiger reserve, you will find yourself in the presence of ancient hills covered in dhau that appear like curling purple smoke pulsing in the heat. Looking at the trees, you realize you are looking at a refuge of resilience. And yet, dhau, that hardy, undulating slope survivor, was hard to grow, particular in the way it wanted things. Initially, germination of dhau seeds was at a low 1 per cent (this figure has now gone up to 7–8 per cent).

'We realized that it is not possible to replicate many microclimates the trees like,' Vijay says. So there was still a lot to learn as to what could be done. Everything was hands-on.

As the team explored, they reflected on what they had found. Long considered unbeautiful, many trees of the Aravallis were revealed to have a galaxy of flowers. Those who live in Delhi or other cities know the flowers from other parts of the world better than they know their own. Dahlias are borrowed from Mexican and European gardens; and in 2024, the Netherlands sent 20,000 tulip bulbs to Delhi for a popular spring festival. Very few grow, or even know, native Aravalli flowers which flourish through the hill range.

The shrub adusa has beautiful white flowers which are loved by Indian white-eye birds, Purple sunbirds and a variety of butterflies. Goats don't seem to eat them, a blessing for starting a nectarine ecosystem. The adusa was grown in the park, to invite butterflies. Trees with large flowers in the Aravalli region include the rohida or roheda (*Tecomella undulata,* a tree of desert soil, with large, orange-red tubular flowers), barna (*Crateva religiosa* a sacred tree grown near temples with softly fragrant orchid-like white flowers), gamhar (*Gmelina arborea*, with flowers that have a yellow to red transition), and desi kadam (*Mitragyna parvifolia*, with soft-yellow, ball-shaped flowers). And there were trees with tiny flowers too. The ber tree, from the *ziziphus* genus, has small, whitish flowers. While flowering, the chamrod (*Ehretia laevis*) looks like a shower of tiny star-sparks—each flower is just a few millimetres. Like the bright stars that emerge in the clean sky once it has rained, the chamrod may flower multiple times a year after rainfall. The East Indian rosewood, *Dalbergia lanceolaria,* (while not classified as an Aravalli native) is a large tree with tiny, lovely pink flowers. The kullu tree, *Sterculia urens,* is white-barked and grows forked, like it is lightning on soil. Its bark glistens pearlescent—like a tower of mercury, a liquid thing made solid. And the whiteness eventually yields even more surprising colours: tiny, velvety-green flowers, and a hairy hot-pink fruit.

Every trip, everywhere in the Aravallis, became a mission to find seeds, saplings and new ways of understanding the hill range. Seeds now became more than just a capsule to grow a plant—they thrummed with the weight of ideas. The team learned how to take each idea and line it: they followed the forest, seeing how plants grew and what they tolerated, how composites of matter formed a particular kind of soil, and what kind of soil lay under a particular tree. Were the trees in valleys or slopes, in the shade or in the sun? Did a particular tree like partial shade? Each detail was important. Slowly, the seedbed took shape, blossoming, transforming into a firm bedrock of ideas.

More salai was gathered from Jhir and Mangar Bani in Haryana. In Jhir, Vijay found the *Ficus mollis*—a fig tree growing out of hot, sunburnt rocks. This is a tree he would later grow through cuttings. He found kaim trees growing in seasonal streams at various spots. And in valleys, he found indrok trees (*Terminalia coronata*), which can grow in sandy-loamy places, like lake beds and valleys. In Delhi's Central Ridge forest, he found doodhi, also called kirni *(Wrightia tinctoria)*, a white-blossomed, white-wooded tree. He also found Rohini (*Mallotus philippensis*) trees, the preferred food of elephants. Even though the doodhi is browsed by many animals, it is a hardy plant, a hallmark of many native Indian species that can survive both heatwaves and damage. At a nondescript roadside, he found the shrub *Dyerophytum indicum* with its pale-green leaves, and a handful of seeds were collected. In Haryana, he found the kat-bel, the *Naringi crenalata*, with fruits that are a luscious blueberry colour.

Through the years, I walked in Aravalli Park, revelling in the sights, watching the trees grow taller. There were so many textures to take in—smooth, like the kat-bel leaves, hairy, like the kullu flowers, spined like the dhaula thorns, toothed like chirchitta seeds. I learned new leaf shapes and the words for them: ovoid shapes, like ovals, as many leaves are; lanceolate, shaped like lances, like the dhaula leaves are; pinnate, with leaflets arranged opposite each other, such as on the siris tree. There were other identities the trees had too—their relationships with other beings. The salai tree, that great teacher of the Aravalli Park, is relished by elephants, but it is also hardy and tends to survive browsing. As per M.Z. Siddiqui in a 2011 paper,[6] boswellia is also called gajabhakshya, a Sanskrit word which translates to 'eaten by elephants'. It is fitting that the trees I had grown to love, the ones beyond the traditional mango, banyan and guava, were also loved by our non-human kin.

Meanwhile, the seeds which had germinated grew taller. As plant communities established, seeds were everywhere. The chirchitta caught on my jeans and the skin of livestock with their itchy barbs. Other seeds, such as the khinna and the salai, winged through the air. The same wind that had blown away salai seeds when Vijay went to gather them was now helping establish new salai trees in the park. Even light seeds have weight: they can become volleys, breaking stone-seats in amphitheatres but landing in precisely the place they should be in.

As the Covid lockdown lifted, I visited the park with Vallari. I had just recovered from the Delta variant in the second wave of Covid, when I got Omicron in the third wave. My body felt gutted, my mind turning to mush. The only thing I could think of for recovery was following the wisdom of my ancestors—when people had respiratory illnesses in the generations before us, they went to sanatoriums in the mountains, breathing in fresh air under trees. On an off day, we decided to go out to the trees. The monsoon had just ended but the air was thick with the promise of more rain. This made the air stifling, so we planned to go early. The light was magnified in the way it often is on cloudy days: we were inside a snow shaker, sunlight reaching us through glass. As we entered the park, there were few people in the vicinity. In the parking lot, a goya khair bush was full of furry blossoms, half-pink and half-yellow; each flower like a little paper lamp carrying its own light, reminiscent of the glorious dhaula. The bush had the familiar look of trees in arid areas: scrawny when first seen, metamorphosing into molten loveliness when in flower. If the dhaula was a laughing person, the goya khair looked like it was a tavern—bees hummed in it like they were reciting jokes and comebacks to each other. House sparrows pecked at the ground, chittering, a sound familiar from the garden of my childhood.

A little ahead in the grasses in the park sat various kinds of bugs. One was a striking red-black, a red body with black portions that resembled ink stains. It also had markings resembling white water-colour daubs. The legs were muscular and spiky: it looked like a ladybug on steroids. This was the flower chafer beetle, the *Oxycetonia versicolor*, on a jhad ber branch. The leaves of the ber, the *Ziziphus nummularia*, had tiny white flowers, even smaller than the beetle. There was moisture everywhere, getting into my eyes as I tried to adjust my gaze for the tiny scale I was looking at. The grasses radiated wet heat, the heat of cooked food when a lid is pressed upon it. On a long grass blade sat another insect, burly shouldered, its huge eyes funky, a film reel exposed to the light. Unlike the chafer beetle that was moving up and down the sprig of a ber shrub, this one sat in complete stillness. It held down the grass strongly, like it was waiting for something. Underneath its muscular shoulders were finely veined wings, and a body covered in hairs. This was unmistakably a predator, in wait to ambush other insects. It was the robber fly, which lives off eating other insects, including the ones we try to kill, often unsuccessfully—the fly and the mosquito. The robber fly possesses a forceful, zooming flight and a strong, biting mouth. Its saliva has neurotoxins. I spotted a male and female, their wings shining, veined like streams in a delta. I wondered how long they had waited for their prey, and how many mosquitos each had eaten. If we had more robber flies, we'd need less chemical repellents in the world. What we need are little assassins in clumps of wild grass.

As we went forward, the heat beat down upon me, a ladle banging on a pot. Sweat had made rings on our shirts. On the ground ahead, pansy butterflies seemed to look at us from markings on their wings, designed to imitate eyes. I wanted to take photos, but suddenly I was out of breath.

I couldn't even reach my favourite kullu tree, one which always had birds on it.

'I can't go on,' I gasped to Vallari. 'I just can't walk anymore.'

'What happened?' she turned around and asked kindly, as if it was a problem that could easily be borne.

'I just can't put one foot in front of the other … I just … I just can't walk.' I was breathless. She looked at me. I waited for her to say: have you eaten enough? Did you drink water? Why are you walking if you had Covid? And the best, most entitled question: why do live in Delhi if your lungs can't take it?

Amitav Ghosh writes in his book of essays, *Wild Fictions*, how living in polluted cities for some South Asians is like a rite of passage: a hardship that must be endured for progress. Yet sometimes you stay where you are not for muscular reasons of progress, but because your family—found and biological—is there. Sometimes, the choice to stay is not inertia. It's just a choice life made for you. All these thoughts chased each other in my head as a cough hacked at my chest. Fresh sweat bloomed on my face and chest. I had spots in my vision. Perhaps both of us knew I wasn't yet ready to walk in the wet heat, but there were no recriminations coming from Vallari.

Instead, she said: 'That's okay, we can stop.'

'But we have so much ground to cover!' I was apologetic and quietly furious, an odd, warring combination. She had come because I had asked her. She had come, and we had hardly covered any distance. I was disappointed, vaguely with the world, but specifically with my body.

'Yes, but you can take all the time you need. We can rest.' She looked at my disbelieving face and continued softly. '*Arrey*, we don't have to go anywhere. This is also a place.'

She held out her water bottle to me, wordlessly. I looked at her, steadying myself. We were so different, and yet she always seemed to understand perfectly what I was going through. She studied trees, and had imbibed patience through them. There was another indescribable thing she had taken from trees too: instead of counter arguments, she provided shade and refuge when her friends needed them. At that moment, in that hot place, I felt something germinate. We were like pinnate leaves, mirrors of each other, growing in opposite directions but coming from the same stalk.

We stopped. I closed my eyes. Green-gold light from under the trees touched my eyelids. The light came to me through a double filter, green through the leaves and pink through my lids. It felt like honey going slowly down my ragged throat—a trick of the light and shadow, a healing trickle. I wondered if my great-aunt with tuberculosis had felt like this, standing under a tree in a sanatorium in the Himalayas. A sort of peace crept over me then. This was a special place because it had turned a degraded, littered area into one with proud trees that didn't need us anymore. It was a special place because it was a showcase of thorny beauty with no artifice—just a naked passion to live, interconnected and enmeshed with the chafer beetles, robber flies and warblers who lived their lives like bright short-lived sparks. But it was also a place of safety. So many times, women go to places with plans clasped in iron. There is usually no chance to tweak schedules. One can walk, but not loiter; one can stop, but only very briefly. One must be a river, always flowing, getting out of the way of harassers, possessing a kind of pace that signals a universal, urbane urgency.

And yet, we had stopped. Here in safety, with a friend, we had the luxury of changing plans; the luxury of time itself. As Vallari had pointed out, we were already in a place, and there was no hurry to get to another place.

Under the tree, my throat still burning, I decided it was going to be all right.

In a few months, I returned.

The Aravali Biodiversity Park is one of the few places in NCR where one can get a really good look at a kullu tree. There are many trees in the park. But there is one kullu here that grows on the brow of a hill. Around it lies undulating land. It looks like the wild kullu trees of Central Indian forests—of Pench and Kanha and surrounding regions in Madhya Pradesh, bursting out through waves of rocks. In the forest, it is hardly easy to see a thing well, unless it's in a rare clearing. You snare a glance of a tiger's stripes slinking through tall grasses, or between trees. You see a piece of solid grey moving a little differently between the trees—and that's the Indian elephant. You see the pert nose of a hog deer, but not its rump. And you see the kullu shine between other trees like a spill of silver, many other trees in the way. Someone thought the silver sight looked like a ghost, and thus it has another moniker, the ghost tree. The tree's bark is papery and aids it during drought. In the dry season, the leaves fall off, and it is the body of the tree, the trunk, that photosynthesizes light. The kullu is also a tree that loves growing on solid rock, holding the ground down with command and charisma. The roots splay out over rocky substrate like an octopus of the sea, or a spider holding down a vast, interconnected web. The kullu on the hill in Aravalli looks like a cousin of the huge, utterly singular trees I had seen in Central India. And like in those old forests, this tree too gets covered in a way, not fully visible. A huge male peacock sits on the bare boughs of the tree, his long tail cascading down pale branches in a dizzying combination of iridescences.

In Central India's Pench tiger reserve in the years before, I had seen a leopard under a kullu—a ghost under the ghost trees. The sight in Aravalli Park was so different, but also similar. There were many peacocks in Pench, and it wouldn't be a stretch to see them on the ghost trees. That day, the peacock's tail in Aravalli looks botanical, composed of kullu leaves. And the tree looks like it would sprout feathers. The ease that the tree and the bird has with each other mirrors the ease of the leopard sprawled under the kullu; it is the ease of love ... an ease I desire, for me and my friends. But urban life is always prickly, always triggering. There are no easy drives, no easy walks. 'Freedom, I am told, is nothing but the distance between the hunter and its prey,' writes Ocean Vuong in *On Earth We're Briefly Gorgeous.* Vulnerable people in cities—women, the elderly, children—hasten to make sure they have freedom, widening the distance between hunter and prey. They sprint across roads, wide-eyed; they rush home after dark. To have freedom in the city is to build communities that fortify you, whether human and more-than-human. Rings of native trees that survive anything, the warmth of friendships, birds to watch together, places to walk in without getting molested are all part of this sense of freedom. A safe native park is a net of the best kind—a net of climate resistance, time-and-drought-tested, a safety net that women can go to when they need space, with the luxury of pausing time when their lungs give way.

Looking at the kullu tree, at arm's length from the Mehrauli–Gurgaon Road, white boughs spread out in majesty, turning light and water into glucose, I feel history being formed. It is an ending and a beginning. The ending of the idea that only foreign trees can build parks and places of value. The beginning of an intimacy with native trees: learning how they can grow and what their intricacies and idiosyncrasies are. Learning that even the toughest of trees—growing in literal dust—are particular, for a time. They grow if they choose to, and then they spread as plant lords. They can be appreciated, and they can't be underestimated.

From the kullu, Vijay takes me to a part of the park which now has an established dhau cover. We are in a depression, looking up towards quartzite rocks that rise like cliffs. Under a particular set of jutting rocks, white splotches shine. These are the tell-tale signs of a family of Indian eagle-owls, also called Rock eagle-owls. These are big birds, with plumage that resembles pebbles and stone-dust. They have large, glowing yellow-orange eyes, the singular colour of lava. When they turn towards you, you are jerked by an ancient, serious scrutiny. Residents of cliffs, Rock eagle-owl populations may have declined because the habitat they favour—cliff sides, strewn with rocks—are under pressure from rock and boulder mining.[7] Here in this place re-built from mining, we climb the hill from one side, hoping to spot the family. There is a dhaula growing on the brow of the slope, and a dhau on its hairline. We clamber to the top, and as we look below us, the dhau shimmers purple. For a second, I am back in the hills near Sariska, clothed in wild dhau. We search for the owls, but we don't spot them. Nothing can puncture our cheer though. The hills and cliffs of the area are not 'natural'. They have been mined out. We are standing in a landscape gouged and depleted by machines, and it is fitting that this has since been corrected, colonized and covered by native vegetation.

We stand there, breathing, looking over the rise and fall of the land. It's fine if there are no owls, I tell myself. Just spending time out here means something. At that point, I believe it. As we gaze out, eyes half-shut in the heat, a large bird circles the sky. It makes slow, languid motions, hardly flapping, looking like a shimmer in the heat. We bring our cameras out; and just then, the bird makes a decision. It stops circling. It makes a gentle dive and alights on a bare tree. It is a large bird with a crest on its head, yellow facial skin and a powerful beak. It is a Crested serpent eagle, a raptor that specializes in eating snakes. 'Do you know, I've never seen this eagle in the park before!' Vijay says.

'Really? The owls took us to the eagle then. I knew we would see something!'

The eagle sits on the bare boughs, holding its position with the insouciance unique to the apex predator. It has barely perched for a minute or two when the first House crow appears. Crows mob other birds, but they have a particular aversion to predatory birds. They attack owls and eagles with enthusiasm, pull their tail feathers and caw indignantly, even though eagles are much bigger than them. Another crow appears to join its friend. The first crow inches closer to the eagle. The second one watches. The eagle shifts. It will soon be gone, more willing to face the heat than corvid harassment. I think of the city then, how it always takes and takes, chipping away at green areas, proposing plans to build roads through biodiversity parks with regularity, taking one bite at a time, remaining insatiable. I think about the crows, those generalists, eating both wild bird chicks and potato chips, taking and taking what they can get, and how they will be fine no matter what. But the eagle, with its heft, its size and its nature—something like a salai or a kullu—is particular, and it requires habitat and stewardship.

The eagle flies off. We decide to come down the hill.

I walk next to the kullu for the last time that year, feeling it stretching its boughs in the heat it loves. Near the auditorium I see a leafless creeper, scrambling over hot rocks.

I feel again the surge of plant lords around us. I feel their tenacity and wide-rootedness, their resilience in the face of pollution, their no-nonsense aversion to too much water or meddling, their irrepressible nature. I can only hope we will inherit this power: the strength to meet and subvert expectations, to think beyond office or garden rows, to find the gravitas and spread of the native, to uncover peace at the centre of storms which break over us.

Slowly and surely, the wild has nudged its forehead closer to Gurugram, the Millennium City. It is a fierce and beautiful thing to behold, a poem hidden in the seed of a thorny plant.

If the people of Gurugram are resilient, so are its new, old trees.

NEHA'S FIELD NOTES

July 2021: A Purple sunbird, olive and yellow and female, balances upside down on an arni plant in Aravali Biodiversity Park in Gurugram. The plant has small white flowers which could remind you of miniature hibiscus. A painted grasshopper sits at the very top of the plant, a colourful king. In the background, the metro train whizzes past.

A blue-banded bee dives into a wild sesame flower. The flower is baby-pink with a touch of fuchsia. The bee is small, with neat bluish bands on its body. But there are even smaller things to see. Below the flower sits a brown moth which is a few millimetres in size. This is the *Eretmocera impactella*. A black ant clambers up the side of the flower, its head turned up, sensing the world around it. There are three green flies with orange eyes on furry *Cenchrus ciliaris* grasses. These are very small things on the small things, living at a scale that is both vibrant and overlooked.

September 2021: A *Tephrosia strigosa*, an Indian plant with grass-like leaves, has produced the most delicate lavender flower, a few millimetres wide. Two Tarucus species butterflies, white with black dots and dashes, are perched on another tephrosia, the *Tephrosia purpurea,* with hot pink flowers. The marks on the butterflies are morse code for 'small is big'.

Found Spaces

Tughlaqabad

The Nilgai stands on the edge of the fort wall, his powerful neck muscles bulging. The bulges remind me of hills—of ridges that are still, yet watching us. He tosses his head and the ridges move; his funny, black beard twists in the air. If you have ever been close to a Nilgai, you know they are nervous, skittish animals—they erupt like a flock of bees, streaming forward. Students in Jawaharlal Nehru University in South Delhi watch out for Nilgai not because they attack you, but because they run away from you in a way that can tear down your clothesline or topple a biker. Asia's largest antelope, almost five feet tall, the Nilgai is like a tropical tornado with no fixed path. At this moment though, the Nilgai isn't running, because distance saves him from us.

That distance is because of a fort and the park in the fort's shadow. We are in Tughlaqabad Fort, looking out from Tughlaqabad Biodiversity Park, and the scene looks like it may have looked hundreds of years ago. A fort, a Nilgai, a valley of plants, and the luxury of a vista—a vista that is a sweep of distance. If he has to run, the Nilgai knows he has the time and space for it.

The fort has the casual timelessness that heritage buildings wear like a shrug. Like the building has always been here and will continue to watch over this place. I think of government-built housing that can't make it thirty years without cracks, and then I look at the Tughlaqabad Fort. It has been vandalized, but it is also proud and upright, lustrous under a weak sun. Its stones are differing shades of mud—the orange of a Yellow-eyed babbler, the yellow of an Ashy prinia, the brown of a Jungle babbler. At that moment, seeing the cold, bluish-grey of the Nilgai against the warm stones of the fort, with no other buildings visible—feels like a kind of time travel. Hundreds of years ago, Delhi had wolves. They too might have stood like a painting against this building. Perhaps a girl like me watched them and wondered if Delhi would always belong to Nilgais and Indian Grey wolves.

As I walk closer, I look at a mighty tree gripping the sides of the fort wall. Rather than growing upright, it is splayed like an octopus. This is the lannea,[1] rare for this region. To remove the tree would be to break the wall. The tree and the wall are one.

We come to a small wetland, and it is crowded with birds standing like they're waiting for a conference to begin. A majestic large bird, its feathers glinting metallically in the sun, walks slowly on the soggy shore. This is the Red-naped ibis. When it opens its mouth to call, the sound is primal, keening—like the call itself has a long neck and head that carries itself above us, circling. A Red-wattled lapwing cuts a jagged path through the sky. There are Pond herons, statue-still until they start loping through the grass on the side of the wetland. There is a bird with a back the colour of mossy old pond water and a white, vanilla ice-cream belly, probing the marshy lip of the wetland with some urgency. The beak is a needle embroidering the ground. This is the Green sandpiper, a migratory visitor from the Palearctic.[2] Time slows down, then loops back. I think again if these birds always visited the areas around the fort. How many generations have visited this old place? The sun is glowing brighter, burning off the patina of fog, and I am again struck by the feeling that we are in a Delhi of yesterday. In a way, Delhi is both of this time and the time before. Birds have been migrating to Delhi for longer than centuries. And some creatures look like they are wearing time themselves. There is something near the water that looks like ancient wood, mottled with not just age but also experience. It moves then, a fast motion which wood doesn't make. It detaches itself deftly from the rest of the marshy pond. The animal is now the main focus, the rest of the setting a blur. I wonder how I didn't see it before. The legs become visible, long and gangly, and out comes the beak, long and tough. This is the Wood sandpiper, another migrant to Delhi. It moves with so much energy and speed that all thoughts of it being ancient are quickly discarded. In the way that wild creatures have, the sandpiper is both ancient and a youngling.

I shake my head at what I am seeing and feeling—nature is a moving picture with pixels changing colours, shifting between time periods I can't immediately grasp. Things seem both formless and possessing shape, old and young, complacent and hungering. The wetland itself has recently been made to clean dirty water and provide an ecosystem for the birds. Yet, though it is new, the scientists at the park have mimicked the feel of an old place. There are no flashy tiles or boards, and the edges of the water are jagged with grasses and reeds. Aquatic plants float on the surface. It seems like it's been around for years. I am the youngling now.

Here, like the sandpiper forages peacefully with other year-long residents—impossibly long-legged birds that look like they're wearing tuxedoes. These are Black-winged stilts. Their legs are so long and with angles so sharp, that their body resembles a sail that may fold up and topple. They move in a curious, hesitating walk. You can feel their long feet sinking into velvety, marshy mud, making footprints that fish, not humans, see. The water is imprinted hundreds of times a day.

The way we measure such places cannot just be in budgets spent and trees grown: it also has to be in the wealth of footprints and beak-prods by birds, by an understanding of the innate value of freshwater and mud.

Some distance from the wetland, there is another shore of grasses growing in a pit. These are dry, golden strands, interspersed with sharp green blades. A little thing is moving through this universe of grasses. A round shape, wet, lively-eyed: the female Red-breasted flycatcher. She too is a winter visitor, propelling her tiny body from the Palearctic to Delhi in winter each year. As I look at her, the grasses move again. This time, it is a Nilgai, a female, resident to the visiting flycatcher. She has leaped in to the grassy pit and no doubt will leap out if we go close. She seems shockingly big compared to the flycatcher. Indeed, she seems the biggest thing in the area.

Everything else is miniscule, and it demands perfect attention. I discard the many layers of expectation one has from parks. The first layer to discard is the expectation of size. This is a new restoration site, and there are no huge, dramatic swathes of green. The second is the expectation of flowers. There are no masses of flowers. Instead, the restoration is gentle, slow and steady. Saplings try to become trees. The wetland laps the ground, trying to get cleaner. I don't see the flowers at first. But looking at the flycatcher has trained my eyes to see the small things; and looking at the camouflaged sandpipers has taught me to look again. Dotting the grass—cross-stitching it with motifs—are a set of tiny blossoms. They are the size of the letters in a child's notebook, and they have a message. Wildflowers can grow in dust, and they should not be overlooked, even if they are tiny, barely a few millimetres in size. There is a blue flower, a brilliant blue, the colour of school-time Chelpark ink. This is the shankhpushpi (*Evolvulus alsinoides*). I have found the flower from the garden of my childhood. Another flower grows, the colour of rooh-afza or rose syrup mixed in milk. This is the *Indigofera linnaei*. A little further ahead, there is a simple, mango-yellow flower, smaller than a hook on a dress. This is the gokhru, *Tribulus terrestrias*.

I remember the story of Thumbelina, the tiny little girl who slept inside little flowers. If she were here, she would have many beds to choose from. These are the little blocks of colour from the garden of my childhood—building blocks at scales which are small, which nevertheless shape the world.

A little distance ahead of us, Dr Vivek Choudhary, the scientist-in-charge of the park, points out Blue pansy butterflies, looking like petals on the wind. On the ground, there is a creeper with things on it that look like eyes.

Blue pansy butterflies fly everywhere, looking like petals on the wind. There is a creeper with things on it that look like eyes. They are the eyes of an angry thing, perhaps a goddess with an opinion. They are black-and-red, seeds of the rati creeper, poisonous, and each weighing the same. A rati signifies a unit of measurement, and traditional jewellers still use rati seeds to weigh tiny, specific amounts.

I pick up a bead of rati and take it home, tucking it into my jewellery box. I hope for a rati of patience. A bead of tolerance for small, growing things from older times.

Found Words

Bittern-Grass

The sun hadn't yet broken out of the horizon when we reached Chandu[1] on a humid September day. The place is a mosaic of agricultural fields, wetlands and grasses merging into one entity—a microcosm of some parts of the Indian countryside.

It was a time of change. The weather was turning from explosive heat to simmering warmth, now glazed over with moisture. New smells were in the air in the city—the heavy, intoxicating smell of the flowering saptaparni—a fragrance that is intoxicating to some and hateful to others, and the beginning of the blossoming of the sweet-smelling shuili. There was also a sense of transformation in this transitional time—September was when the first migratory birds would arrive, making local places into a global pitstops.

Gradually the sky turned orange, and the sun struggled up, a molten coin that autumn had touched and softened. From where I stood, the coin had tossed itself between two bushels of extravagant, flowering grasses. These were *Sachharum spontaneum* or kaas grasses, with puffy white flowers that the wind would grasp in handfuls and carry away. You can cut your hands on the blades of the towering kaas grasses, but its flowers feel like silk. Silk with little coarse bits, reminding me of semal cotton full of firm seeds. It's how much of nature feels—frequently beautiful, with gritty spine.

The birds were ready to make the most of the seasonal bounty. In the path ahead of us, a beautiful bird tugged at green grasses. It had a black head, brown wings, and a white neck and sides. This was the Tricoloured munia. It held a strand of grass and pulled sharply, spraying grass seeds on the ground. And this, too, is how forests and natural areas are made. Through birds building nests, each tiny beak and pair of wings shaping the world around it.

We went closer to taller grasses, hoping to see bitterns. The area was lush with typha and saccharum grasses, and the first thing I noticed were places where the grasses seemed glued together, part of a larger sculpture. These were the efforts of Black-breasted weavers, who had taken green, living grasses and pulled them into a structure which was to be their nest. The main nest chamber looks something like an upside-down vase, or a single inverted comma—roughly an oval shape with an entrance shaped as a tube. The bird lashes tall adjacent grasses to the main structure of the nest. This gives the effect of an octopus-like art piece, stabilized by its 'tentacles'. It is a testament to a bird that manages to balance its family in between nothing but the whisper of grasses.

Apart from a sense of parental duty, the weaver birds also have a sense of beauty. In a 2020 paper, Diwakar Prakash, S.L. Niangthianhoi, Ram Kumar and Faiyaz A. Khudsar write how Streaked weaver birds complete nests only when the females approve them. The female has the last word, so to speak, and we guess this depends on two things. In order to attract females, the male makes a good nest, but he also decorates it. And the weavers seem to like the colour yellow. In the northern districts of Tamil Nadu, M. Pandian documents Black-breasted weaver birds bringing bright yellow cucumber flowers to decorate their nests. And near Hyderabad, Aasheesh Pittie, Siraj Taher and C. Tom Hash found that the Black-breasted weaver brought yellow acacia flowers to their nests. Is it because the male weaver birds themselves have bright, mango-yellow caps, and yellow is a favoured colour in the weaver bird world?[2] I don't know the answer to that, but the idea of a bird on a supple cucumber vine, or a thorny, heat-battered acacia tree—picking out the perfect yellow flower which will retain its colour despite being dehydrated, is enormously charming. And in our cynical lives, we need this charm.

So here is the second thing about nests—nests shape bird worlds, but they also shape a nicer world for us through their art.

Some of us looked in the skyline for bitterns, while the rest peered at the reeds.

I was part of the reed-staring group. The reeds looked very different from the trees. They were tall and erect, but they moved with even a whisper of wind. As they swayed, gaps formed, and one could see very far into them. And then the curtain returned, and you were looking at grass, not gaps. The movement was constant, making the reed-world look ephemeral and more than a little psychedelic. To find a bird in between this shifting scape was like looking at the memory of a thing rather than the thing itself. I stared some more. A waterhen called. The grasses were hypnotic. Swish, swish, sway.

The reed patch had Yellow bitterns, Little bitterns, Cinnamon bitterns, and rumoured Black bitterns, the latter also frequenting the nearby Najafgarh lake, but I couldn't see any of them yet.

Bitterns look a lot like herons. They often have a hunched pose that seems like the bird is in deep thought. This is actually a deep strategy. Both herons and bitterns stay motionless while hunting their prey, appearing still and unthreatening. But when a fish appears, the bittern's neck will spring out like a harpoon, and its beak will spear the fish. You can almost hear the coil of muscle as you watch a bird's neck become a weapon, the point just before a fish becomes a meal. After swallowing its prize, the bird becomes still again, resuming its wait, and its hunt. And when surprised, bitterns employ the same strategy—they freeze.

My first Yellow bittern sighting was in Mangalajodi near the city of Bhubaneshwar in the East Indian state of Odisha. The sun beat down on our backs, pooling at the sides of our eyes, while we went silently through the reeds in a hand-rowed boat, feeling like an ancient alligator in her swamp. Mangalajodi once suffered from immense local hunting, until several interventions—with the pioneering involvement of the NGO Wild Orissa—encouraged hunters to turn into bird guides. Now Mangalajodi's story is that of the abundance of wild resident and migratory birds. This is the place where elegant, rustic boats rowed by an ex-poacher take you right in the middle of the reeds, and where the captain stops and lovingly tells you bird names. That day in Odisha, the reeds towered over us, solemn, making flute-like sounds when the wind rustled them. It wasn't just a place of reeds: it was a reed-forest. For me, it was just the beginning of learning to see through tiny gaps between reeds.

An ecologist on our boat suddenly cried out, 'What's that, something's there.' We frantically followed her eyeline, wondering what treasures the reed-forest would reveal. I looked once, roving through the area with a torchlight-like sweep. Then I looked again, up and down, left and right, imagining I was covering a grid. There was nothing to see. Except, there was a reed that looked just a little bent. I thought the wind and waves had broken a single reed, leaving it a stump. A little break from the vertical symmetry.

Nothing here, just reeds, I told her. She was still looking intently at the bent reed. She pointed. I looked again, and as I focused, a beak appeared in my comprehension—angled in the way of a broken stem mouth. Its body had soft-brown marks down its front, like it had been lovingly caressed with chocolate fingers. Those marks made the bittern's body so identical to that of a wind-swept, sun-baked reed that it was nearly impossible to tell them apart. We gazed again, the sun in our eyes. A slight moment, a twitch and a turn. The bird changed its position near the beginning of the water and froze again. We watched bird become reed, and imagined the bittern's 'kakak' call threading through the fluted reeds, their voices becoming one.

Sometimes when looking intensely for birds, one's vision seems to alter. While looking at Amur falcons in the sky in Nagaland in October for ten years of my conservation project, I had to squint to understand their true numbers. There were so many they filled the sky, from corner to corner. And they were so high, they looked tiny. A flush of falcons had become a swarm of mosquitos. I used to track the falcon flocks, and at dawn, they would fly up in spirals, making heaving columns that kept going higher. These were gyres that seemed to be shaping the sky and the surrounding world itself—the birds crying out with high-pitched, keening sounds, raising goosebumps on my flesh. Their swift wings would take them higher than your neck could crane. The gyres too had layers. Behind one spiral column was another, filled with more screaming, rapturous falcons. I had counted close to 100,000 falcons on one occasion, considered the world's largest congregation of raptors. When I closed my eyes, I'd still see black dots flitting across my vision, ecstatic and shrieking.[3]

A researcher who studies warblers, tiny birds that love trees, tells me he sees leaves when he closes his eyes. Particularly, the long, elegant and bottle-green leaf of the mango, a tree preferred by many warblers to sally on for insects.

In Chandu, as I watched for bitterns in the tall green-golden reeds, it seemed the whole world had become divided into vertical stripes. The landscape was lineated—submitting to a slicing of the world into bittern-size snapshots. Bitterns have an ingenious way of gaining height while they perch in the reeds. They grab a strand of grass in each foot. This makes them look splayed between the vegetation but they are perfectly at ease. They instantly remind you of the cool power of martial arts: how a painful-looking pose masks strength and relaxation for the master. That day, we waited for the bittern, and its cool powers of freezing and repose, but did not see it. It was time for me to leave. But when I closed my eyes, there were grassy streaks behind my eyelids, gold bars of meaning which I could return to again and again.

During the Covid lockdown, I had experienced a different set of bars. I watched the world from between the bars of my kitchen window, spaced four inches apart. There was a neem tree outside my kitchen, another one outside the bedroom. In the lockdown, we were trapped. But the birds were free, perhaps even made bolder by our absence. They did various things as I watched, slack-jawed (or with onion-tears, while cooking in the kitchen). Common mynas would bicker on the neem branches. Rose-ringed parakeets visited, their coming heralded by loud screeching. Rufous tree-pies arrived too, looking for nests to raid. And in spring, the neem changed completely. It opened up thousands of tiny, star-shaped white flowers. They had a subtle shine, like looking at a light through water. On these flowers, delicate Red pierrot butterflies would alight. The kitchen and bedroom were filled with a lavender scent. Nature had reached out to me, though I experienced it through bars that lay like stripes on my vision. I'd fix one eye between one set of bars and close the other to be able to focus my vision. I'd angle my camera through the bars too—I managed to get some close shots, but more zoomed-out shots were impossible. Sometimes all I got was the eye and beak of a bird, staring out of the photos like a huge dinosaur.

As my frustration grew, I spotted movement in the neem outside the bedroom. Whatever was moving became immediately invisible. I slashed my head from right to left, desperate to see, but with hardly any space to do so. The bars poked my forehead, and the neem leaves cloaked the bird, April winds whipped the tree. I was looking through, and at, miniscule spaces. Squinting my eyes, I finally grasped a glimpse of what was moving on the tree. It was a Yellow-footed green pigeon.[4] She perched serenely on a flowering branch, now completely unmoving. I tried to see her without blinking, wondering if she would vanish, absorbing the sight of her. She looked like an extension of the leaves, green and yellow and soft. One more movement, a little nudge, and there was an outsized beak next to her. It was a fledgling. The wind puffed and the flowers nodded, a cinematic spotlight, before they turned into camouflage again. It took me a few minutes to comprehend that there were actually two chicks, flanking the mother on each side. They had beaks too big for their faces, their fronts covered with grey-green downy fluff. Through my lens, I saw the colour of the mother's eye: pink-rimmed and purple-irised. The chaos of the pandemic seemed far, far away from the family's colourful, dreaming eyes. I noted the gentle way they stayed in their private bower of flowers, heads tucked low. How the mother occasionally preened her young ones but also provided an example by staying hidden. A wind rose, buffeting the branch sharply. All three bodies were jostled, but they did not move their positions. They seemed to have a deep acceptance of their life, and their situation. They seemed to know more than us restless pandemic souls. It was like looking at a forest pool, still, pellucid, and secretive, yet with more depth than what met the eye.

I watched them every day till the chicks flew away. The tree pigeons had taught me two valuable lessons. One, you may not be able to see perfectly—through bars or reeds. But even an imperfect view is an important view. And two, if you can't see things at once, you wait. Birds reward patience.

And so I return to Chandu on another autumnal day. I stand at the same spot as before, looking at the reeds, their opening and closing gaps, their shifting nature and their sheer numbers, my vision slashed into vertical stripes. There are warblers calling from the reeds. Streaked weavers and Red munias flit around me. My friend Anita turns and smiles at me. I look through the grass gaps. There are no bitterns standing like statues, no bitterns holding one reed in each foot. And then: in the air, flying out—a Cinnamon bittern. We see it clearly, floating away from us, and then we don't see it again.

It isn't exactly the hours of bittern observation I wanted, but it is an important moment. The focus, sliced in vertical pieces, has paid off. My friends and I smile to each other. Birds like patience.

As I go forward, there is a Siberian stonechat, setting on a celosia clump, just like I had seen in 2022 with Pankaj. Many birds show preferences for certain sites, what we know as site fidelity. Satellite tracking of Bar-tailed godwits migrating from Russia to Australia showed the birds visiting the same site—Roebuck Bay—every year. Looking at the stonechat, I wonder if it is the same bird returning to the same bush, even if it crossed hundreds of kilometres on four round trips to do so. A little ahead, a dragonfly sits on *Dactyloctenium aegyptium* grass. This is a grass with a seed head that looks like a cross. It reminds others of a crow's foot and so is also known as crow's foot grass. A Pond heron sits next to the water, holding saccharum grasses in its clasp. It looks just like a bittern. There is just so much happening among the grasses—in the reeds as well as the drier grasses—that it can be hard to accept that most grasses are undervalued by managers.

Farmers with livestock cherish grasses. But horticulturalists abhor wild grasses, and wetland managers would prefer water lilies to reed clumps. This is why the 'development' of so many wetlands, in cities like Nagpur or Bengaluru, has meant a forced, manic neatening by removing grasses. For most managers, grasses become too impenetrable far too quickly, too spear-like and savage. And in revenue records, grasslands—with native grasses that often look browned—show up as wastelands.[5] The Wasteland Atlas of India, 2019, has a map of alleged 'wastelands'. These have categories like land with open scrub, barren rocky areas, land with dense scrub, marshy land and underutilized forests. These areas are analogous with natural features—yet they sit in the same categories as devastated sites which are closer to the 'waste' category, such as mining and industrial wastelands.

'A reduction in wastelands area was observed in the categories of Land with Dense Scrub, Waterlogged and Marshy land, Sandy areas, Degraded pastures/grazing land and Gullied and/or ravinous [sic] land,' says a press-release on the release of the Wastelands Atlas.[6]

And because grasslands aren't doing well, neither are many birds connected to wet and dry grasslands, such as the Lesser florican and Bengal florican, the Great Indian bustard and the Black-breasted parrotbill. It has today become imperative to identify grasslands and reed-lands as ecosystems with their own character, integrity and needs. I think the easiest way to do so is to view grasses from a bird's perspective. This is a secretive world which you can't see all at once, but provides food, shelter and nesting sites. Grasses also make an astonishing world, because frail-looking grass actually has a spine of steel—holding up entire nests of weaver bird babies.

Meanwhile, the bittern stills itself, and then climbs reeds, holding down hard, attempting to hunt. And then it tries again. It knows how to save its energy and make the most of a reed-forest.

On difficult days, I think we have a bittern in all of us: holding precariously on to things that have personal meaning. Grasping at shoots that look frail, but which turn out to be lifelines.

NEHA'S FIELD NOTES

The Chandu-Budhera complex, with its astonishing variety of birds, is the favourite of many birdwatchers (for more, see 'Growing a City We Love'). In March 2022, we were looking at a solitary Open-billed stork, a snail-eating specialist named after the gap between its beaks (which helps it grip snail spirals). Behind the stork on the unpaved road, the ground seemed to scurry. It was a group of small pratincoles, exactly the colour of the soil. On another tree close by, Spotted owlets snoozed, while a Woolly-necked stork (with a bright, white, fuzzy neck) patrolled for pickings. There were many different guilds of birds, all in one place, some close enough to walk up to, some further into the distance, all going about their business.

July 2022: Just like we searched in bittern-grass in Chandu, we went looking in the grasses in another part of Delhi-NCR. The Rain quail is assumed to be a local migrant, and it calls from agricultural fields in Jhanjhrola, Haryana, in the monsoon. This is a small bird, richly streaked and marked, camouflaged for a life in scrubland. During the monsoon, the fields are covered in new, green grasses, where the quail hides. It takes many visits and plenty of waiting before one can see the bird, and when you do, it's usually because the bird is calling, head up and beak thrown back, its streaks looking like dry grasses swaying in the wind, its call a passionate cry for a mate.

Found Places

Firefly-light, Owl-light

'In the North-west of England, dusk used to be known as "eawl-leet", "owl-light".'—Robert Macfarlane on X (formerly Twitter), 2 April 2017

That day, he was wearing a striped shirt. I noticed because he rarely wore stripes. They were considered too racy for his government office job.

He had his cuffs buttoned, and his shirt tucked in a straight, sobering line, horizontal to the vertical stripes. The smooth lines meant he was just about to go to work, but something extremely important was keeping him seated. He sat at the head of the table like always, his neat, half-moon nails smoothing down the clear plastic sheet which sheltered the tablecloth crochet from food stains and naughty toddlers.

'Did you go to the park alone?' he asked me, his warm voice burred by something I couldn't place.

I was six, and had grown up mostly in our large garden. Behind the wall, a wild tangle of a park spread out. In a sense, the park was like an extension of the garden, but it meant opening our gate, going out, and slipping through another small gate to get into the park. The gate was my size. It is only now that I realize that in my present size, I would have to duck to enter that gate. But because going through the child-sized gate was no effort for me in my girlhood, going to the park had an informality which 'going out' did not have. But my father continued smoothing the plastic sheet with an intensity which made me believe he was not proud of my presence in the park.

'Yes, I did,' I squeaked, instantly swallowing all the other things I wanted to tell him about my visit—a dark brown mammal that had streaked into the underbrush, a black-orange bird with a long tail sawing out its urgent calls, a bush covered with tiny white flowers, crowned with a ladybird.

'You can't go to the park,' he said. There was finality in his voice, a feeling that he had convinced himself.

I swallowed and stared at him, hoping my eyes would immediately make him change his mind. Why, my eyes asked. My toes dug into the ground. I was assailed by the familiar feeling that the adult world was unfair, and worse, firmly against fun. I wanted to kick and scream. I wanted to nurture a ferocious tantrum, a fierce pet which answered only to me.

'But—' I breathed.

'You can't go to the park, because,' my father's fingernails bit down into the table cover with a pressure that rivalled the force of my despair, '... because you could get kidnapped.'

I felt physically struck. Why would anyone kidnap me? I was six. There couldn't be any reason to be kidnapped, because I wasn't of any particular use. It seemed unfathomable, and my heart rapidly sank, tracing a line through my body, puddling near my feet. I realized this diktat would apply not just to the next park visit, but to all visits outside. Like putting my father's unlit cigarette to my mouth, it would henceforth be illegal in the eyes of the set of laws that ran the household.

Looking back, I realize now he used the word kidnapped because he did not want to use the words 'sexually assaulted'.

The message was clear, that time, the next time, and the one after—it was not safe for me to go to wild areas in Delhi by myself. I could also not go with someone my age. If I went, ever, it would be with older authority—approved, safe figures, he told me. I looked at the tablecloth, grooved with my father's nails, and understood this was an issue that deeply worried him. Perhaps that is why it drew a line inside me, neat like his tucked-in office shirt, a line that every woman learns to transcribe, scored on her soul and under her skin: the boundaries of safe and unsafe, the order of 'borders' in the world. Lines that shouldn't be crossed, of places that are dark or remote, lines that get frequently re-established, lines which feel like a heavy toll to drag through life.

At the lip of Sanjay Van, where the darkness bleeds into the lights from nearby caravan eateries, I hesitate. That line I mustn't cross—inherited from my father, discussed with my girlfriends, hated and accepted, crawls over my skin.

Light pools like dull paint near the forest entrance. Behind that, the road appears as a tunnel—a walkway flanked by darkness so black it could be solid, subterranean walls. And beyond the tunnel, the darkness gets thicker, more intentional, the kind of darkness that is the umbra.

I have been in many darknesses of the forest before—sometimes chequered with moonlight, sometimes spattered with a faint starlight that feels silver, or pink, a feeling not so much of light but whimsy. But those wildernesses have been far away, in places that count as untrammelled, pristine in a way. This is the heart of a city, the heart of a city of violence, a city where the size of your car matters more than the size of your service, where crimes against women break records just like its high air pollution does.

I step closer and see that the darkness tunnels even further back, a worm becoming a huge king cobra.

This isn't the small stripe of darkness of Hauz Khas park. This is bigger, wilder, sprawling. Something needs to challenge the darkness. Maybe today that will be us.

My friend Nikhil is leading a night survey in Sanjay Van, so we have special permission to walk in the forest at night. I am still pausing at the entrance. I have been here many times, just not at night. Behind us, a tree with feathery leaves stands outside Gate No. 3 of the forest. A sound emerges from it, throwing itself with full force against the night. It is hoarse, like a bark. It also sounds thrilled. There is an owl on the tree, a bird with what looks like triangular horns on its head. We watch it looking at us with all-seeing eyes. It is an Indian Scops owl, found in many parts of Delhi, yet not commonly seen.[1] Scops owls are lovers of old trees, and that stirs something in me, a recognition, a relation. If we could all spend our lives near old trees, we would be happier. In that, the owl and us are the same.

'There will be more owls inside,' Nikhil says, perhaps knowing, in the way of old friends, that I need the nudge.

I listen again to the Scop's cry, turning it around in my mind—how wild it is, bucking, so unafraid. It is an all-or-nothing sort of cry, the sort that moves the entire being, of the bird's and the observer's. It has no decorum; it is instead all declaration. If we listen in the right way, it is exciting rather than petrifying.

There will be more owls inside. Their calls will be torchlights in the dark for me. They make me want to step inside and explore, to see if the dark could be a blanket rather than a snare. It is, after all, violence by people that has made the dark frightening, not the non-humans of the night. It wasn't the park that my father warned me about, his nails scoring into the tablecloth, it was the people: their hands, their black intentions.

Sanjay Van is a site for violence, crime, stashed dead bodies. But tonight, we have good people with us. I hope new stories can be written. On this night, being afraid can be optional.

We step in.

Nikhil is a big guy with gentle eyes, and he has walked thousands of hours in the forests and arid lands of Delhi. He looks like the guy from the movies who beats up people, but he's the exact opposite in real life. He refuses to take me to places he doesn't deem safe and yells at me when I don't pay enough attention while crossing the road. He has been held up in many parts of NCR, but he carries with him the eternal candle of hope all birdwatchers carry: despite the dangers, there might be a great bird. Once, while following vultures, he chanced upon an unlicenced group of people extracting hides at a carcass dump. He had been walking for one and a half hours in Haryana, and while looking up at thermal air currents being used by vultures, he found himself in the middle of rotting carcases in an abattoir. Sweat ran down his face and back, and there was something like blood and viscera on his field shoes. Another person who was with him threw up. It was worth it for the vultures, he told himself, turning his gaze back up at the sky. All of a sudden, he was surrounded by a group of tough-looking men. There were four. They had been extracting hides—messy, difficult, illegal work. One of them shouted at him, another gestured at his country pistol. 'Why do you have a camera?' he yelled. 'I am here to see birds,' Nikhil shot back. What followed was a low and urgent conversation. The men thought camera-toting Nikhil was a journalist. 'I explained my history to them, even my geography. That I lived not far from here, that I watch birds, that I have binoculars and cameras not to report these guys, but to document birds. They were unconvinced. So, I called a local friend who placated them,' Nikhil grins.

In the presence of wildlife, he is quieter. He communicates using low sounds or hand gestures. His first gesture is to tell me to switch off my torch. '*Ei,* listen. We will only use one torch, one only,' he says. I switch mine off, and someone else puts off her cell phone light. We are walking on a sandy path now, inside the tunnel of darkness, and there is forest on both sides. Our eyes blink. There isn't enough light to see ahead of us. Nikhil halts. There's something he is looking at. The single torchlight pools on the ground, the very edge of the pool touching a small black shape that's moving. Nikhil is fully alert. 'No one will step forward,' he hisses. He takes a tiny step ahead. 'That's an Asian palm civet,' he whispers. 'And it's gnawing at the base of the amaltas tree.' We look again. The animal is indeed gnawing at the tree, and it doesn't seem to mind us.

It raises its neck, its tail like a plume behind it, its movements as graceful as an otter in the water. It has the fuzzy cuteness all small mammals have—the face is like a raccoon's, the body like a well-set mongoose, the tail swishing and thick like a Madagascan lemur's. In the greyscale of darkness, it also seems only half-real. Its colour appears predominantly dark. We can make out a clever, masked face and little paws. Civets are able to run on the ground as well as to dart vertically up trees. They have an enviable lack of effort in their bodies. We are looking at a piece of night snatched into a streamlined shape that can cut through tunnels of darkness.

Civets, often colloquially called civet cats (though they are not cats, they may appear catlike in their grace and tree-climbing ability), are nocturnal. The night is a pall, and people don't like being blindfolded. Perhaps that is why creatures of the night have various superstitions tied to them—be it owls, hyenas or civets. Unlike the rumours about civets—that they are bad omens which dig up graves—they are sleek, harmless mammals that eat a wide variety of things—scavenged dead animals, plants, and as it now appears, amaltas bark.

The monsoon has just ended. The air is sultry. Most of the amaltas has finished flowering. People may have lost interest in the tree once its stunning golden blossoms drop. But the tree is irresistible for the civets.

Nikhil is watching, transfixed. 'I always stop near this tree. You know, it's a favourite for the civets. So I have to stop too.' In other Indian forests, I have seen trees gouged by claws of much larger predators—confident two-foot long marks made by tigers who don't have to fear a bigger predator, wicked scratches made by leopards with knife-like claws, and zig-zag marks left by the nails of sloth bears, like a game of noughts and crosses. Here, a much smaller animal—the size of a week-old tiger cub—has marked a favoured Indian tree. Somehow this leaves a deeper impression on me than the tiger did. Perhaps it's because I didn't expect to see it in Sanjay Van. Perhaps because it is breaking the taboo of the darkness. The tunnel is widening, the night falling away: it is still dark, but the dark is full of dazzling things. It seems standing in a wood in almost-complete darkness, rainwater fresh on the sand below my feet, soaked in sweat and a desperation to shrug off my fear, I can feel the wild all around me more intensely.

It is uncomfortable, and it is cleansing.

We walk forward. A call knocks on the dark. It rises higher, kicking down the door, no longer asking. It is unmusical and onomatopoeic: not a sound but a screech. It is a Spotted owlet calling from a tree. Like the Scops, this too seems to be a declaration, an announcement that there are animals all around us, and they are awake. This is one more torchlight in the dark. I exhale; I am no longer scared.

The world has narrowed to shades of black and grey, plentiful in their variety. Our senses are sharper now; the world becoming clearer as our eyes adjust, ears pricked like that of a wild animal's. Something loosens in my chest. I can feel the group shedding its urban skin of apathy and numbness, learning to be a little more animal.

There is a very light drizzle coming down, almost like a sodden mist. We are free now, part of this place, our toes dug deliciously in the metaphoric sand. There is a feeling of abandon in moving ahead without being able to see each other well, a freedom which would not have been possible in the studio blaze of sunlight.

What looks like a pile of boulders emerges on the left. These are actually vestiges of the Aravallis. A papdi tree explodes from between the rocks, gigantic, marking itself not just at the spot, but also the inside of my head, like a flagstaff. The path ends in a T-point after this flagstaff, and we take a left. A little ahead of us is Delhi's oldest fort, Lal Kot. The Tomar kings made this many centuries ago. Now, it is an irrevocable part of the forest. We amble up a gentle slope, going up both rock and worn-down built structures. Now we are on Lal Kot. There is something on a tree close by, giving off a gentle light. It's the dusky light of feathers, of fur, of fine, closely compacted things. Like a moth wing at twilight, or an owl's wing at gloaming. It is in fact a Spotted owlet, sitting perfectly still on its tree. Its eyes are trained on something, something far far away, and I know it is looking at what is far beyond our senses. 'Two dark, serendipitous orbs gazed down at me, riveting in their serenity,' writes Aasheesh Pittie, on the eyes of the Mottled wood owl in his book, *The Living Air*.

On top of Lal Kot, a small wind nudges us. The rain has stopped. Nikhil tells me the fauna changes here. 'It's drier here. This is the forest's highest point. And, it's a hidden world,' he says with excitement. 'The fort is mimicking a rock face, you see. We will find bugs and other animals that we don't find down in the forest.' Nikhil has seen geckos, nightjars and Delhi's smallest frog, the *Microhyla nilphamariensis*, here.

We stand there, some of us sitting, watching the ground. In the horizon, there is a faint, smudged line where the forest ends: light from buildings, the city-line. Moths emerge around us. The Spotted owlet, which has moved away, must be having a great time snapping them up. In the daytime, the space around Lal Kot has Grey hornbills flying low. There is also a Sirkeer malkoha that lives here, a large bird with a yellow-tipped red beak so vivid that it's also called a lipstick bird. The lipstick bird is a resident of Delhi, but it is so shy, most people consider it a visitor.

The night feels completely unknown because none of the familiar birds and animals are here. The hornbills are resting, the Sirkeer has retreated. Instead, we spot something on the ground, near our feet. It's large and confident, and it is moving. The insect is black, and irrepressibly chic. It has six large white spots on a burnished body which is the hue of a cracked-open amaltas pod. This is the Six-spotted ground beetle, *Anthia sexguttata*. It has fearsome mouth parts and will spray you with formic acid if you get too close. It moves at a pace that is quick, scurrying, purposeful. It covers a foot in a few seconds. This isn't a lot for a person, but is a high speed for insects—a high count of body lengths per second. In Greek, anthia means 'tyrant'; the rest of the name refers to its six bold spots.

Some beetle eyes change between conditions of light and dark; in the dark, the spaces between eye cells get larger for clearer vision. I look at the large, compound eyes of the Six-spotted beetle on Lal Kot. For a second, I feel he is looking at us with all his eyes. Each eye is perfectly in sync with the other in the dark, something which has been described as 'mutually coupled' eyes.

The beetle also keeps good time.

Many beetles have what biologists call 'circadian pacemakers', ways of knowing the difference between night and day, which tells them when to emerge. The Six-spotted is nocturnal, and his body has told him the time to come out is now. There are other beetles in Sanjay Van too, like dung beetles that roll balls of dung larger than their own bodies. Like the Six-spotted, they are enmeshed deeply with the world around them, and have impressive skills. Dung beetles like to roll their dung balls in straight lines. Studies have revealed how they do this.

In an experiment conducted on African dung beetles, a group of scientists tested how dung beetles navigated themselves—by watching the stars. If the full starry sky was not visible, they were also able to orient themselves with the belt of the Milky Way. And they managed to roll their dung balls in straight lines, keeping the stars as pathfinders.[2] It is humbling to think of a tiny creature, smaller than a hand's palm, looking far, far into the sky—much further than people used to looking at phones do. The dung beetle stargazes so it can continue to be particular, rolling its food in straight lines; the Six-spotted ground beetle follows its body clock, being able to see much better than us at its chosen nocturnal time of emergence. I look above me, at the stars, with my newly adjusted eyes.

A sense of peace, and with it, a sense of deep time, washes over me.

I am on Delhi's oldest fort, now home to a creature that looks ephemeral but is ancient. Beetles came much before bees; I think of the magnolia tree that evolved to be pollinated by large, clumsy beetles rather than delicate, whirring bees, or diaphanous butterflies. The beetle I am looking at prefers insects to flowers. In the torchlight, it looks like a complex tin man that appears deceptively like a toy. It rushes forward, carrying within itself reserves of acid which it will squirt at me if I dare stop it; it rushes forward, onwards, further, its little legs now a blur, dashing out of the circle of torchlight. I lose it to the darkness, blinking with blindness and a touch of frustration.

Lal Kot seems so old, so knowing. And yet, the beetles were here much before the fort. Looking around me at both the peace and the pall of the night, I know in my bones that it is right that beetles, not kings, have recolonized this place.

Nikhil's voice breaks my thoughts. 'Yes! Yes! I knew we would see the Six-spotted. They are always here.' He thinks for one second, and then carries on. 'They aren't afraid!'

Now he drops to one knee, and is looking for other things, or the signs left by other things between the rocks. In a café in Delhi overlooking a saptaparni, the *Alstonia* tree, he told me about his favourite wildlife sightings. I wondered if Sanjay Van would be in his list of favourites. It is. In the monsoon of 2023, he spotted a pair of eyes in the same Lal Kot area. Then the eyes were gone. Nikhil waited; he guessed the eyes would look out again. A little later, a creature emerged from a crack in the rocks. It was a gecko, black and slippery-looking, furtive like an eel in the sea, covered finely in dots. It was a leopard gecko, the first time Nikhil had seen one in Delhi. He would soon spot it again, and again, making Sanjay Van unforgettable.

That night, we walk on through the Lal Kot, no leopards or geckos in sight. We spot Pioneer butterflies, dormant on a leafless shrub, looking like snowdrops in a winter forest. There are Plains cupid and Pea blue butterflies, using grasses like they are vertical mattresses. They are so silent, so still, it is as if they are moths in the daytime—unmoving, sunk in thought and rest. I know I will never uproot grasses from my pots again, because butterflies use them for rest when I am sleeping.

As we descend the Lal Kot, a sound rises around us. It is like a chuckling, audio frisbees being thrown at us, woo-woo-woo. Two girls walking in front of me stiffen. I understand their trepidation. It wouldn't be eerie if it wasn't dark. As I listen, nostalgia plucks at my sleeve, then settles all over me. The sound is from childhood, from a time rife with monsters, unbearably happy days in the garden, sticky fingers, and the dusk air full of calls. The sound is that of a small dog-like animal that laughed at night. I remember this as the singular call of jackals in Delhi's air, keeping time even through the rude blare of horns and the summer drones of air coolers.

They call woo-woo-woo again, and I know they aren't far from us. I imagine three or four of them gambolling, building bonds through play in the way dogs do. I think of Pradip remembering jackals in Central Delhi, and think how sound joins us through different eras.

'It sounds like laughter,' I tell Nikhil.

'No, it doesn't. It sounds like a hooter,' he says immediately.[3]

This is our relationship: we bicker like siblings but likely will dive in front of a car to save the other. I smirk at him. He walks on, and I follow.

We leave the cackling jackals behind. The air is now full of the hum of insects. They sound content. It's a symphony I have heard in the past, in the garden of my childhood: a scratchy, polyphonic rising sound insects make when they become active at night, and when it stops raining. It's the best kind of white noise—a hush, a calming. Over the years, as insect populations have crashed, I have felt keenly the absence of this sound; its silence has been deafening and deadening both. Not so in Sanjay Van. Like the Central Ridge, the forest has fresh soil and a chitinous soul, crawling with many kinds of insects. I hear crickets, and perhaps frogs might be calling too.[4]

Nikhil is now leading us to a waterbody, an old one. We come to an open place with stair-like levels. At one time, this might have been used for bathing. That's the thing about Delhi—so many places are connected to empires and power, whether they have to do with humble ablutions or grand court hearings.

We stand in the middle of Anang Tal, now whiskered by bushes and bracketed in place by the surrounding trees. There is no water in this step-well of yore, but I imagine bathing in the tal, ringed by the jungle, protected as I was in the Old Fort's semal fortress of flowers. It would be a forest immersion of the best kind. A herpetology enthusiast from the group wanders to the edges of the tal, looking for frogs. As he edges forward, the frog he was looking for quietens, sounding like a withheld breath, a pause between heartbeats. Other frogs from the bushes pick up the beats and begin calling loudly. It's a passing-the-parcel, a necklace of connected sounds. There is that feeling again, the one I had standing on Lal Kot, looking at a beetle that perhaps looks at the stars—of great breadth, of a sense of relation between us and the habitat, of a chain forming between frogs that were here before the eleventh century and still exist in the twenty-first, of deep connection across deep time.

In this wild capital, the mighty exists next to the mundane; and sometimes politics is the connective tissue between the two.

On a recent daylit visit to the Anang Tal, Delhi's Lieutenant Governor declared that the monument should be restored and protected. A 2022 notification followed: 'The central government is of the opinion that the ancient mound including Anang Tal, Tehsil Mehrauli, district South Delhi, National Capital Territory Delhi … is an ancient site and remains of national importance … central government hereby gives notice of its intention to declare the said ancient site and remains to be of national importance.'[5]

And so, Anang Tal is set to be famous. Perhaps it can avoid being infamous like the rest of Sanjay Van, which is known for being the capital's most haunted place.

In the path ahead of us, a tiny yellow light flares for a split second. On its left, another fizzes, then disappears. These are signals. They are made to each other, and to those who can appreciate them. Fireflies. Soon, there are more along the path, some on bushes, and others in the air. As we walk towards a stream, the numbers of fireflies climbs higher, achingly higher, a reminder of sights that have vanished from city lives; a reminder that perfect darkness is a natural and desirable state. We don't see the stream, surrounded by foliage as it is, but we feel it, because the fireflies congregate in dark, wet places, and they are bedazzling us here.

At the edge of the damp area, skittering frogs call, their voices like dried leaves rubbed together. The necklace of sounds has another link now, of skittering frogs. We keep walking, revelling in the rich sound and light show of the Van's darkness.

A colleague cries out at something ahead, and we spot movement.

Edged by the light of a torch, we see a pair of eyes over a whitish mass. It is like the palm civet, but its markings are different. 'Wait wait wait wait,' Nikhil hisses. He looks ahead eagerly, his jaw tensing. Then he relaxes. It's a Small Indian civet, he whispers, a rare record for the area. Nikhil waits for it to leave and goes ahead to see what it was doing. He returns to tell us the civet was eating an unusual creature—a black-and-white furry animal, a domestic rabbit. We walk closer. The rabbit's head is to one side, and its eye is open, glassy, staring up at the stars. The civet had just started eating its hind legs, but the rabbit looks entranced, not dead. Its fur is still immaculate; I wonder if the civet hunted this domestic creature, or whether it died of exhaustion amongst the shard-like wild grasses, possibly abandoned to die here by its owner.

'You know I was told Sanjay Van is haunted,' Nikhil tells me later, while we are near the *Alstonia* tree. Dead bodies are routinely found in the area. Sanjay Van is a place where the unwanted is stashed—garbage, enemies, pet rabbits. 'But Sanjay Van is beautiful. For me it's always been a place of discovery,' he says. In 2022, he first saw his leopard gecko, and then when he knew where to look, he saw it again in 2023 and 2024, each time on Lal Kot. In the daytime, he would also see a Sirkeer malkoha there, sitting on the same rock at seven in the morning. In September during a dragonfly survey, when the air was wet and the dragonfly wings looked like pieces of stained church glass, his volunteer heard a loud flapping sound. A large yellow and black bird was on a goolar tree. He told Nikhil that it was a hornbill, but much larger than the usual Grey hornbill seen in Delhi. It was the Pied hornbill, a bird of deep forests usually sighted in the Himalayan foothills. It was a rare sighting in Delhi, but Nikhil was not surprised. He walks in Sanjay Van in dragonfly, moth and butterfly seasons after the monsoons. 'Over time I have encountered so many unusual things.' He doesn't discriminate between sightings of rare animals versus common ones. His interest is in animal behaviour, in the magical way wild animals pop up in the right habitat, moths to a flame, ships to lighthouses. In the Van, he's spotted Yellow-footed scorpions—black arachnids with yellowish feet;[6] he has ducked the venomous krait snake, and its banded lookalike, the non-venomous Russel's kukri snake. He has found several Indian paradise flycatcher nests, which is special because this striking bird—the male with a long, ribbon-like tail, the female being rufous brown—comes to Delhi from other states to breed. He has seen between fifteen to twenty Oriental honey buzzards at one go and found seven active nests. Honey buzzards are birds of prey with an unusual quarry: they attack swarming bee hives and eat bee larvae. While larvae are the main prey, they are not averse to eating pollen and honey, and thus their nomenclature. The bird has a pigeon-like head with dense, scale-like feathers; this prevents stings from furious worker bees. 'You know what so many Oriental honey buzzards mean?' Nikhil asks. 'It means there are many beehives in Sanjay Van. And that's the sign of a good forest.'

But his most interesting sighting was at the amaltas tree. 'You know, civets usually bite at and eat bistendu,' he says, referring to the orange-like fruit native to the

Aravallis. 'But I waited near the amaltas, and I found the civet appearing. And guess what? A porcupine was already there. It was gnawing at the base of the amaltas tree. And the civet stood there, waiting its turn. He was so patient. It's like he knew he would get his chance.'

Porcupines are rodents, with incisor teeth that grow lifelong; these need to be filed by gnawing and chewing. But the civet quietly waiting its turn was an insight into the secrets of the Van, a record of the behaviour of small creatures living alongside each other, unseen by us. In moth surveys in Bharatpur in Rajasthan, Nikhil had seen two other similarly sized creatures—the jungle cat and palm civet, digging holes in one place. The sympatry burnt itself in his brain—the manner in which animals live next to each other, often peacefully, their paths crossing like village roads meeting highways, sometimes heading in the same destination.

In the *Gazetteer of Delhi*, 1912, there is evidence of much more abundant wildlife in the capital. It notes the presence of pigs, leopards, hyenas, wolves, hog deer, foxes, jackals, hare, monkeys and porcupines. Wolves were common in Faridabad's Ballabhgarh, and in the Yamuna river, there were tor mahseer fish, gharial and mugger crocodiles. Many of the animals were viewed as pests (such as porcupines, wolves and leopards) or as game (bush quail, partridges, Bar-headed geese). Rewards were offered for hunting wolves and leopards—a princely amount of five rupees was given for the leopards, three rupees for male wolves, and five rupees for female wolves. Between 1908–10, the average amount of rewards was Rs 143, suggesting at least thirty animals were hunted each year.[7]

Now, the abundance of wild animals is missing. The wolves are gone from the semi-arid land of Delhi, and the mahseer and gharials have vanished from Yamuna's waters. What we have now are the clues remnant populations leave us. How important the most basic things are to wildlife—a mature tree, a patch of chemical-free earth, clean amphibian-filled water, dark and damp places where fireflies can light up the way.

We walk onwards. The bark of another Scops owl breaks the hum of insects. We are now heading towards a moth trap, a sheet of white cloth lit by a bright light, which will attract moths and give us an insight into the diversity here. As we walk, the moths are everywhere. Their eyes shine in the torchlight, catching the light at certain angles. Their furry flight makes scallops in the air, cutting through the moisture in beautifully sharp swipes. Someone with an imagination may think ghosts are following us. Ahead of us on the wet pathway, something glistens. We look again, and the shine seems to intensify. It's a huge, bulbous Indian bullfrog, and he's in nuptial colours. His skin gleams a wet lime-yellow, the most cheerfully gaudy colour I can think of. And his vocal sacs, one on each side of his face, are cobalt blue. Then he calls, and each sac expands, the call flashing blue-blue. The colour-burst is like the Van's fireflies leaving a glittering tail: a split-second incandescence, a beauty you want to clasp with bare hands and hold, because it's gone before you can comprehend it. You remember it, rather than grasp it, and if you're lucky you see it again. And so, fireflies and mating bullfrogs are freezing time for us—they take and stretch a split-second into something valuable, something colourful and rare, something that illuminates the dark, that sheds light on frequently forgotten places. The bullfrog evolved this way to attract a female frog, and I am reminded that both frogs and humans see similar colours, but frogs see better than us in low light. The female sees his blue-blue and lime-yellow more vividly than I in this poor light; their frog nuptials don't require human witnesses. As we go even closer, the bullfrog is still in the middle of the path, straddling it like an emperor with a ripe confidence in his finery. He reminds me of chital stags in mating season, their antlers full of grass, strutting their decorations and wares, unmindful of danger, no longer shy. The frogs and stags know that gaudy risks may often bring rewards.

We have edged forward, and the bullfrog now hops nonchalantly aside, as graceful as a drop of water plinking into a stream. His call joins the other frogs humming, chuckling and clacking from the waterbodies around us, their sounds tributaries that have now become a solid stream of consciousness. Ahead of us, we see the faint light of the moth trap. The flow of frog-calls, the white noise of the insects, the occasional owlsong, the feel of water in the air: it is a multi-sensory experience. It is like all the creatures here are combining to create the forest and engraving their imprints on it: the equivalent of a blister beetle walking on roses in the garden of my childhood and leaving his trail, methodically and indelibly. Sanjay Van is alive, and it sings to prove it.

Once at the trap, we look at the variety of insects on the white cloth. There is a fruit-piercing moth, a patch of yellow at the bottom-centre of its wings looking like a colourful fold, a children's book's pull-out with a hidden message. There are other small moths too. There are also some things that are not moths. An insect with what look like tweezers on its rump explores the sheet. This too, is an insect from the garden of my childhood. It is an earwig, I know now. There is a mole cricket, a burrowing insect with an interest in architecture—it makes special burrows when it projects its song to attract a mate.[8]

Afterwards, we go to Sanjay Van again and again, in the night and in the day. We have learned to walk in very little light, and have learned to push back fear a little better. Darkness doesn't just mean the time for assault and criminals; it is also owl-light, where owl calls are torchlights in the dark, it is also firefly-light. It is a place where the forest recognizes how it lived years ago, where beetles now rule over forts and frogs take over step-wells, where time is a path that winds like a circle. And sometimes, if you're very lucky, you find yourself at the very centre of that circle.

NEHA'S FIELD NOTES

February 2019: Reading old Gazetteers of Delhi is a reminder of how much flora and fauna we have lost. Yet, there are still many things to see in the city, and the urban and wild lap against each other in interesting ways. In February 2019, I counted Greater flamingos in the Okhla Wildlife Sanctuary in Uttar Pradesh, situated on the Yamuna. The water was blepharis blue, and the flamingos shone white and pink. Behind them in a settlement, India's national flag flew, and I could see the board for a gym called 'Fit You'. I am waiting for a city which can fit in its wild birds and animals even more comfortably.

August 2022: Sanjay Van is unbearably hot, but that doesn't deter walkers. People jog past me, kicking up the red sand on the trails. A tailorbird chitters, sounding like it is throwing pebbles on a glass window. A restored waterbody, Neela Hauz, has two Spot-billed ducks in it, the spots on their bills reflecting faintly in the mossy-green water. For a second, there is alchemy and the water turns verdigris.

November 2022: I have come to Neela Hauz again. Close to it, the water smells, and there is industrial-looking foam in it, a poor copy of ocean waves crashing into the surf. I breathe from my mouth, determined to enjoy my post-pandemic freedom. It's only as bad as the overflowing gutters in some of our swankiest, most expensive markets—the middle lane in Khan Market, or the Vasant Vihar Priya Market, where visitors walk in designer heels, dodging the sewage-puddles. It's reminiscent of patten shoes in nineteenth century Europe, meant to avoid stepping in sludge. Any birdwatcher can take a bit of sewage, and because apart from being a birdwatcher, I am also a market veteran, I step closer to the Neela Hauz's dirty water like it is of no concern. There is a coot in the wetland. A Little grebe is there too, and it goes round in circles, its patience seemingly infinite; its world that dirty pool I was sniffing at. I am looking for winter visitors, and finally, I see one. It's a Green sandpiper, prodding the Neela Hauz bank with its long bill. As I watch, a keen call rends its way across my head: a Grey hornbill, perched on a *Neltuma juliflora* tree. Next to it, a Chiffchaff, a small migratory bird, hurtles from branch to branch, looking for insects, stitching the whole scene together with energy and meaning.

July 2023: we go to Sanjay Van in the morning, just to be outdoors. It is the hottest, most humid time of the year; I know we will sweat, but I want to expend my sweat specifically for Sanjay Van. Oriental honey buzzards fly overhead. From a clump of grasses, a Zitting cisticola calls wildly, 'Zitting, zitting', like its name.

August 2023: We have caught a glimpse of Nikhil's Sirkeer malkoha at Lal Kot, and it was close to 7 a.m. when we saw it, as he had promised. From the trees nearby, the machine-gun call of the Plain prinia ricochets. I am bitten by insects, something like ticks, and it feels good, like I am earning my stripes in a forest that is feeling mine with each walk, one bite at a time.

June 2024: The forest is full of dry summer heat, the rocks feeling like ovens. The streams have become smaller, like shreds torn from a larger ribbon.

December 2024: The Green sandpiper is back in Neela Hauz. It seems to appreciate the water, which is not foaming now but still looks unclean. The sandpiper reminds me of people visiting bars that are well past their expiry date, moving from chic to seedy as steadily as we dirty the waters in a city. The Spot-billed ducks take off from the hauz, flying above my head like an Olympic shotput throw.

May 2025: I watched a TV show where murders took place in Sanjay Van. Fiction had copied real life, and this is not how I want Sanjay Van to be memorialized. I go for a walk in the forest again, slightly resentful of how people usurp places when the places should be writing their own histories. When I enter, everything seems covered in yellow. Amaltas blossoms cover trees and the ground. Gales have struck Delhi with relentless force this month, and the flowers on the ground seem like tree-tears. Still, there are much fewer fallen trees in the Van than there are in the roads outside. The forest knows how to gird itself, and in the absence of concrete, the trees fare better. And forests also like fallen trees, trunks getting colonized by ants and mushrooms, and with little mammals and reptiles looking for refuge. Outside Sanjay Van, on Aruna Asaf Ali Marg, a fallen tree is an obstacle. In here, it will be a feast.

The woods are ringing with the 'Brainfever! Brainfever!' call of the Common hawk cuckoo, a bird that visually imitates the Shikra. There are amaltas pods on the ground, and I crack them open, seeing the burnished but glossy texture of the Six-spotted beetle staring back at me. I trace the whorls of amaltas tree trunks with my fingers. In deeper places on the trunk, the wood is very dark, almost black. It looks like lava pools burned and cooled down, with their own ridges and black lakes, bordered by lighter-colour wood, a map of time and memory. When cut, tree rings tell time and the passage of years. But so do the scars on a tree's trunk—holding memories of civet and porcupine teeth, human and animal graffiti both. 'Brainfever!' the call comes again, and I laugh. The closer I go to the cuckoo, the quieter it gets. As soon as I walk away, it explodes into its call again, like it's saying: 'Ha! I got you. I choose if you get to see me.'

June 2025: An eighteen-year-old girl has been murdered in Sanjay Van, her body stabbed, strangled and burnt. She was found not far from where we last walked. 'Brainfever,' the cuckoo calls in my mind, 'your civilization has brainfever.'

June 2025: In *The Wild Places*, Robert Macfarlane writes about how the wild isn't just out there. It is sometimes right where we are, though 'menaced' by us. Walking in the night in Sanjay Van has changed me. I still feel its danger, menaced by us as Rob puts it, but I also know the night belongs to good creatures. I might not always be able to witness them, but it feels good to know they are there, that they choose their paths and the turns on these paths, navigating by starlight and the ultraviolet shine of flowers. It is correct that we don't own everything, certainly not the clever ways that creatures have made the night their own. It lights a lamp of hope in me—the feeling that the night is not just danger, that darkness is not just the absence of light; but it can also be hope, the presence of the living. For the first time, a little moon-touched, star-struck wildness grows in me.

The Found

How to Become a Butterfly

'The archaeology of grief is not ordered. It is more like earth under a spade, turning up things you had forgotten. Surprising things come to light: not simply memories, but states of mind, emotions, older ways of seeing the world.'

—*H Is for Hawk*, Helen Macdonald

'Normality is a paved road: it's comfortable to walk, but no flowers grow on it.'

—Vincent van Gogh

The days stretched on like the lectures of politicians—unending and ringing with false promises. It was still the time of the Covid pandemic. I had just begun to get interested in butterflies. We had known that if you plant a flower, a butterfly would come; but I now knew this was only one part of the story. Adult butterflies will procure nectar from most flowers, but they are very particular about which plant their caterpillars will feed from. You can plant flowers for the adults, but you won't have butterflies flourishing unless you nurture host plants for butterflies. The links between host plants and butterflies are the links of life—the patharchatta or *Bryophyllum* is the host for the small but spectacular Red pierrot butterfly, the lime plant hosts the eponymous, gaudy Lime butterfly, the *Calotropis* (aak), also called the milkweed plant, is home for Plain and Striped tiger butterfly young, the vajradanti for the Yellow pansy butterfly, the *Salvadora persica* (or the meswak, used as a woody toothbrush) for the Little orange-tip butterfly, the *Salvadora oleoides* (the jaal) for the Pioneer butterfly.[1] Pioneers are thought to migrate to Delhi each year, and they likely come from drier, desert-like places with jaal trees—places like the ones we found in Mitraon.

In my little garden during the pandemic, I waited for the promise of butterflies. It was June 2020, and all other promises were broken—that the pandemic would end soon, that friends wouldn't die, that the government would take care of it, that we knew what we were doing. The final promise lay outside our human machinations, in the very alienness of being a butterfly. I had sowed plants for them. And now I hoped they would come, carrying colour and whimsy into my bleached, sanitized life. When the sun climbed the sky, a blazing yolk with sunlight streaming from it, the birds would retire, but I knew the butterflies would be active. Butterflies are cold-blooded and they need the sun to get their day started; they will sit still in sunlit patches to 'recharge' before their long, quivering day flights. My house, with its little flat, its terrace, its balconies and windows, was quarantined—and my prison was my empire. I had planted rows of patharchattas, of grasses, of curry patta plants for the butterflies. And now, I waited on the terrace for butterflies to come and drink nectar, to come and lay eggs after the monsoon, to start new life, to thrive better than we were doing.

The sun climbed higher, impossible to look at, the sky a heated metal plate above my head. A dead wind rustled the grass that ran in leaps through my pots—grass that looked like weeds, unkempt, strangling other tamer plants, there for the singular purpose of being desired by butterflies. The heat of the terrace radiated into my thoughts, making me feel weaker, a little more alone. In the distance, the semal tree shimmered with leathery leaves which were a few months old. And as I watched, as the moments went on, tick tock, a Common grass yellow butterfly sailed through the terrace, floating in like a child's kite on a slack string. It was a bright, lemon yellow, coming towards me with little puffs of effort. I logged it as the pandemic's first butterfly. It felt like a tiny sign that the world was still carrying on. The butterfly floated a bit around a pot, and then, just like that, it was gone. Though I was prepared, I couldn't take a picture. It had vanished like it had never been there. I had no evidence of its existence but memory, a split-second view of a yellow that didn't burn my skin. I waited a while longer, acutely aware the butterfly did not know I was waiting; aware that it might return when I wasn't on the terrace, that I would wait for it in my mind anyway.

I trudged back to the cool of my flat, feeling oddly punctured by a little butterfly. I realized butterflies value moments. They stretch microseconds, where a lot is done—flowers inspected and discarded, danger darted away from, decisions made and enforced, patrols and recces made in jagged lines and curves which are so alien to our expectations of something small moving in straight, simple, unimaginative lines. If I expected a butterfly to come to my terrace and land on a flower or rest on a blade of grass, I was wrong. Instead, it would take the path of its own choice. Sometimes, a butterfly would alight on a terrace ladder, completely avoiding the flower and leaf buffet I had ready. Sometimes, it would pause on vinca flowers—blooms with pink or white faces—and then leave just as they looked comfortable. Butterflies on the terrace fluttered, dashed and dived, and when I was really focused, they danced away into the gaps between pots, and into the wider unknown. They weren't mocking me—though they looked like they did. Their behaviour was outside the realm of prediction, their decision-making completely singular, derived not only from a different sense of time, but also space. They navigated the stillness of the hot June air in a way that exhausted us, and they were attracted both to fragrant flowers and rotting things. The world was dangerous for them, but it was a space they continuously explored. If I was looking for predictable comfort and reams of photography during the pandemic, butterflies wouldn't be the source. I learned to keep my camera aside and look at them just with my eyes. I learned that if I wanted to learn from butterflies, I would be in their hands, and not the other way around.

In September 2020, Vallari and I decided to test the bars of our cages. We were allowed to walk outdoors, so we plotted where we would go. 'Sanjay Van?' I asked. 'Too far,' she said. 'Neighbourhood park?' 'Too many people,' she replied. The pandemic felt like childhood again—lines drawn on the ground, strict rules for where we could and couldn't go, Cinderella timings for venturing into parks and the wilds, masks which hid our faces, not unlike school uniforms that turn individuals into cogs of a wheel.

We decided we would go to Aravalli Biodiversity Park, a site that had been restored from invasive tangle to curated tangle, from weeds to native Aravalli vegetation. Once a site for 'bad things', not unlike Sanjay Van which routinely ended up as a crime site, Aravalli Park was exactly the kind of park my father wouldn't have let me walk in as a young girl. He wasn't the only one. 'You know when we were growing up, we never came here. This was where men played cards, you know, where people stabbed their enemies and left them to die,' Vallari said. We were walking side by side, step by step, like schoolgirls walking to school, hair pinned up, masks and pinafores neatly turned out. The lure of Aravalli Park wasn't its horticulture. It was the fact that the area was now restored into a wildness, a microcosm of the dry Aravalli forest. Bushes merged into trees in impressive, impenetrable masses. Grasses lengthened their blades with pride, gleaming in certain lights, like canine teeth in a delighted smile.

We had come early in the day, 7 a.m., but the post-monsoon forest was sultry. The trees pressed down, the air was liquid; our faces had melted into a morass of mask and skin. By this time, a year into the pandemic, we were mask experts, learning how to twist the elastic near our cheeks to relieve pressure on the back of our ears, made frequently sore by repeated mask-use; we knew how to wear spectacles with our masks in a manner that they didn't fog over. We had learned to alternate between the arsenal of masks the average Delhi person had: heavy and synthetic N95 masks were for the outdoors, and lighter masks for the indoors which never came off. There were new variants of masks with 'fans', which kept faces cooler, and we already owned vog masks for air pollution, since we were the children of a city that gets slathered in unbreathable air every winter—but those masks were tucked away for now. 'Should we take our masks off?' I asked Vallari after we had walked a little. I looked at her sideways, the way you turn slightly towards someone you know well and feeling you know what they will say before they say it. For a second, she shimmered and changed into Shakuntala, my childhood companion.

'No, keep them on till we see no people,' she said.

We ambled on. The red path below our feet, made of bajri sand, glittered in the bright sunshine, crushed jewels when the sun was at a certain slant. I wondered if there would be butterflies, or whether they would dance away the way they did on my terrace.

We wanted to get off the path, get into the real wild and the real park, to flex a little against our childhood taboos, shatter some of the pandemic bars.

We walked for about a kilometre. The sound of insects was in the air, but there were no butterflies. Birds called, a Rufous tree-pie buzzing and sawing to the backdrop of the insect hum. A female koel trilled, her sharp jewel-red eye looking through us. Near her perch, we spotted an overgrown, tumbling path next to the main path. It snaked away in curves, nearly indistinguishable from the thicket around it. It looked like Robert Frost's path less taken. It was beautiful.

Vallari and I looked at each other. 'We're going there,' she said. Yes! I agreed.

We entered the trail. On the ground in front of us, mushrooms blossomed from a dead log, looking like the whites of eyes, the dead wood a springboard for life. Already, this was more exciting than the red sand path.

A little ahead, the path opened out into a clearing. Grasses rose here in flourishes, seedheads glinting golden in the sunlight. On one side, there were scraggly bushes. It was a mini grassland.

On the edge of a grass, something was poised, a droplet about to fall. Its wings were grey, with a smattering of fine black dots. It was a butterfly from the blues subfamily, the smallest group of butterflies. The blues are part of the *Lycanidae* family, which has some incredible ways to survive. Caterpillars secrete a sugary substance that ants love to eat; in return, ants protect the caterpillar and the pupa.[2] That day, the butterfly was very, very still. I expected the butterfly to vanish, to fall off like the drop of water it resembled, to be gone, just gone in the magical way butterflies disappear into memory.

But it didn't move. It had the solemnity of a larger creature, a raptor on a bough during a storm, a thing that feels magnetized to a certain place of refuge in the way animals deeply know the right places of rest.

'We should look for more unmoving butterflies. They are soaking up the sun,' I whispered to Vallari. There was, in fact, no need to whisper. When we looked for stillness rather than movement, we realized there were butterflies all around us, and they were all sun-basking, eating the sun before their days began. From that state of restorative stillness, they wouldn't have moved with the sound of my voice.

A Little orange-tip and a White orange-tip sat together, wings partially opened, revealing white wings brushed with orange forewings. A Leopard butterfly, orange with black speckles and a fine wrought-iron trim on the edges of its wings, perched on a shami plant. There was a brush-footed butterfly, with the first two of its six feet curled up, hairy and brush-like, used for tasting food. A female Yellow orange-tip butterfly, blackly veined on egg-white, sat on a lantana bush. Then, there were butterflies with fake eyes—designs that are meant to stare back at you, to command you into fear. There was a Lemon pansy, brown with orange 'eyes', on the ground, and a Yellow pansy, with cobalt blue 'eyes', on a lantana bush.

On another thicket there perched a male Danaid eggfly butterfly, large and black, its white 'eyes' chased with cobalt blue. The blue didn't just captivate, it positively sizzled, as if the butterfly was glowing, not just being. Perhaps for a second, in that generous morning light, I was seeing as a butterfly does. We see blue, green and red through cones in our eyes, and we see in the dark through rods. Butterflies are able to see blue, green and red, but they also have ultraviolet vision. This means they can see patterns on flowers which are invisible to us; altogether they see more than us. Flowers appear so colourful to us, like they were meant to enchant people. But they are in fact advertisements for butterflies—for the latter, they glow. In the quirks of rich, deep morning sunlight, I was seeing the Danaid eggfly glitter. Perhaps I was seeing for a few seconds exactly how the butterfly wanted to be seen.

'It's so incredibly beautiful,' I said after a while. 'This place is a wonderland,' Vallari responded. 'To think we always see the Orange-tips flying away from us, and here they are just sitting still. You can really see their patterns. You can really see *them*.'

We had stopped walking. We stayed in one position to just look at the soporific butterflies around us, paused but still poised, so uncharacteristically comfortable they could be dreaming. If butterflies could dream, here they were safe, warmed, and dreaming.

At the edge of a bush, a Blue tiger butterfly perched. He had wing patterns of cerulean blue shot through with veins of liquid black. His body was a delta of tributaries, flowing with a longing to live. But the ends of his large wings, and their rivers, ended in softly jagged lines. These were battle scars: the place where rivers evaporated. Something had tried to make a mouthful of the butterfly. The butterfly had escaped, life intact but wings shredded. Young caterpillars of moths and butterflies will sometimes hiss and squeak, but as adults, most butterflies don't make sounds.[3] The tiger wouldn't have cried out when he was attacked. The only evidence of violence, struggle and triumph was in the softness of his wings, and in the damage to them.

I felt a realization in me. A little insect with glorious wings was attacked and left scarred. Still, it was here, and it was enjoying the sun. There was no evidence of its woe, only its desire, quiet and strong, to carry out the act of living. It did not complain; it endured. I had not derived comfort from butterflies, because I had pursued them and they had eluded me. Once again, I was in the metaphoric hands of the butterfly: I could derive strength from the fact that they would appear on their terms, at a certain time of the day. I had to go to them, not in pursuit, but in pilgrimage, and they would tolerate me. Between their heartbeat-like flutters and periods of deep linear rest, they escaped a warming world where everything else was designed to crush, displace and eat them.[4] These were not comforting nurses. These were warriors.

We returned the next day to Aravalli, and the day after. The trail we went to seemed ours, and ours alone. This was the biggest luxury during the pandemic—a slice of the wilds, plated for us, served with the sides we liked—safety, privacy, and wander.

On the second day, we saw a Common evening brown butterfly flying over the undergrowth with damaged wings like the Blue tiger's. It was like watching a poet go to war; here was a creature that made its tattered flight a poem. Above our heads, a Skipper butterfly, brown and muted, perched on a gangeti plant. It looked like a lioness looking out over her territory. A Common lime butterfly hovered near a flower, displaying astonishingly complex patterns—eyes of black and orange-brown, spots of brick orange, lines of swirling black—a mesh of calligraphy curves and paint splatter that nevertheless came together in a way which was giddyingly aesthetic. It glittered in the sun like the Danaid eggfly had. Close to it sat an emigrant butterfly, its proboscis[5] coiled up, waiting to be unfurled to spear the heart of a flower.

That coil was like a film reel—it would sense things, sending sharp 'images' back to the butterfly. With its ultraviolet vision[6] and tactile 'tongue', the butterfly was seeing and tasting the flowers much more than we were. Watching the butterflies be still was an invitation to look more deeply at the refuge around me—at its spill of flowers, the clamber of vines, the scramble of leaves, the steady rising of the grass. There was so much energy here, and a deep power in that energy. During a time of sickness and worry, this was an invitation to slow down and unspool, to watch the grass grow, to allow nature to vaccinate us against chronic loss.

We sat there for a while, not speaking. The air was charged. This was a place where our ambition of sitting undisturbed in nature was being realized, where our childhood parks with games, innocence and leaping wildlife had seismically risen up to meet us as adults.

'Some people say history moves in a spiral, not the line we have come to expect. We travel through time in a circular trajectory, our distance increasing from an epicentre only to return again, one circle removed,' writes Ocean Vuong in his book, *On Earth We're Briefly Gorgeous*. That day, a spiral heaved and moved and met us, our childhoods looking at us with kind eyes.

We had gained something. It was not something easily articulated, but we both tasted it and knew it. We had come here depleted and were leaving restored. There was a connection with the place and its silent butterflies which fell softly on our skin, the dapple of morning sunlight through the trees, hot but nourishing. We needed time to absorb how the place now felt ours, and to paste its picture in the scrap book of our minds. It was time to leave.

We got up, wiping our sweaty faces, and began walking through the grass. Ahead of us, there was the sound of rustling, the vegetation moving with increasing urgency. The back of my neck prickled, as did my ankles, chafing with blades of grass. Something I didn't want to see or hear was ahead of us. It was a man, sweating and in a uniform. 'What, what,' he cried, 'what are you doing here!'

'We came here to see the plants and butterflies,' I replied.

'But it's not safe here! You can't walk off the path. What if ... what if ... there's a *kaala saanp* [black snake, signifying a cobra],[7] what will you do then!' He paused here, sputtering and spent.

'*Aap kaun ho,* who are you?' I asked.

'I am a security guard. You can't be here!' he responded. His voice was growing firmer with his conviction.

'The path was open. And we study trees,' Vallari said. I had heard this before. I had heard her say it, or had heard myself say this, when men had stopped us, and I listened, bracing for the rest of the exchange.

'You can't go just anywhere,' the man said. 'You could be bitten, you could get into trouble.' He said this aggressively. The heavy implication of his words was: because you're female.

Wordlessly, I opened my camera and showed him pictures of trees, flowers, bugs and butterflies.

He watched. He softened a little. 'I have seen this,' he said, pointing at the photo of an emigrant butterfly. Here were creatures he knew, though he didn't have names for them. They were all titli, butterflies.

'I've seen this titli, I've seen it in this park! And this ... and this too ...' he went on, now speaking more to himself than to us, lost in the photos.

I told him we would take permission to enter the trail if we needed to, and that we didn't know we were transgressing. I added, for the sake of both of us: we were perfectly fine, we had common sense, and we did this for a living. He didn't say much more. He insisted on escorting us to the gate, to make sure we departed from the area, and his responsibility.

The spell had broken. It really was time to go home. '*Kaala saanp*,' I whispered to Vallari. It was sad but also a little funny. We laughed. No matter what our achievements

Top left: Flower bower: a Yellow-footed green pigeon teaches stillness to her fledglings.

Top right: For one moment, a Yellow orange-tip butterfly alights on a passiflora on the third floor of a building.

Middle: A Shikra trains her eyes on a prey in Asola-Bhatti Wildlife Sanctuary.

Bottom: A bat flies against the moon on a COVID-lockdown evening.

Top: An Oriental honey buzzard pauses against the vestiges of fresh laundry.

Bottom: A Spotted owlet looks at the world from a flowering palash tree.

Top: A Rain quail, plaintive, calling and looking for a mate in Delhi-NCR.

Bottom: A Red munia, in breeding plumage, is crimson against golden grasses.

Top: Visiting from Central Asia, a Siberian stonechat in Chandu.
Bottom: On the banks of the Yamuna, a Striated babbler hops on a bushel of wild grass.

were, we still had to prove ourselves again and again, like raising our hands in class for an always-churning report card, like trading in a run through a meadow for cataloguing butterflies so we could establish our worth.

A caterpillar never wants to be seen. It looks like the leaves it eats. It camouflages itself in various stages of growth, called instars, which look like versions of leaves: fresh new leaves, decaying ones, dead ones (and sometimes, bird droppings). It then enters its chrysalis and becomes a kind of soup. It emerges as a butterfly that can not only fly but snares the eyes, capturing attention and admirers. The butterfly is contrary to the caterpillar: appearing reckless, toothless, capable of migrating long distances—an advertisement as opposed to camouflage; an adventurer whose entire body is dedicated to living its weeks-long life fully.

So far, in my lepidoptera journey, butterflies had taught me a kind of ragged endurance. Unintentionally, they also had taught me patience. And now, they were about to test that patience. In my little garden, I had pots with beautiful *bryophyllum* (patharchatta) plants in them. These are kalanchoe succulents, with fat, fleshy leaves full of water. The leaves are a tender, translucent green, appearing luminous in the way something underwater would. The *Kalanchoe blossfeldiana* produces bright pinpricks of red flowers that look the sun in the eye, flourishing even in extreme heat. As is the case with many heat-adapted succulents, the plants don't need much, just a sprinkle of water. In the 1970s, astronauts successfully grew kalanchoe in space—with ambient lighting and without gravity. This was part of a project to improve astronaut mental health and explore food options with other plants.

Back on earth, in my little balcony garden, my *bryophyllum*, which had brought me so much joy, looked ravaged. In contrast, little critters seemed very happy, and very hungry, on the plants. The leaves were covered with caterpillars which were green with black dots and little hairs, and they were on the leaves, under the leaves, and in them.[8] I shuddered. I loved butterflies, but that didn't mean it was easy to watch hand-grown plants being eaten alive. If the butterflies filled me with a sense of nostalgic, light-limned delight, the caterpillars crawled under my skin.

'Oh my god, how hungry can you be!' I said out loud. Maybe it was meant for the caterpillars, maybe it was meant as an existential comment—if you're a gardener, you learn to embrace the cyclicality of both life and death. But I was conflicted: delighted that Red pierrot butterflies had found my plants and chosen them to lay eggs on, and more than a little surprised to see how many caterpillars there were. Little dots of their faeces gave them away, with poop trails inside the leaves. I counted seven caterpillars on two small plants. I touched one. It bucked, as if electrified, offended by the contact, and went back into its leaf-tunnel. With their little hairs, the caterpillars were like caricatures of something that are meant to scare you.

On behalf of every gardener and farmer concerned about their vegetation, I had the same question: would insects using my plants kill them? I started looking for evidence of other insects using plants. The aparajita, the butterfly pea flower, revered and used in the Durga puja in autumn, had leaves with a strange crochet pattern of holes. Neat circles had been cut out of the leaves and taken away. I imagined the leaves as flat beads being used for a pillar-monument, or as a flying saucer for a little creature. This was in fact the art of a mother leaf-cutter bee. These solitary bees make nests in decaying wood or holes, and they line their cells with circles of leaves. Each leaf-circle makes one cell, with one larva. Sometimes, the leaves are stacked in a row, 'a badly made leafy cigar', as naturalist Karthikeyan S. describes them. The mother bee had taken from the aparajita in order to sustain new life. She had also taken in a manner which left the plant with enough healthy leaves. I was confident it would survive—it was just a question of sunlight, water, and time. The Red pierrot caterpillars lived a short life. Perhaps that was why the caterpillars were so hungry—they needed to fill their bodies with as much fuel as they could, as fast as they could, in preparation for their metamorphosis, that stage of stillness, staging and vulnerability.

And in the big picture, the time of their hunger was short. The caterpillars would be on the leaves for a week, maybe ten days. During this time, most would become the host for the Wolbachia bacteria, which kills male caterpillars or feminizes them.[9] The Wolbachia gets transmitted from mother to offspring; the bacteria attempts to feminize the entire population.[10] Studies show that some butterflies develop suppressors for male-killing Wolbachia, which the latter surmounts, leading to what scientists have called an 'escalating arms race'.[11] Not only did the grub not have much time till the next stage in their life cycle, they also waged wars both visible and invisible—with birds that would pick them off their leaves, with chemicals that stunned their soft bodies, with bacteria that killed or changed them from within.

I decided it was time to pause the pity for my plants.

The caterpillars would learn to become butterflies. The *bryophyllum* would learn to endure. This too, was a game of patience, of waiting, of the ellipsis between decay and regeneration. There wouldn't be a full stop for the plants yet, nor for the lives they hosted.

April 2021. We cannot breathe. We both have Covid, and there isn't enough oxygen in the air to make us feel better. It feels like our lungs are getting eaten alive, and he is worse off than me. A pneumonia grows in his lungs, like the male-killing Wolbachia in the caterpillars. I am pained and stupid, having contracted the infection before him, guilty that I infected him, ravaged from coughing, feeling slow, like moss is growing on my brain. We have a decision to make. No, *I* have a decision to make, on his behalf, and our behalf. He is not getting better. We might have to leave the quarantine of our home to go to a hospital where he will get oxygen and expertise. The world outside is burning. There isn't enough wood left in Nigambodh ghat cemetery, next to the Yamuna river, to burn the dead. Bodies litter the Ganga river in other states, and perhaps the Yamuna in Delhi too. People have died under shady trees, waiting to be admitted to hospitals. In death, we return to water and tree-wood, the same things we build over in our cities.

It will not be easy to go out, to fight through crowds, to struggle through the infection, to find a bed. We could die. He could die.

I think the decision has been made, because when I see him, he is stooping, unable to even sit up in bed. We have to get help. Now the question is of finding the energy to enforce the decision.

My eyes burn with fever. I don't feel strong enough to lead or even to walk. Like a compass, my head turns towards my favourite thing, the neem tree outside the kitchen window. The tree is covered in thousands of tiny, star-shaped flowers. It is about 9 a.m. The flowers are gently warmed by the early summer sun, which still rises despite human suffering. As I watch, a Pioneer butterfly, white with black markings, alights on the white flowers. I look a little closer. There are more butterflies on the flowers, flapping their wings to stay alight, an entire constellation of lanterns. The shadows of the flowers fall on the butterflies, drawing grey lattice-patterns on their wings.

They are, as usual, quiet. They look, as usual, like they are delicate, while masking great strength and endurance, afloat through sheer effort. The neem's flowering is a once-in-a-year phenomena, missed by many because it is so often above the eyeline. But the Pioneers don't miss, their visit to Delhi sweetened by the neem's nectar. They have reached here after what we assume is a long migration, and the kitchen tree, where they flutter each year for an hour or more in the season, is a favoured pitstop. Butterflies know when to be still and when to fly for their lives. I know that for us, it is now time to leave, to fly to survive.

We mask up to leave the house. I know I won't see the butterflies on neem flowers anymore this year. I want to see them again. I hope I can see them the next year.

We lived. Or maybe I should say we survived. We learned to breathe with cardiovascular marks in our lungs, counting days with blood pressure levels, hours of fasting before blood tests, and the time it took to stabilize critical Vitamin B12 levels. After the Delta strain came the Omicron strain. And then came long Covid. Like so many others, our hearts and lungs were run ragged, our confusion mixing with panting, a thick braid that fell heavy on our backs and comprehension. Our sense of smell vanished and then returned slowly, but the return to a sense of self was even slower.

It is 2025. Vallari is recovering from the death of her cat Disco, who was run over by a car. Disco was a calico street cat who had adopted Vallari as her human family, though she remained an outdoor cat at heart. She wanted to go out for long periods every day, fighting with street dogs from her vantage point in the letterbox, and exploring the branches of Vallari's moringa tree. During Covid though, Disco was gentle and considerate in the way animals always are when their people are sick. She checked on various members of the household through the infection and the depression that often followed. This was a time of minimal demands from her. It was like she was a nurse that didn't want to be touched but was nevertheless always at hand.

When she passed, Vallari sobbed: Maybe I shouldn't have let her out that day. Grief is so often mixed with regrets. What if I had shut the door? What if I had loved her harder? What if I could get just one more day with her?

I told her: She spent her happiest years with you. She died like she wanted to, outside. But the words sounded tinny, hollow.

It is April 2025, four years since our first Covid infection.

I am on the terrace, looking at my plants. The larkspur flowers I have planted have exploded in a purple column, solid enough to form a tower, feathery enough to still look floral. It's a generous flower, seeding and germinating with little care. As I watch, a butterfly I don't recognize flies over and settles on the larkspur. It is large, off-white, and has smart black dots on its wings. The forewings are chased with black, like metal edging on a grand, leather-clad book. I turn to my pup, Gypsy, who is waiting patiently for me to play with him. Look Gypsy, look at this beautiful butterfly! I say. He has that patient way of cocking his head, trying to understand every incomprehensible word I say. He sees the butterfly and notes its presence; I hope that he views it as a friend. The wind rustles the flowers, and the butterfly darts, almost like a hop, to settle on another flower column. 'The flowers are vestigial,' I write on X. 'The main thing is a butterfly came.'

It is a beautiful day. It seems perfect. I am glad to be alive, and glad that a butterfly whose name I didn't know found us.

June comes. It is unbearably hot, the sudden cool winds that sprang up in April and gusty May having dried up completely. Gypsy is vomiting foam, and we rush him to hospital. He is bloated. The doctors are incompetent and delay his surgery. He is sinking, and we make a sudden decision to take him to another hospital. He is operated on to untwist his stomach. For the next three days, we wait in limbo, in the ellipsis between healing and necrosis. We have become soup, a muddle of tears, unable to lift our limbs to do anything other than visit Gypsy and then wait near the phone once the visiting hours are over. Gypsy is confused and in pain, surrounded by dogs and doctors he doesn't know. A little beagle comes and piddles outside his ward and he watches, lacking the energy to do anything. The hours drag, waiting for the healing that time brings.

On the third day, he is better. He raises his head and he wants to come home with us. He has survived his surgery, and a critical forty-eight-hour period. He should emerge soon from the chrysalis of the hospital. My brother and his wife are hopeful: 'He is a fighter!' they write to me with familial pride. On the third day, all heat records have been broken. I remark how hell is global warming and heated concrete. Still, we are smiling when we leave the hospital. It seems Gypsy might be okay. It seems the 'critical' label in red felt pen outside his ward might be erased.

Time passes. The heat tapers a little. Unexpectedly, the phone rings. A man tells us that Gypsy has gone into cardiac arrest. We get into the car, shooting towards the hospital, faces white, blood pounding. Nothing matters but getting him back. We will take care of him forever. We will change everything for him. We will do anything to have him in our lives.

Gypsy dies before we reach him. In the end, he could not see us. When we see him, his eyes are still open, but they are not bright. They are stars behind a cloud. They are the eyes of a domestic rabbit dying in an unfamiliar forest.

There is no meaning to the days that follow. I had looked for signs everywhere when he was in hospital. If I would finally see the myna who is raising a nest in my kitchen ventilator, he would live. If the amaltas tree was still flowering the next day, like O. Henry's 'The Last Leaf', we would bring him back home tomorrow. None of the signs have amounted to anything. I am unable to separate my anger from my sadness. I know the first hospital was negligent. I know an innocent dog died because of veterinary apathy, and a lack of care of consequence.

I enter days of deep inertia. I can't leave my bed. I can't write, or taste food, or look at my flowers. Gypsy's food is still in the fridge. His toy is under the sofa, where he left it. I am still, but I am not peaceful. I feel I am more soup than woman. Boneless, formless, incapable. The grief follows me everywhere. It can see me. It is like tropical sunshine, stealing in from the cracks under doors, inescapable and stinging, there for all the hours of the day that count.

I have stopped searching for acceptance. I cannot accept his death. But I am still searching for meaning. 'He didn't want you to see him die,' my friend whispers to me. Many people have experienced the same with their dogs—their pets go to a corner to die alone, detaching themselves from their pack. Perhaps this is an act of consideration for the rest of the pack, perhaps it is a pursuit of peace. In his book, *The Inner Life of Animals,* Peter Wohlleben writes about his beloved goat, Schwänli, who went to a quiet place and settled into her favourite position—legs tucked under her—to die. I know Gypsy and Disco died painfully and violently, so this is little consolation.

Still, I look for meaning. It is chilling to consider there is no warmth but that of my grief to keep me alive, to keep me feeling.

Author Oona Robertson suggests becoming more animal to live life. 'My favourite thing about humans is that we are animals,' she writes in her *Orion* essay, 'Towards an Architecture of Belonging'.

I am trying to be more animal. I don't believe in signs anymore. I do believe that time is a thief, having complicated my pup's stomach and recovery, having chipped away at the walls of his immunity. I am sitting on my balcony with a self-destructive cigarette when a butterfly flies towards my pots. By now, I know this is the Large cabbage white butterfly, off-white with black dots, forewings edged with black. The purple larkspur flowers are gone. But the visitor stays on the pots, a tad longer than usual.

The butterfly is not a sign. It is a fact. It lives in a different cycle of time, stretching the time given to it. What are days to us could be weeks to the butterfly, in proportion to its life span. It hastens to make up for its lack of time. I sense it is the same way with dogs. They have seven years to our one; their daily cycles of play and acts of waiting with, and for us, likely feel longer than a day to them.

Here is the Large cabbage white, Gypsy's butterfly. Here it is, living. Flight by flight. Day by day. Day by week, till it is done living. Butterflies have pushed me to explore, towards hospital and recovery, towards happy memories. Here they are again: living for themselves, and so, teaching me. They do not give speeches, they do not stand on ceremony, they fight invisible battles, and they just live.

I open my eyes to the world. I look at the sunshine of my grief. I note the colour of the sky, the torpidity inside me and of the day. I wait. I wait to pupate.

NEHA'S FIELD NOTES

June 2020: I observe an Arjuna tree daily. It is visited by Rosy starlings in winter and Brown-headed barbets in summer. The observations are most interesting when the tree is flowering in May and June. The tree covers itself with off-white blooms that look like electrified bulb filaments. Butterflies descend on them to feast. There are Plain tigers and Pioneers. On one day, a Paper wasp comes to the same cluster a Plain tiger is on, displacing the butterfly. Wasps have carnivore reputations, but like butterflies, adult wasps often spend their time between flowers, sipping nectar. For feeding their young, they kill small insects.

September 2020: We spot a Plain tiger butterfly sitting on a barbed wire in Vasant Vihar. It feels inherently wrong, like an image of beauty masking militarization, a butterfly's scales sugarcoating the violence of the lockdown and the forced isolationism imposed on migrant labourers. Or, it seems like the butterfly will get hurt by the fence and its jaggedness, by the urge of humanity to be fencing, to be building over, to be 'mending wall' as Robert Frost once lamented.

In the same month, I notice something on my pale-green *Syngonium* plants. It is the gloaming, and the sun has gone down. The *Syngonium* seems to have appendages. The leaves grow downwards, in a weak-stemmed tumble, but the appendages point upwards. They are Mottled emigrant butterflies. They are exactly the colour of the plant. I wonder if the butterflies know their own colour, picking the plant that matches them the most for their nocturnal rest. This is not a question with an easy answer. We don't know if butterflies have a sense of what they look like, but they do know how to camouflage, and how to mimic others. For instance, the female Danaid eggfly mimics the toxic Plain tiger butterfly. A bolder chain-link pattern on wing-edges is a good way to identify the eggfly.

April 2020 and 2022: I missed the Pioneer butterflies on the neem during the Delta phase of Covid in April 2021. But there are many butterflies to see, photograph and sketch in 2020 and 2022. I watch the butterflies skip through the air, landing from flower to flower, entranced by the generous neem. In one photo I take, the butterfly looks like a naughty sprite, sticking its proboscis out at me, looking at me with its compound eyes.

September 2021: A Plain cupid butterfly comes to nectar on my jatropha flower, a Grass yellow on my vinca. Since the pupation of the Red pierrot on the *bryophyllum*, I know the tangle of my garden is the right way to go.

If you want to attract butterflies to your garden, plant a diversity of flowers without the use of any chemicals. A chemical-free garden will get pests, but there will also be predators (such as wasps and ladybugs) for the pests, and with diverse plants, you will have more floral success than losses. Also, grow butterfly host plants (*bryophyllum*, curry, vajradanti) so the butterflies have a chance to raise their young.

A Skipper butterfly, like the one I saw on the gangeti plant in Aravalli Biodiversity Park, alights on my yellow allamanda flower. The same flower is also the target of a honeybee, which makes a beeline for the flower despite the butterfly. The butterfly takes off like a curl of smoke.

June 2024: A Yellow orange-tip butterfly pauses on my *Passiflora*, the passion vine. The vine is scrambling and untidy, and its blossoms are a radiant, purple shower of sparks, like the charkha, the wheel firecracker from childhood. The flower is usually pollinated by large bees. I like to think the butterfly sat there not only because it would get food, but because it preferred that spot.

April 2023–25: We have moved. The neem outside my window is replaced by a gulmohar tree. I see a Pioneer butterfly on the red blossoms. On butterfly surveys, I find emigrants on amaltas and Plain tigers on daisies. In the parks of Delhi, Blues butterflies skip through the grasses, as tiny as the length of mowed-down grass. A butterfly list in the post-monsoon season yields more than fifteen species in biodiversity parks and the Ridge forest, a reminder that though butterflies like gardens with planted flowers, they are wild creatures that also cherish the native wilds.

Found Rivers

'Muscular, wilful, worshipped and mistreated, rivers have long existed in the threshold space between geology and theology. They give us metaphors to live by, and they decline our attempts to parse them. Unruly, fluid and utterly other, rivers are—I have found—potent presences with which to imagine water differently. We will never think like a river, but perhaps we can think with them.'

—*Is a River Alive?*, Robert Macfarlane

In 2023, the Yamuna river rose to meet the Ring Road. An old bridge joins the iconic Red Fort with the Salimgarh Fort over this road. Anyone driving on the Ring Road—and that is at least a hundred thousand vehicles a day—

may wonder why a bridge is needed when a road already exists, and you can cross it to get to the other side. This is because once this road used to be water: The Yamuna river flowed where the road now lies. When it rains excessively, the Yamuna decides to move, reclaiming her old haunts. Sometimes, we go searching for the river, and the river finds us instead. The river has 'crossed the flood line', 'the Yamuna is in spate', the authorities announce in the monsoons, like Yamuna is a wilful child who left the nursery while her nanny was not looking.

In 2023, the Yamuna went for a roll and a swim. The river inundated several houses, streets and hospitals in North Delhi. This had happened before: in 1978, the Yamuna flooded areas in North Delhi, following which the river was girded with embankments. Amiti Sen remembers both floods. A business journalist with roots in North Delhi, Amiti spent all of her childhood and much of her adult life in Model Town. She recalls the water flowing through her house in 1978. Her uncle came up to the family home, floating on a raft. She was around three years old then. 'My family was so worried, but I was so excited,' she recalls. To escape the flood, they moved to a friend's place near Delite Cinema in Old Delhi for a few days.

When they returned home, the imprints of water were everywhere. 'There were fish. There were so many fish, they were everywhere.' For a Bengali family, this was an exciting prospect. Her father, along with a friend who she remembers as a mysterious Mr Mukherjee, used to go fishing earlier. This weekend activity was revitalized after the flood. Next to their house, a man-made lake called Naini lake was now jumping with fish. This is a regular process for rivers—they rejuvenate riparian wetlands with fish and other creatures as they inundate floodplains. The difference was that the Yamuna had never come up to Naini before. 'Now on Sundays, it was serious business to go fishing. It wasn't just timepass. We were, after all, eating the fish!' Much to her excitement, Amiti was given a fishing rod too. A corner was dedicated in the house for storing the rods. When she reached the lake with her gear, she solemnly cast the line and waited. It was the first time she had been given such responsibility. To her delight, she did catch a fish. A small one, but a fish nonetheless. In her mind then, the Naini lake registered as a living place, a place with living creatures.

As the years passed though, Naini lake began degrading, a slow but certain loss of character. It started with a smell. A sour stink drifted from the water, and Amiti recalls the water now had moss in it. The walls of gentrification too were rising—the area became hemmed in with walls, the sides marked with rails, soon to become a commercial location for boating. This also marked the demise of the lake as a wetland. Even as access to the lake was controlled, the garbage in the water went up, pooling at the corners. Fishing, and spending hours near the water with gentle, restorative attention, sans fees and frills, became a thing of the past.

She was nine when she was first allowed to go near the Yamuna river, for the annual bhaashan, the immersion of the goddess Durga in the river after the Durga puja. She wasn't allowed before this, for reasons which will not resonate with today's nine-year-olds—because the river was too deep. Her mother feared the little girl might get too close to the water and get carried away. When Amiti first saw the Yamuna, she remembers: 'The water was so deep. There was so much of it. The people immersing the idol did not have to go far from the shore to place the goddess in the water.'

As the years passed, the distance from the shore went up. People had to go further in for immersions. The water in the river had shrunk, the banks sticking out like bones, and the idol would get stuck, sinking no longer. Like Naini lake, the Yamuna too became smaller and smaller—in the imagination, and as a thriving, living place.

The 2023 floods brought memories of the river back. 'The Yamuna wasn't as big as the Ganga. But the Yamuna was still a river. It was a river, and a place. When I see the Yamuna now, I feel an intense sadness. It is now a place of dirt and squalor. I feel we had something, we had a beautiful thing, and we squandered it,' Amiti says.

There are still many official plans around the river—restoring stretches of the floodplains with vegetation through new biodiversity parks, building ghats and immersion areas, cleaning the water. This is a mix of commerce, rewilding and a further commodification of the river. Still, there is another task that needs to be added here: to rebuild the Yamuna in the imaginations of the people of Delhi, to make it a place from the un-place it has become.

For memory too is like a river, near the high tide at sea. Sometimes you go forth in a rush. At other times, the river tugs you against the flow, as the sea tide backs up. Sometimes, the water breaks all over you with no particular warning. You are hit with its immediacy and plumpness, left gasping. When the ripple retreats, you are left with questions.

I have many questions connected to my memories of the city. Was the orange bird with a long tail in the garden of my childhood a rare Indian paradise flycatcher? A pair of vultures nested on a majestic eucalyptus tree opposite my school on Hailey Road. The nest was big, untidy and strewn with colourful things. It had a single woolly chick in it, alone but animated. Were these White-rumped vultures, or perhaps Slender-billed vultures, returning to their tree each year?[1] I wondered at the housekeeping of these big birds—all the other bird nests I had seen so far were small, woven, and most of all, tidy. The nests were there every year, until they were not. Was the cactus tree in my garden a thor, an Aravalli species, or was it an imported Mexican variety?

I remember too the Yamuna, and its specific kind of dust. It wasn't the dead burnt-rubber dust of the highways. It was a feathery, fine dust, thick but also remarkably slippery. Like the river, it had a fluvial quality.

I didn't know it then, but the Yamuna's velvety dust would become part of my core memories from childhood. Each year, with my parent's permission, I would be part of a troop accompanying the immersion of the Durga idol in Yamuna. This was no easy thing. The idols were huge—over ten feet tall—and the fact that the goddess had ten arms made holding the structure a fine art. We held her from the back and hoisted the entire thing on our shoulders, taking care that no limbs (that of the idol, and after some consideration, also our own) broke in the process. The weapons carried by Durga and her children, part of the same idol, were stacked away for use the next year. Meanwhile, dhakis, ceremonial drum beaters, would beat their drums, stomp their feet on their ground, and spin in circles, the veins in their necks straining. Fine dust dervishes would shoot up, becoming one with our clothes and skin. We would feel rather than see the dust getting into the roots of our hair. Our clothes became russet—to remain a faint off-white afterwards. It's hard to imagine where else one would wear this stained kurta, this tunic which looked like it had been rinsed in paan[2] water. That particular item of clothing was marked henceforth as the bhaashan kurta, to be taken out once a year. By the time the clothes became russet, shoes would come off and bare toes would grip the sandy banks in some approximation of how our ancestors walked the earth.

Each puja samiti (or committee) had a designated area for their drums, dancing and dust infernos, and this was marked with a rope boundary. Behind us would be thousands of people, dancing, praying and crying.

This was like a Bombay restaurant moment: the creation of an intimacy amidst crowds of people, a bubble for the individual and her loved ones despite the clamour. Behind all the human frenzy, the river glimmered, tired with our offerings, but still moving, eternal, imbued with the patience that nature has.[3]

Those days, I never thought how the water was glacial, that it came from a remote place in the mountains, and that Delhi changed it forever, becoming the greatest burden on a sparkling river. I always thought that the river was a celebration.

At some point in the day, the crush of people became one mass, an anthill with many ants, all rope boundaries crushed. Everyone would move in a single direction towards the Yamuna. The goddess's eyes—her face had three—stared at us. Her gaze seemed baleful. It was time for goodbyes. We all knew it wasn't a goodbye just to the goddess. As the sun slipped over the horizon, the goodbye was an agreement that our togetherness was over. We'd head back to our individual lives, jobs, romances and cities, an outward migration of heart and head. It was a going away from the puja but also from the river. The Yamuna was right in front of us, but already so far away. She never appeared in our conversations during the year. An amnesia fell over us, thick like a dust cloud.

Perhaps it is time to wade back into forgotten rivers and pick up riverside dust again. We are older; death has touched us all. Yet, the Yamuna, like the city, is not dead. The thing about nature is that it has the potential to revive, to be rewilded, to be restored. And love gives us a way out: if we care, we can do great things.

I sit on my memory river, and drift to another part of the city. As a child, I remember a flash of electric blue above storm water channels near Delhi University. These were White-breasted Kingfishers, brown and blue and white, zapping through the air and fishing in the storm channels. Over time, these channels degraded both in language and reality. They are now referred to as ganda naala (the literal translation is 'dirty drain'). The city has a wide network of storm water channels. But solid pollution, litter and effluents have turned them into dead zones. They stink so much it seems they were born because of cities, not because of rainfall. Areas like Defence Colony in South Delhi have covered the channels to reclaim land, and remove the smell from hell. Yet, storm water channels remain in the public imagination. While asking for directions, you may often hear someone say, take a right from the ganda naala. People cheerfully cover their faces when they walk next to the naalas, like carcasses that birders skirt in remote areas.

Our rivers and our storm water channels are ripe for restoration. This requires both political will and ecological insight. The shores of the channels can be planted with indigenous plants, suggests environmentalist Bharati Chaturvedi. 'People seem to hate them, but really, we should value our storm water drains. They can be waterways and their sides can be walkways,' says conservationist Sejal Worah, who is the co-founder of Jabarkhet nature reserve. A resident of Mussoorie and Delhi, she remembers freshwater channels in Dehradun. 'The water was white. The water would gush. You felt invigorated just looking at that water.'

Not far from the storm water channel of my memory is Yamuna khadar near Wazirabad. Nikhil Devasar is an old hand at birdwatching. The Yamuna khadar used to be his haunt every other weekend. Till 2005, the place was full of wings.

'The Yamuna khadar was wild and open and unpredictable,' Nikhil remembers. His face softens with fondness. 'It was a patchwork of wetlands and grasslands right at the city's edge. We saw incredible rarities there: Short-eared owls in fields of marigolds, Horned larks at the ash pit. Sand larks called from dry patches, and we once recorded a Grey-headed lapwing, a single visitor. On winter mornings, small groups of Northern lapwings would drop in, and in the right season, Greater flamingos, pelicans, and even cranes would grace the floodplain. An easy morning would get us a checklist of 125 species. It felt like Delhi's hidden wilderness.' I ask what has happened to the area now, though I already know. Still, I want to hear it from him.

He tells me the ash pit has become a housing colony. There is illegal dumping in the area. To see birds, Nikhil visits Chandu-Budhera now, where he has seen remarkable creatures: Little gulls, White-winged terns, Red-necked phalaropes, Bar-tailed godwits, Ruddy turnstones, Caspian terns, even a Lesser white-fronted goose. But he still remembers Yamuna khadar from twenty years ago. 'Places don't vanish overnight,' he says with emotion. 'They erode in silence. Unless someone speaks up.'

At the other end of the Yamuna's journey in Delhi, at Okhla, memories from winter are full of flamingos and fog. Journalist and author Ananda Banerjee has lived in Delhi since the mid-1990s. He describes dramatic sequences of seeing hundreds, sometimes thousands of birds near Okhla. 'At the turn of the century, I joined a newly-formed group of birdwatchers, which often took me to the banks of the Yamuna river. Our frequent morning haunt was a "dhobi ghat" (laundry washing site) near the Kalindi Kunj barrage on the Delhi side.' But of course, birders have their own names for places—for birders, the dhobi ghat was the 'flamingo point'. 'At dawn, it was a surreal sight to witness hundreds of these avian ballerinas in close proximity. Once, I counted one thousand Greater flamingos,' he says. The water was full of life.

And so were the skies. In April, Delhi's skies host groups of Rosy starlings migrating Northwards. In the evenings, they fly in what are called murmurations. Diving and turning and dipping and pulsing, the murmurations look like underwater shoals of fish, choreographing themselves as if in a hive mind, never bumping into the other, a team sequence of incredible beauty. In the early 2000s, Ananda witnessed murmurations of thousands of migratory Black-tailed godwits near the Yamuna. They would rise from the water into the air rapidly, filling the sky with their manoeuvres. He hasn't seen the same murmurations since, with tremendous habitat loss around Okhla.

But in May 2025, nineteen-year-old Gurnoor Dhillon found Black-bellied terns,[4] an endangered species, next to the Yamuna in North Delhi. And in June 2021, then nineteen-year-old Maitreya Sukumar spotted a Black-bellied tern near the Signature bridge in Wazirabad. The birds have not forgotten the haunts of their ancestors. The river of memory is especially strong for the Yamuna, not just for people, but also for wildlife.

I want to go back to the Yamuna at Wazirabad, the point where the river first enters the city. Like millions of other Indians, I suspect it will be like a pilgrimage. Over the years, I have visited Yamuna Biodiversity Park, near Wazirabad, several times. Now I want to return, again and again, to the main stem of the river. I am with Akash Gulalia, who regularly walks the river shore. We go through the dense colony of Jagatpur, like our ancestors who stayed close to the river. Furious road manoeuvres follow through crowded streets. Finally, we reach a place thick with velvety dust, and we know the river is close.

We park and begin walking slowly through the thick soil. The Yamuna stretches in front of us, the entire horizon taken up by her. On one side is a Delhi Jal Board water treatment plant, swallowing the Yamuna's water so we may drink it. Further ahead is the Yamuna's Signature bridge, where the Black-bellied tern was spotted. Near the bridge, the Sahibi river meets Yamuna, but no one would call this a confluence. Both reduced and dirtied, the Sahibi's other name is Najafgarh naala, a drain. This is contagious. Naala is also a derogatory name for the Yamuna now.

We stand on Shank 1 at the river. Ahead of us, parting the water is a River lapwing and three Pied avocets. Closer to us, people are fishing. There is a solitary man in one corner, and another man with his pre-teen son sits close to us. I remember little Amiti and her fishing rod. This is the only stretch of the Yamuna, before the confluence, which remains relatively clean throughout the year; this is the stretch where you may in fact catch fish that is safe enough to eat.

It is silent and hushed, like being underwater. Yet, a lot is happening. On a far bank, buffalo carts are waiting, each tethered with a single buffalo, to cart away precious river sand. Below a peepal tree, there is a makeshift temple, suffused with religious banners and cloths. A squirrel has taken one of these cloths, red edged with bright gold, up the tree, and it shines from the ball of her nest. A man sits silently in his methi field, surrounded by acid-green, iron-rich fenugreek plants. His fingers move deftly, picking the crop and tying it in small bundles. A black-and-white cow suddenly emerges from a clump of saccharum grasses, looking like a rhino coming out of a grassland in Kaziranga. Our phone pings with a 'Welcome to Uttar Pradesh' message. 'The cow is from Uttar Pradesh,' the farmer grins.

A pair of Striated babblers bounce on the saccharum, the seed-heads their personal trampoline. You can hear the trees growing and the fish plopping in the water.

Next to the shore, on the Jagatpur bund, stands a board displaying the Yamuna's flood levels. It is squat and blue, like a report card. In 1978, the year of the great flood, the water levels were 209.5 metres. In 1995, 2010 and 2013, they were between 209.3 and 209.7 metres. 2023 is too recent to be on this old report card. But in 2023, the river crossed 206.34 metres, triggering evacuation plans.[5]

We remember the Yamuna when she floods.

Before my Yamuna pilgrimage came the Sahibi pilgrimage. I have gone to Najafgarh lake countless times. The jheel lies splayed on the Delhi–Haryana border. Most of the water today is in Haryana, a state that seems more interested in the 'land' part of the wetland. A century after the lake was described as inundating 80 square miles, wildlife still endures here, depleted but not dead. At the jheel, I have counted more than ten dragonfly species named after the water they love—the

Ruddy marsh skimmer, the Crimson-tailed marsh hawk, the Long-legged marsh glider. I have watched Greater flamingos traipsing delicately through the water, their pink and white bodies glowing against grey sludge. On one morning I saw a jackal, on another a Black-naped hare bounded away.

In the 1980s, conservationist Vivek Menon spotted Indian skimmers at the jheel. And before that, birder Usha Ganguli reports that A.O. Hume, ornithologist and co-founder of the Indian National Congress, saw the now nationally extinct Siberian crane in the same jheel.[6]

'In the mid- to late-1980s, birdwatching at the Najafgarh drain and jheel was the thing to do for Srishti, Delhi's nature protection group that I had founded,' Menon recalls. He describes the place as full of water and life, a flood water channel. 'The water was channelled by the confines of its earthen banks and bounded by dense scrub. Flamingos and pelicans abounded in winters, and ducks and geese spread till the eye could see.' And he observed Indian skimmers there, an endangered bird now mostly confined to the Chambal river system. 'The splendid stars of those days were the pied Indian skimmers, flying swiftly into the river with only the lower beak skimming its surface for prey. The skimmers no longer have four inches of clean water to slice its beak into. They have disappeared, along with my teen years.'

Najafgarh lake now is full of effluents. Housing flats rise on the Haryana side. And while the flats appear to be sinking in the marshy land, they are still growing.

Close to Najafgarh jheel is Basai wetland, the same place mentioned in the 1912 *Delhi Gazetteer*, a place historically held in the grasp of the Sahibi river. It is now a shadow of its former self.

Pankaj Gupta has birded in Basai for years. Like the erstwhile Najafgarh jheel, there was abundance there, thousands of waders and geese on their winter migration each year. Pankaj and his friends opposed the destruction of Basai by poorly planned projects. But a construction waste demolition plant, full of chunky solid material, was placed in the catchment of the wetland. When rubble meets water at scale, rubble often endures. Basai is run over now, with cars, people and activity.

This should not be the fate of other liminal areas, around cities and their rivers. Pankaj suggests setting aside at least 10 per cent of Delhi-NCR for wetlands and another 10 per cent for grasslands; habitats that are ignored but vital. If we restore the Yamuna and Sahibi rivers, Najafgarh jheel, Chandu and Budhera, which are fed by the Sahibi, will also flourish. 'The Yamuna and Sahibi aren't drains. They are living systems. They deserve to flow freely and cleanly. They deserve dignity,' Gupta says.

If we were to make an atlas of important places in Delhi, all we need to do is look at the wildlife. Through their songs, their tracks, their beak prods and their choices of refuge, wildlife already show us the places of value: Yamuna river, Sahibi river, the Najafgarh jheel and wetlands in their present and paleo channels, along with the veins of various storm water channels in the city.

We know the places. What we require now is an ecological imagination. It is possible to zone land in a manner that the ecological integrity of these systems is maintained. Author and birder Anita Mani suggests regulating land use around the Chandu-Budhera and Sahibi catchment, preserving their pastoral use and preventing concretization. Birder Kanwar B. Singh has a list of wetlands that dot areas in NCR: Surajpur, Dhanauri, Beel Akbarpur, Mandothi, Dadri, along with assorted waterbodies along the Yamuna, which need protection from land-use change.

The dumping of rubble on riversides has to stop—floodplains with their velvet dust are soft mouths waiting for flooding, not hard containers for waste. Floodplains act as seasonal wetlands, and they require cyclical thinking which can imagine how they look in monsoons, not just how they look in the dry season. Simultaneously, we need a rigorous cleaning of water before it reaches not just rivers but storm water channels. It is unbelievable that this hasn't yet been achieved, but it still can be done. We need to remove invasives and plant the right vegetation on banks.

It is raining as I write this, an early June monsoon. I have searched and searched to answer the questions raised by my memories. In an old, pencil-underlined book published in 1975, I find some answers. In her seminal work *A Guide to the Birds of the Delhi Area*, birdwatcher Usha Ganguli mentions many White-backed vulture (or White-rumped vulture) nests in Delhi. At one point, she notes a single nest placed high up on a leafy tree. She also observes the birds taking over a crow's nest; the chick being woolly and playful and playing with sticks, just like the one I saw. Neither the adult Ganguli, nor I as a child, would have ever thought that this scene would become so rare that decades later people would wonder if seeing a vulture in Delhi was just a trick of her imagination.

The rain patters on. In my mind's eye, I can hear the rain falling on the Yamuna, the river my mother paddled in, others held swimming races in, the one that became untouchable, yuck, yuck, in my own generation. The river of memory flows forwards. If I were to cruise into the future, I would be reminded that in the present, the Yamuna and Sahibi are still living, as evidenced by their avian, odonate, botanical and mammalian industry. If we do what is right for these rivers, there will come a day when we view the confluence of Yamuna–Sahibi as a place to visit, as an embrace as fitting as the jaal and *Capparis*, as a reminder: *This is Delhi too.*

Growing a City We Love

'New York City in the late afternoon, shining in the sunlight. It did my heart good to see it again, its jolies-laides streets both generous and mean, so much talent in the air, so many rats underfoot, its people striding forth in summer shorts, its parks brightened by young girls in flower, its rusting metal bridges, its pinnacles, its terrible road surfaces, its everything-at-once-ness, its inexhaustible abundance, its crowded excess, and construction sites and music everywhere.'

—*Knife*, Salman Rushdie

'And on turning the last page, we found the first.'

—*The Elsewhereans*, Jeet Thayil

Why do we like cities? Surely, it's not just the commerce, or the limelights and floodlights. It is, I suspect, the potential for being surprised. In cities you will certainly meet people you don't like, but it's equally certain you will meet people, and experience places, that you will never forget. You will locate your creative kindred at a metro station or on a tree walk. You will find someone who likes exactly the weird and specific thing you do—bonsais in ceramic pots for tiny balconies, a retrospective movie screening where everyone is a stranger but nevertheless feels familiar, an astro-group that meets only on a few days of the year when there are clear night skies. You will also find someone who hates the very same thing you do—a punitive rent lease, a badly placed and noisy wedding venue, a new law that shuts down establishments early—and this too builds friendships. You will find opportunities for life and your preferences, the headwind of the city bucking with a bewildering array of smells and tastes. You can order in gochujang paste while eating idli for breakfast, and you will find rare herbs, banana flowers, and hope in markets, just when your life needs them.

Cities are also surprising because spaces are dynamic, often in the way of black humour. Things are hodgepodge and next to each other anyhow. A nightclub wedges itself between the Indian Statistical Institute and the Department of Scientific and Industrial Research (this indeed is a real place on Shaheed Jeet Singh Marg in Delhi). At Bhandwari in Haryana, a garbage landfill, visible from Mangar, stands taller than the surrounding Aravalli hills. In various other cities in India, old monuments, dignified and neglected, tower next to new but already rickety e-vehicles.

Things are anyhow, but 'development' here is always both a promise and a threat. Exhaustion and excitement are always a knife-edge away from each other.

So how do we save these bewildering places?

We can start with growing differently, and growing things differently.

The first thing to do is to seek out water and land and pay attention to small scales. Plants are the foundation of ecosystems. It is no exaggeration to say that life begins with plants: they are the first place to look. There are approximately 400 plant species which are native to Delhi. Some are very small, and some grow in water. The wetlands around Chandu still have tiny, old growth vegetation. There are little things in the water that eat mosquitos. These are bladderworts, carnivorous plants with little, underwater bags (and so, the name's reference to 'bladder'). Yellow-flowered and cheerful looking, bladderworts prefer slow-moving water and grow in seasonal wetlands. Insects trigger the bag-like mechanism in the plant and they get sucked in; pest control (such as mosquito control) is just one of the wonders the plants offer. Unnoticed by us, they do their work underwater, like whales filtering plankton.

As we notice the bladderwort, let us forget for a minute the huge dahlias and chrysanthemums in winter gardens, the conical 'Christmas trees' lining houses, and the disastrous vilayati kikar. After the announcement of the shifting of the imperial capital to Delhi in 1911, the British planted many trees in the Delhi Ridge, a bid at afforestation, and a control over nature and who could access it. They described the hills of Delhi, the Ridge forest, as stunted, bare and thorny. As an ostensible 'correction', among the many trees they planted was the green vilayati kikar, a miscalculation that still costs the capital. Instead of looking at forests as tools of ceremony, let us populate our minds and gardens with the native, simply for the plant's own sake. There are Indian plants waiting—for the shade, for the sun, for creeping under trees, as windbreaks—that need our patronage. We don't have to carry on with the horticulture we have inherited. We can create our own local cultures. For instance, author Madhulika Liddle's favourite place in Delhi is Sunder Nursery. This charming area close to Humayun's Tomb is full of trees, which she loves. But she also cherishes the wilderness zone there, which has little water bodies, and untidy clumps of grasses and shrubs, many of which are native.

I am asking, then, for a decolonization of our thoughts. I am asking for a recolonization by the native.

'I like the small plants. I like what people dismiss as "ghaas-phoos", grass and other untidy things,' says plant researcher and PhD candidate Vikram Iyer. In the wetlands around Chandu grow assemblages of such ghaas-phoos plants—at least ten varieties of grasses and ten to fifteen kinds of herbs that can no longer be easily found in other parts of Delhi. These are remnants of the Sahibi river's original seasonal vegetation. In his childhood, Vikram would be in the kyaaris (the rows where plants are grown) in public parks rather than elsewhere. Life in the soil fascinated him. Years later, he found something unforgettable in one of the fragments of the Delhi Ridge. The plant *Dipcadi montanum*. The *Dipcadi* is found growing occasionally from rocky crevices in the ground, and has clusters of pale green flowers, each about 2 cm in size. This is a bulb-forming ephemeral endemic to the Indian Subcontinent. Its range includes the Western Ghats, the Aravallis and the Western Himalayas, and in Delhi, it is found on the Ridge.

In J.K. Maheshwari's *Flora of Delhi* (published in 1963, for which the fieldwork was carried out in the 1950s) *Dipcadi* is described as uncommon. Decades later, Vikram found the same plant. 'Usually, such bulbous plants are the first to go when human activity increases, so it is very heartening to see that in spite of everything, they are still around. And not just a few scattered individuals, but reasonably large populations,' Vikram says. I ask how many plants are locally extinct now.

Around thirty species described in Maheshwari's book have become locally extinct in the seven intervening decades of urbanization, he responds. I am hushed. Likely, we never noticed these extinctions. And so, we didn't mourn them.

And yet, somehow, the *Dipcadi* made it through the chasms of our apathy.

'There are so many reasons why seeing *Dipcadi* in Delhi was a big deal for me. There is the sheer beauty of the plant,' Vikram enthuses. And then, there's the wait for that beauty. 'This is a spring ephemeral in Delhi. It flowers for only around a month in early spring before producing very generic leaves for another few weeks, and then goes dormant until next year. So being in the right place at the right time is very important.' Delhi felt like the right place.

The *Dipcadi* proved that the soil of the city, in parts, still had memories of yore, and that plant bulbs are a promise, and a legacy. Plants are capable of writing their own history, and their own future. If only we let them.

Decolonization is allowing, no, encouraging, the forgotten to run through the land and waters again. It is learning to appreciate the slow over the showy, for valuing plants that make us wait till they flower, or appreciating a different aesthetic from the ones we were taught to choose. It means reassessing why a dry-looking, thorny-looking plant was so unappealing to the British and why it continues to appear 'ugly' to us.

Instead of lawns with thirsty grasses, one can grow native grasses of Delhi, like *Oplesminus burmannii*. We must nurture small Indian plants like *Commicarpus chinensis* (with pink-white flowers), *Boerhavia diffusa* (pink flowers), *Convolvulus arvensis* (candy-striped pink and white flowers). Instead of chrysanthemums or plumerias (the first is visited ruthlessly by aphids and needs chemical help to stay alive, and the other is not visited by birds), one can plant hardy Indian shrubs and vines you have read about in this book, like gangeti, arni, kair, ghatbor (*Flueggea* species like *Flueggea virosa* and *Flueggea leucopyrus*), vajradanti, adusa and *Vallaris solanacea.*[1]

Apart from parks and gardens, road dividers and roadsides also have the promise to become more biodiverse, more *jungli*, a little more wild, just overall a little *more*. Road dividers can have more than one tier, mimicking a natural landscape. We could have adusa and vajradanti growing below moringa and ber trees. We could have native grasses on road dividers with less soil. Decolonization also is recognizing the real diversity in a native forest, and learning to mimic that diversity.

In my pots, I mimic the tiers of a forest. I grow yellow, prickly vajradanti. It needs nothing, just some moisture every other day. I grow the blue-blossomed day flower, the commelina *(Commelina benghalensis)* in one pot, and it leaps from pot to pot with no assistance, forming impenetrable ground cover. In larger pots, I grow shiuli *(Nyctanthes arbor-tristis)*, which reaches for the sky but showers the ground with fragrant white flowers. The flowers are a mental note for re-stringing daisy-chains from childhood. I also grow makoi (*Solanum nigrum*), a plant with little red berries, loved by Red-vented bulbuls and Common mynas. The yellow sorrel, *Oxalis procumbens*, just jumped into my life and my pots, and I let it thrive ever since. They shoot upwards, delightedly, every day of the year, and on some days they produce yellow flowers from the garden of my childhood.

These hardy plants ask me for nothing but water. And it is a joy to watch them live with no assistance, brave and independent and mostly pest-free. I draw from the rati of patience from my mental purse every day, and I draw energy from the phloem of the native. I thought I would have to give a lot of time to my garden, but instead I have become the recipient of its generosity.

Finally, decolonization is learning forgotten words, planting their seeds in our own hearts and language. It means asking for lesser-known things, the vajradanti and aak and gangeti and makoi in our nurseries so they can be planted in our lives. It means giving them our attention till they can establish themselves. And after this establishment, we can leave them to their own agency.

'Native plants are less water hungry,' Vikram reminds me. 'They are also less attention hungry.'

I have found in gardens and forests an order that is missing in human society: the capacity to feel challenged by physical difficulties, yet never oppressed.

I remember a part of the city where my friend was groped by a stranger. It left her furious with anger but unable to speak about it. That place was splotched in red for us ever after, a shrine to the girls we used to be. I think of the adjoining place I went to—Sanjay Van, where

I walked in the day and night, and how timeless it felt, how removed from grasping crimes by men. Cities are places where absurd things happen to everyone, every day. Life can seem meaningless here, bordering on the cruel. No person is left untouched by how vast and unending the world seems when something is stolen from them, and how small and shrunken it appears when one is searching for a sense of belonging.

Yet, despite the sourness broken city systems and people can bring, I am suggesting not an inward retreat, but a movement towards the outwards. This is harder to do for women, and thus more valuable. We can find purpose, and we can find ourselves, in the outdoors. Perhaps this is because in a sea of extractive relationships, our bond with nature is non-commercial, one of immersion. Nature doesn't ask us for reports, payments or untruths. It asks for little more than our attention. Being out in nature has gifted me with a rare thing—a sense of time, of having time.

Even if my visits or spells in nature are short—a brief walk, a few minutes of looking out from the window, spending lunchtime near a tree—being attentive restores my steadiness in breathing. Plants produce phytoncides that help us with our immunity, and watching something that is as far removed from Excel sheets as it can be is also exciting in its otherworldliness. The bushes that spring up on my terrace garden keep hosting insects that are so outside my imagination that I get instantly involved—a baby weevil, miniscule but with antennae waving; a bee-fly, a fly that mimics a bee, buzzing into a flower again and again like a boomerang video; a shield insect that looks like it is wearing a shield with another insect drawn on it; an ant farming an aphid for honeydew on a heart-shaped, tapering peepal leaf. Even the familiar can be seen differently when a creature interacts with the world around it—with a sofa, a plant, a person, a predator, its prey.

There isn't always time to pay attention to nature every day. But I have learned even a little time is good time. It restores the attrition of the quotidian, it restores a sense of self. I have found nature to be a paradox in a good way—it is both calming and exciting, renewing and heart-thumping, the best kind of tea blend. If life takes away little bits of ourselves, being out in nature brings little bits back to you—birds homing at twilight, the tide leaving a tapestry of shells on the shore, a wind dropping seeds from a tree or a flower at your feet. You are left with little jigsaw pieces of meaning which you can place in an order that is of particular relevance to you. Perhaps your order is reclaiming the parks of your childhood, or foraging for a dish your mother made, or finding calm in a plant when multiple battles rage in the world. Everyone's puzzle will be different, dizzying, a time capsule into storied lives.

A sense of purpose in being in the outdoors can also come because of the way our animal kin allocate meaning. Wildlife values places which we already know, places we share with them; and they show us repeatedly how important cities can be for their life cycles.

Birds that migrate to cities like Delhi have often flown hundreds and sometimes thousands of kilometres.

They carry with them memories of their routes. I have watched a lone Greenish warbler on the same shahtoot (mulberry) tree each February, and a group of Rosy starlings alight on the same section of a semal each April. Migrations transform local spots to international ones; they demonstrate physically what nature-lovers sense intuitively—that the world is connected, that we are small parts of the larger world. And that the world is made more vital if we understand the links between tree and bat, bug and bird, person and creature.

In 2016, Hemant Kairola, a birder who spends hundreds of hours outside each year, found something extraordinary in Mangar. It was a Song thrush. This is a singing bird that breeds in Europe and the Western palearctic, and its winter migration is mostly to the Middle East. 'I saw this graceful bird just perched on a tree. It had come from thousands of kilometres away,' Hemant says. And just then it wasn't far, it was in fact quite near Hemant, just like a favourite tree. 'It was where I was. It was simply extraordinary.'

Birder Mohit Mehta's friends asked him what he wanted to see in Delhi. In 2024, he had seen the Little gull, Falcated duck and Marbled teal in Gurugram, all thrilling rarities. Without hesitation, he responded: 'I want to see the Baikal teal.' This is a duck that breeds in Siberia. The male has striking green and yellow patterns on its head, drawn in curves that look like commas. It migrates southwards in winter, but mainly towards the region around South Korea and Japan. It would be exceedingly rare to spot one in Delhi-NCR. But in December 2024, Mohit did, in Sultanpur National Park. 'Spotting such a rare bird in the same year you wished for one is special,' he says. 'But so is the fact that it was so close to me!'

So here is the second thing we can do for our city: explore the outdoors, preferably with the like-minded, in small groups of people who can ensure mutual safety.

It might seem daunting to find such people, but more often than not, people who share similar interests are people you can get along with.[2] My birding group comprises an Army colonel, a tech guy, a botanist and me. We are very different and yet bound together, tied by birds who don't even know we are watching them. With these friends who share my obsessions, we have endlessly debated things that would make no sense to a third person—almost an emotional, private vocabulary. Such as if the warbler we saw was Green or Greenish, if the faraway eagle in the sky was White-tailed or not, whether Picture wing dragonflies, looking like bits of camera film flying, gather only at one time of the year, and what is the best way to parakeet through life. We have walked in scary places and easy places. We have prepared for a good time but faced adversity together. We have walked in complete silence, hisses or full-throated conservations. We have co-created a language of camaraderie.

We have also gained confidence in the very act of walking with a single bottle of water to share, changed flat tyres in places that still are not marked on maps, and tried going to a petrol pump that is on Google maps but doesn't exist in real life. Going into nature has meant a going out of comfort zones, and a growing inward for rootedness. It has helped us find our voice and locate what we really care about. For some of us, it's not the birds or the plants but the camaraderie that's valuable, for others it's the feeling of being under a big sky on alternate weekends. For each one of us, it is a coming home with a set of adventures where no two days are the same, of being able to say that on a particular day, the plant or bird or bug we wanted to see was close to us.

In 2013, ornithologist Surya Prakash went with a group of twenty-five birders to see a migratory bird that hadn't been seen in the region for an estimated forty years. In a wetland called Dighal in Haryana, the group saw the Marbled teal, a rare migrant to North India. Surya remembers the soundscape from that day—the calls of hundreds of birds, but also the snapping sound of his friend's cameras taking photos. Together. He remembers it as a thrilling sound.

There are also memories of animals as flag posts.

'Which city in the world has so many trees? Where do you get entire avenues of old trees?' asks Ravi Singh, the CEO of WWF-India. He is a kindly man who lights up while talking about birds. His memories of the city are like a drawer full of postcards from different parts of the region, full of birds ... and fish. Two decades ago, he remembers giving directions near Mathura Road. For a long time, the direction was: take a right from the semal tree with the vulture nest. Sitting in Kaka Nagar colony, he would see birds wheeling in the sky—Painted storks, Openbill storks, three species of vultures. At Garhi Harsaru near Sultanpur in Haryana, he saw thousands of waders in the wetlands on one side of the area's railway line. In the 1970s, in his years in college in Delhi University, he watched freestyle swimming races in the Yamuna river near Bela Road. Canals were drawn from the Yamuna, towards Civil Lines. These were flushed periodically, and were full of water and fish. These areas have now been built over. He remembers the skies from the evenings, pierced with black dots—droves of birds returning to roost from agricultural fields around Delhi.

'Cities don't just get built,' he muses. 'They evolve. We must evolve in a way that is conscious of water, wildlife and forests.' His face is lit up as he tells me this. He also suggests a better usage of water in Delhi, with a reclamation of wetlands and storm water channels.

And so: the last thing we can do for our cities is really for our own selves.

It is to *allow* ourselves to be surprised, especially in our urban lives, where liveliness can drain away quickly. In 2021, during the pandemic, Ajay Kumar saw a flash of blue he didn't recognize. He didn't just turn away. He looked again. Birds come in various blues—the Ultramarine flycatcher is an electric, detergent blue. The Tickell's blue flycatcher is cobalt blue. And the Verditer flycatcher is a baby blue, powder blue. The bird Ajay saw was powder blue. What he was looking at was indeed the Verditer flycatcher, visiting Delhi from the Himalayas. He had seen it numerous times during visits to the Himalayas, but spotting one unexpectedly, and bang in the middle of a bustling urban environment, was something he did not expect, and could not forget. Ajay and I correspond daily on little things that move us—the charcoal-black tips of a dragonfly's wings, a bright orange fungus in the monsoon, he and I noticing the same Kanak champa tree blossoming near the India International Centre in summer.

Studies show how important awe is for our life—engendering a diminished sense of self, an increased sense of meaning, and greater social integration.[3] Experiences in nature create awe, and awe makes us aware of something larger than us—whether it is an ancient jaal tree, a sparkling Yamuna, a bird building nests in the rain. It humbles us, and it moves us, and this ultimately is good for us.

And awe in the ordinary is achievable, because small is so often big.

In the gathering dusk near Gurugram, birder Arun Kamath and I wait near a well-hidden pond for a dry-land bird to arrive. The Painted sandgrouse is a quiet bird that is so well camouflaged it seems to melt into the ground. Because it is a bird that prefers rocks and arid areas, both the male and female are patterned such that they resemble sand, pebbles and scree. Arun had found the birds visiting a secretive watering hole every day, at a quarter to seven in the evening. We have been waiting for about an hour, since 6 p.m. It is a hot day, and we imagine the birds would be thirsty, and we stand there, frozen in the heat, not wanting to startle anything. The sun has almost set, and it is now too dark for pictures. I wonder aloud if the birds will come. 'Maybe they found another source of water,' I tell Arun. But he has been visiting every other day, and he knows the birds will keep time. It almost seems like he is talking about a family member. 'I am telling you, they will come,' he insists.

And they do. Just as it turns seven, three birds arrive for their daily drink. They land near the water and immediately became invisible. But we know where to look, and we see through our eyes, the dusk too dark for camera lenses, lapping up the sight: birds with site fidelity, birds that know the time of day, birds that keep good time. Animals have their own schedule, and it seems a miracle when our times together coincide.

We need more miracles.

In a vitiated atmosphere, with countries at war, with overstimulated screens with polarized speeches, with an inability to differentiate between propaganda and fact, we often ask for our governments and systems to step up. And nearly always, they don't. What we do control in our lives is small. Yet it is not to be frittered away. We can keep the spark of compassion and curiosity alive in us. We can seek a glimmer of joy every day, we can parakeet through moments. To be humane in a cruel world is resistance; to be open-minded is a superpower.

We are taught to chase the rare, and the rare is precious—whether a promotion, an uncommon gem or an exclusive experience. But there is also wonder in the more ordinary every day, a kind of luxury in making our own happiness through this wonder. The creature that endures and survives, that carefully builds nests and the bridges of our own understanding, is a kind of miracle to behold. As Harsha Vardha Mandava, an Indian Police Service officer, found. Harsha's eyes flash with intelligence, and his speech is precise and mathematical. But when he speaks about birds, he veers towards philosophy. He was thirty-one when he started birding. In a city full of challenges, birds grounded him in a manner that taught contemplation rather than competition.

On a rainy July day in 2024, he went birding near Mangar. He was with Colonel Pankaj Sharma. It had just rained, and the forest was moist and inviting. Buffaloes wallowed in little pools. They had to keep a distance from the buffaloes, who can be aggressive towards tripods. The men tiptoed around the forest, looking at the explosion of birdlife around them. There were nesting Indian pittas, Golden orioles and Indian paradise flycatchers. There were Common woodshrikes and Black drongos. They observed a female Golden oriole feeding something, looking suspiciously like eggs, to her chicks.[4] That day, Harsha also saw something that remained etched in his mind. It was an Asian brown flycatcher, a bird that comes from the Himalayas. With a brown body and large, dark eyes, the bird is the textbook definition of a sweet little bird. It is a rarity in Delhi. That day in July was the first and only time Harsha saw it.

'I told my Additional DCP officer I won't have signal that morning. And as I entered the Aravallis, it was like stepping into another world. You know, at Chandu [Budhera] you see rarities. But in the Aravallis, you see nesting. The monsoon is such a vulnerable time of the year for the birds. Imagine, birds come to Delhi-NCR to nest. That is miraculous in itself,' he says.

On balconies and windows too, there is life waiting for us to pay attention. At home in Greater Kailash, Sejal Worah looked out of the window. There was a big monkey, a Rhesus macaque, sitting outside. 'You know, he had an egg in each hand,' she laughs. 'And I thought, someone is going to miss her eggs today.' A little later, she opened her own refrigerator, a large model with a heavy door. The fridge was lighter. Her eggs were missing. The monkey had slipped in and taken them. 'So here was this guy. He had quietly got into my house. He had efficiently opened the fridge and taken only what he needed. Then, he slipped out. It felt like a real moment. I am living in a place where so much happens in the real world, where the wild is almost always cheek-by-cheek with us.' From her balcony, Sejal has counted thirty-six bird species.

On a hot day during the pandemic, Sukumar Ranganathan, editor-in-chief of *Hindustan Times* newspaper, opened his window on the erstwhile

Hindustan Times office on Kasturba Gandhi Marg. In hopped a one-legged Common myna. It was initially shy, but grew bold enough to sit on his table and watch him work. 'A Shikra must have been watching, for one afternoon it flew into my room and sat on my coat hanger, glaring at me angrily, perhaps because it realized there was no quarry on offer. I let it be,' Sukumar says. 'We have moved office since but I loved that building. When I was working at the *Mint* newspaper in the same building, my room was on the sixteenth floor. During winters I could see the pelicans from Delhi zoo's open-air aviary riding the thermals outside my window. And on the terrace of the next building were a pair of nesting Egyptian vultures.'

Decades ago, Ravi Singh saw three kinds of vultures over Central Delhi; now, another man looks out of his window to see the vultures that remain. In the intervening time, *Gyps* vultures have gone locally extinct; yet the two men are connected by their interest in birds, looking at the same sky, searching for and locating something they value in it.

'If you're holding public or important positions, you tend to lose track of yourself,' Harsha says. 'You feel you are doing things for people; you become attached to your titles. Birding is a reminder—the world has been going for many years, and you too will be recycled. And it doesn't matter who you are, you still have to go looking for the bird.'

We can go out to look at what has been around for centuries—small beetle or big quartzite, floating seed or tree monument, Yamuna or Sahibi, firefly or moth, frog or leopard, longing or belonging. We can go outwards, and this will also mean going inwards. We can search on occasion, and we can search every day, in the flickering light of fireflies and in the flaming lights of our desires, and I hope we always find what we are looking for.

I look every day for the wild in the capital. I look at my body and its minus places with kind eyes, sensing the things it has survived, knowing my spine has semal grafted into it. I have seen death and felt its presence whisper near me, and my eyes are suddenly those of the Yamuna, carrying ashes, but also life. I see the wet humid monsoon air that is curling the page I am writing notes on, and I am reminded of rain coming down in needle-sheets as I walked Sanjay Van one night, the place full of freedom and the rain-sound beloved, like that of a thousand Coppersmith barbets calling. I feel rather than see the needles growing out of my skin, my armour to defend me and those I love, learned and inherited from the thorny trees of the region. I hope a bird will come too, amidst the thorns, and make her nest there. And so I carry forth, heart soft and body strong, waiting for life.

NEHA'S FIELD NOTES

The number of times nature has surprised me in the city are too many to count. Here are just a few. Little damselflies—tiny, delicate relatives of dragonflies—shining in the sun, some of them mating, revealing many as I learn to see one. Jewel-green Senegal golden dartlets and green-and-yellow Coromandel marsh dartlets, gleaming, balancing on a tiny water lily leaf, which balances itself in the water at Dhanauri wetlands in Uttar Pradesh. When the damselflies mate, they form a heart-shape. A jackal raising his head right next to the busy Aruna Asaf Ali Marg, sniffing the air under an amaltas tree. A Nilgai antelope sitting at the side of the road like domestic cattle. Leopard tracks in Asola. A white Barn owl blinking at me from a lamppost in my girlhood, and later, finding an owl with cat-ears, the Indian Scops owl, on night walks in my adulthood.

There are surprising, wondrous ways to tell time that are not connected to mechanical clocks. The male Purple sunbird changes his feathers as per his breeding season. At the beginning of the year, he sports bright red and gold epaulettes and a brilliant, iridescent purple plumage. Towards the end of the year, he sheds his colours and begins to resemble the yellow-olive female sunbird. What gives him away is a neat line down his front, which is still purple. This is his 'eclipse plumage', and you can guess what time of the year it is by looking at it. The other way to tell time is to look at Indian trees—the semal, palash and amaltas will drop their leaves and put out flowers in North Indian spring, summer and monsoon respectively. Watching sunbirds nest near me, and watching Indian trees flower year after year, is my own way of understanding seasons, a reminder to think in longer timeframes, and to slow down. To surrender one's arms to the flow of the natural world, to breathe air sweetened by wild grass and cut by cream wave moths, to both see and smell as we breathe in. To be part of the world, and not a competitor with it.

Appendix

Delhi Flowering Chart

Code		Description
N	Native	Native to at least one of Delhi's ecoregions (mostly northern Aravallis)
E	Exotic	Introduced from a different geographical area
I	Indigenous	Indigenous to some other ecoregion within the Indian Subcontinent
Nat	Naturalized	Naturalized in Delhi (a non-native which is now regenerating on the Ridge)

Notes

- Delhi lies at the confluence of two ecoregions—the Aravalli west thorn scrub forest to the west (also, the northern Aravallis within that), and the Upper Gangetic moist deciduous forests to the east.
- For the purpose of identifying nativity of trees, the focus is mostly on the Aravalli forest. We don't have enough information about the species of the Upper Gangetic Plains, mostly because all the areas have undergone huge modifications due to agriculture and urbanization over the last few hundred years.
- Flowering times are only indicative, and based on personal observations, and information from *Trees of Delhi* (Krishen, P. 2006), *Delhi through the Seasons* (Singh, K. 2015), *Abha Mahal Bagh* (Krishen, P. 2020)
- The flowering of many trees found in Delhi is impacted by the rains, and thus may vary from year to year. Several species may have a second flush of flowering in the rains.
- The changing climate in recent years—warmer winters, hotter summers, and erratic rainfall—has impacted the flowering and fruiting phenology of trees and thus, it may differ a bit from what is indicated here.

Common Name	*Scientific Name*	N/I/ E/ Nat	Jan		Feb		Mar		April		May		June		July		Aug		Sep		Oct		Nov		Dec	
TREES																										
Amaltas	*Cassia fistula*	N								*	*	*	*	*	*	*	*	*								
Arjun	*Terminalia arjuna*	N								*	*	*														
Ashok	*Polyalthia longifolia*	I										*	*	*												
Bakain	*Melia azedarach*	I						*	*																	
Barna	*Crateva adansonii*	N							*	*																
Bottlebrush	*Callistemon viminalis*	E					*	*																		
Chamrod	*Ehretia laevis*	N					*	*	Fruit	Fruit					and whenever it rains!											
Copperpod	*Peltophorum pterocarpum*	I									*	*	*	*							*	*	*	*		
Coral Tree	*Erythrina variegata*	I						*	*	*																
Desi Babool	*Vachellia nilotica*	N															*	*	*	*	*	*				
Doodhi	*Wrightia tinctoria*	N							*	*																
Gulmohur	*Delonix regia*	E								*	*	*														
Harshingar	*Nyctanthes arbor-tristis*	N																*	*	*	*	*	*	*		

Common Name	*Scientific Name*	N/I/E/Nat	Jan		Feb		Mar		April		May		June		July		Aug		Sep		Oct		Nov		Dec	
Imli	*Tamarindus indicus*	E												*	*	*	*	*								
Indrokh	*Terminalia coronata*	N	*	*																					*	*
Jaal	*Salvadora oleoides*	N			*	*	*	*	Fruit	Fruit																
Jacaranda	*Jacaranda mimosifolia*	E							*	*	*															
Jamun/Rai Jamun	*Syzigium cumini/ nervosum*	N						*	*	*	*	*														
Jarul	*Lagerstroemia speciosa*	I								*	*	*	*													
Jhinjheri	*Bauhinia racemosa*	N								*	*	*														
Jungle Jalebi	*Pithecellobium dulce*	E							*	*			Fruit	Fruit												
Kachnar	*Bauhinia variegata*	Nat				*	*	*																		
Kadamb	*Neolamarckia cadamba*	I															*	*	*							
Kaim	*Mitragyna parvifolia*	N										*	*	*	*	*										
Kanak Champa	*Pterospermum acerifolium*	I					*	*	*	*																
Kaniar	*Bauhinia purpurea*	I																			*	*	*	*		

Common Name	*Scientific Name*	N/I/E/Nat	Jan		Feb		Mar		April		May		June		July		Aug		Sep		Oct		Nov		Dec	
Karanj	*Pongamia pinata*	I							*	*																
Khair	*Senegalia catechu*	N													*	*										
Khejri	*Prosopis cineraria*	N						*	*	*	*															
Kullu	*Sterculia urens*	N				*	*	*	Red Fruit																	
Kummath	*Senegalia senegal*	N										*	*	*												
Kusum	*Schleichera oleosa*	I					New Red leaves	*	*						New Red leaves											
Mahua	*Madhuca longifolia var. latifolia*	I									*	*	New Red leaves													
Mango	*Mangifera indica*	I						*	*	*																
Marodphalli	*Helicteres isora*	N						*	*										*	*	*	*				
Mexican Silk Floss	*Chorisia speciosa*	E																			*	*	*	*	*	
Moulshri	*Mimusops elengi*	I										*	*	*	*	*	*									
Neem	*Azadirachta indica*	Nat							*	*	*															

Common Name	Scientific Name	N/I/E/Nat	Jan		Feb		Mar		April		May		June		July		Aug		Sep		Oct		Nov		Dec	
Palash	*Butea monosperma*	N					*	*	*	*																	
Peelu	*Salvadora persica*	N			*	*	*	*	Fruit	Fruit																	
Peepul	*Ficus religiosa*	Nat					New Red leaves																				
Phalsa	*Grewia asiatica*	N							*	*	*																
Pilkhan	*Ficus virens*	I					New Red leaves																				
Roheda	*Tecomella undulata*	N					*	*	*																		
Ronjh	*Vachellia leucophloea*	N																*	*	*	*						
Saijan/ Moringa	*Moringa oliefera*	I					*	*	*	*	*	*	*	*	*	*	*	*	*	*	*	*	*	*	*	*	
Salar/Salai	*Boswellia serrata*	N				*	*	*																			
Saptaparni	*Alstonia scholaris*	I																				*	*	*	*	*	
Sausage tree	*Kigelia pinnata*	E							*	*	*	*	*	*	*	*	*	*									
Semal	*Bombax ceiba*	N				*	*	*																			

Common Name	Scientific Name	N/I/ E/ Nat	Jan		Feb		Mar		April		May		June		July		Aug		Sep		Oct		Nov		Dec	
Shahtoot	*Morus spp.*	E/Nat /N*			*	*	Fruit	Fruit	Fruit																	
Shisham	*Dalbergia sissoo*	I					*	*																		
Siris	*Albizia lebbeck*	Nat						*	*	*	*															
Yellow tabebuia	*Tabebuia aurea*	E					*	*																		
SHRUBS																										
Aak	*Calotropis procera*	N			*	*	*	*	*																	
Adusa	*Justicia adhatoda*	N	*	*	*	*	*	*	*																*	*
Arni	*Clerodendrum phlomidis*	N	*	*	*	*	*	*	*	*													*	*	*	*
Chitrak	*Plumbago zeylanica*	N	*	*	*	*	*	*													*	*	*	*	*	*
Gangeti	*Grewia tenax*	N											*	*	*	*	*	*								
Goya Khair	*Dichrostachys cinerea*	N											*	*	*	*	*	*	*							
Jungli karonda	*Carissa spinarum*	N					*	*	*	*							*	*	*	*						

*Several species of Shahtoot may occur in the Delhi region, including hybrids between them

Common Name	*Scientific Name*	N/I/ E/ Nat	Jan		Feb		Mar		April		May		June		July		Aug		Sep		Oct		Nov		Dec	
Kair/Kareel	*Capparis decidua*	N							*	*	*	*	*						*	*	*	*				
Kamini	*Murraya paniculata*	I					*	*	*	*	*				*	*	*	*	*							
Kanthari/ Heens	*Capparis sepiaria*	N							*	*	*	*														
Neeli vajradanti	*Barleria cristata*	N																					*	*	*	*
Peeli vajradanti	*Barleria prionitis*	N				*	*	*	*												*	*	*	*	*	*
Safed Vajradanti	*Barleria cristata var. albida*	N																					*	*	*	*
Woodfordia	*Woodfordia fruticosa*	N					*	*																		
CLIMBERS																										
Doodhi bel	*Vallaris solanaceae*	N					*	*	*	*																
Flame Vine	*Pyrostegia venusta*	E			*	*	*	*																		
Madhavilata	*Hiptage benghalensis*	I					*	*	*																	
Madhumalti	*Combretum indicum*	I				*	*	*	*	*	*							*	*	*	*	*	*	*		
Shatavari	*Asparagus racemosus*	N																			*	*	*	*		

Acknowledgements

This book would not have been possible without the community of friends and family who have looked out for me and spread their shade.

I'd like to thank Pradip Krishen, Vallari Sheel, Vijay Dhasmana and Vikram Iyer for help with plant identification. If plants grow through every corner of this book, it's because of their help. Thank you to Sohail Madan and Nikhil John for help in identifying birds and bugs. Thank you to Anita Mani, Vallari Sheel, Shalini Umachandran and Arpita Nath for reading the manuscript. Thanks to my birding buddies Pankaj Sharma and Bhrigu, and to my dog-loving girlfriends Megha Moorthy and Rituparna Sarkar, for their enthusiasm and conversations.

For inspiration and friendship: Sumana Roy, Robert Macfarlane, Amitav Ghosh, Hansda Sowvendra Shekhar, Yuvan Aves, Mahesh Rangarajan, Bittu Sahgal, Aasheesh Pittie, Qamar Qureshi.

Thank you to Udayan Mitra, Ananth Padmanabhan and Kanishka Gupta for being wonderful men who I love working with. Thank you Ritu for the lovely, leaping illustrations for *Wild Capital*, and for Bonita for many cover conversations. Thank you to my friends and colleagues at WWF for letting me dream and walk in forests—Ravi Singh (who is responsible in part for me being in conservation), Sejal Worah (never too busy to talk about wildlife, and thank you for the montane shelter), Dipankar Ghose (the kindest man to bird with), Yash Shethia (whose perusal of books and podcasts far exceeds mine: such an inspiration), and to my buddies Priya, Murali, Deepak, Tejas, Sumer, Sanket, Pranav and Nikhil, who put up with me getting freshly surprised on seeing a small Indian mongoose or seed spinning to the ground every day. Thank you to my trainer Nitin for making me stronger during a tough year of my life.

Thank you to *Mint* and Roundglass Sustain for hosting my columns for years—some of those ideas found their way into this book.

To my family: Ma, Baba, Nishant, Gunjan. To my friends, who have seen me through a year of sickness and loss: Bilal, Jenny, Avishek, Bibek, Priyanka, Gaurav, Liza, Pinki, Roshan, Paroma, Noor and Siby.

To you, the reader, thank you for caring, and for walking with me.

To Gypsy: for a love that I cannot put in words. To little Figo, for the mischief. And to Adityan Nair: brightest star in the galaxy, my personal source of daily wonder, thank you for surprising me *every day* (how do you do it?), and also for being so cool.

Notes

Introduction

1. Grade, Aaron, Lerman, Susannah, Warren, Paige. (2021). Perilous choices: landscapes of fear for adult birds reduces nestling condition across an urban gradient. *Ecosphere*. 12. 10.1002/ecs2.3665.
2. From the poem, 'Joy Is the Justice We Give Ourselves', by J. Drew Lanham, published 31 August 2022 in *Emergence* magazine. Retrieved online: https://emergencemagazine.org/poem/joy-is-the-justice-we-give-ourselves/
3. Delhi-NCR or Delhi National Capital Region refers to a metropolitan area around Delhi, containing parts of neighbouring states of Rajasthan, Uttar Pradesh and Haryana. The region stretches over 55,000 square kilometres, and was a move to harmonize development. *Wild Capital* chiefly centres around Delhi and its adjoining towns of Faridabad and Gurugram, because there are no boundaries in nature, and Delhi influences, and is influenced by, the wetlands of Gurugram, and the rocky areas of Faridabad.

Forgotten Gardens

1. This was the small Indian mongoose, a wily predator who has adapted fairly well to urban life.
2. To my great joy, I learned later that all worker ants are female.
3. Ants can make sounds by rubbing body parts, but these aren't easily heard by people. Not only do ants recognize nest mates, but they also identify the 'caste' or the role of another ant in a colony, by detecting odours from hydrocarbons in ant cuticles.
4. Ants are social insects with 'ritualized' movements in communication, which can include dances and jerking. Ants also pick up clues from pheromones, which forms a kind of group memory. This helps in choosing favourable paths and disregarding unfavourable ones, write Jackson, D.E. and Ratnieks, F.L. (2006). Communication in ants. *Current biology*, *16*(15), R570-R574. https://doi.org/10.1016/j.cub.2006.07.015.
5. These were carpenter ants.
6. The touch-me-not plant responds to external stimuli (like touch) by rapidly losing water from its leaves. This causes leaves to droop and close down and may be an adaptation to protect from browsing animals (who may be startled by the sudden movement).
7. Translator Deepa Bhasthi says 'translation is a rigourous act of love'. Bhasthi translated Banu Mushtaq's *Heart Lamp* from Kannada, and the book won the International Booker prize in 2025. In a sense, 'translating' the verbal and non-verbal language of animals also feels like an act of love. For the interview see: https://www.deccanherald.com/india/karnataka/for-me-it-was-important-to-carry-kannada-into-another-language-3570026#google_vignette.
8. The Delhi Parks and Gardens Society identifies more than 18,000 public parks and gardens in the National Capital Territory. But this number does not account for fast-disappearing private gardens, local green spots or avenues, getting swallowed by the city's increasing girth.

Forgotten Trees: The Name of This Tree Is My Tree

1. The neem probably grew in the wild only in a region in northern Myanmar, near the Assam–Bangladesh border (Krishen, P. 2006). It has been transported over thousands of years across the Indian subcontinent (illustrations of the neem have been found in Harappan pottery) and was even introduced to sub-Saharan Africa by the British in the nineteenth century. Due to its cultural, religious and medicinal significance, it has become a much beloved tree, found in almost every city and village in India and now naturalized across the country. Its scientific name *Azadirachta indica* possibly came from the Persian word *Azad-darakht-e Hind*, meaning the 'free tree of India', referring perhaps to the fact that it is usually free of insects and diseases. For more on the neem, see: Krishen, P. 2006. 'Neem' in *Trees of Delhi*. Dorling Kindersely. Pp. 242–43 and *Azadirachta indica*, Plants of the World Online. Retrieved from https://powo.science.kew.org/taxon/urn:lsid:ipni.org:names:1213180-2
2. In 2018, over 16,500 trees were slated to be felled in Sarojini Nagar and nearby neighbourhoods in South Delhi for the development of residential and retail spaces. This led to a large citizens' movement to protest against the felling of these trees. The request was simple: make buildings, but build around the trees. But hundreds of mature trees have already been cut, and new buildings have sprung up where the trees once stood.
3. A jalebi is a syrupy sweet prepared in a spiral shape, consumed hot. For many, jalebis mean celebrations!
4. The Indian Grey hornbill is one of the nine hornbill species found in India. It is the only hornbill that is found in significant numbers in cities and urban areas. As long as we have fruiting trees and large trees for the birds to nest in, the species should continue to make cities their own.
5. Also see the 'Sewage and Semal' section for a similar hornbill mating ritual in Humayun's Tomb.

6. This translates to: 'You can look, but only with love', a rather poetic way of warding off the evil eye.

Forgotten Forests: Jaal

1. We often overlook grass and how important it is, both in terms of resilience and its significance for human civilization. Wheat and rice are both grasses. In his book *The Immense Journey*, anthropologist Loren Eiseley writes about the power of the seed and the petal. Reflecting on the abundance and miracle of plants, he writes: 'The golden towers of man, his swarming millions, his turning wheels, the vast learning of his packed libraries, would glimmer dimly there in the ancestor of wheat, a few seeds held in a muddy hand. Without the gift of flowers and the infinite diversity of their fruits, man and bird, if they had continued to exist at all, would be indistinguishable … the weight of a petal has changed the world and made it ours.'
2. The Sahibi is a historically and ecologically important river of the Aravallis. It originates in Saiwar hills in Sikar district in Rajasthan, flows through Haryana, and enters Delhi at Najafgarh, finally merging with the Yamuna downstream of the Wazirabad barrage. Historically, it formed the Najafgarh jheel, one of North India's largest seasonal wetlands, now mostly drained and replaced by the Najafgarh drain. For maps and more details, see: Rao, R. (2020). 'Sahibi Nadi: How a river was killed'. *Down To Earth*. Retrieved from https://www.downtoearth.org.in/pollution/sahibi-nadi-how-a-river-was-killed-74254
3. Gazetteer of the Delhi district, 1883–84. Page 3.
4. The Peeli vajradanti (*Barleria prionitis*) is a native flowering shrub of scrub and deciduous forests throughout the country, including the Aravallis. It is adorned with bright yellow flowers for several months in the year. It is also an important herbal remedy in Ayurveda—the well-known Vicco Vajradanti toothpaste has extracts from this plant for good oral health.

5. In the Thar desert and other dry regions, the jaal is loved because of its luxurious, cooling shade, gratefully lapped up by people and animals in the unforgiving heat.
6. From the Gazetteer of the Delhi district. Part A, 1912. Page 15.
7. Vilayati kikar (*Neltuma juliflora,* formerly *Prosopis julifora*) was introduced in India in the late 1800s. Alkaloids present in its roots inhibit the growth of other plants nearby, helping it out-compete native species and becoming invasive in the process. In its native range in Central and South America, other plants have coevolved and coexist with it. For more on this, see: Kaur, R., Gonzáles, W.L., Llambi, L.D., Soriano, P.J., Callaway, R.M., Rout, M.E., et al. (2012). 'Community Impacts of *Prosopis juliflora* Invasion: Biogeographic and Congeneric Comparisons'. *PLoS ONE* 7(9): e44966. https://doi.org/10.1371/journal.pone.0044966
8. The flowers and fruit of kair or kareel are prepared as pickles and vegetables (the locally well-known kair-sangri cooked in Rajasthan is an amalgam of kair and sangri, the *Prosopis cineraria*).
9. Kaplan, Stephen. 'The restorative benefits of nature: Toward an integrative framework'. *Journal of Environmental Psychology*, Volume 15, Issue 3, 1995. Pp 169–182: https://doi.org/10.1016/0272-4944(95)90001-2.
10. Many authors have written about our weird penchant for having any type of green, and often the wrong type of green, in planning decisions. 'Now the coastal forest is largely gone; the flatlands are mostly farms and fisheries. But humans long for green, so the trees make their way back to the cities in ceramic pots and roadside verges, climbing the trellis of every back alley unabated,' writes Jessica J. Lee in her 2019 book on her family's roots in Taiwan, *Two Trees Make a Forest*.
11. See the chapter 'Forgotten Forests', to understand how *Neltuma juliflora* should be cleared.

Forgotten Words: Fireflies

1. Fireflies create light through a chemical reaction known as bioluminescence. They have a compound called luciferin in specialized abdominal cells which reacts with oxygen to produce light. Fireflies can control this light production, and use it for communication, especially for mating.
2. All over the world, firefly populations are facing steep and tragic declines. Habitat loss, light pollution and pesticide use are some of the major threats fireflies face, found Lewis et al. (2021) in their survey with experts. For more, see: Lewis, S.M., Wong, C.H., Owens, A.C., Fallon, C., Jepsen, S., Thancharoen, A., Wu, C., De Cock, R., Novák, M., López-Palafox, T. and Khoo, V., 2020. 'A global perspective on firefly extinction threats'. *BioScience*, *70*(2), pp.157–167: https://doi.org/10.1093/biosci/biz157
3. Approximately 2,000 species of fireflies are known worldwide, and about fifty are found in India.

Forgotten Trees: Semal

1. The Black kite (*Milvus migrans*) is a ubiquitous bird of the Delhi skyline. Access to year-round food in the form of meat scraps in landfills and waste dumps, and perhaps the disappearance of the *Gyps* vultures, has given them the space to thrive in the city. The semal, tall with broad, spreading branches, is the perfect tree for this large bird to nest in. Their plentiful nests can be spotted across semal trees in the city.
2. Many seeds have fluff to help carry them on the wind. One example is that of saptaparni, the *Alstonia scholaris* tree, which blooms in October, around the time of the Durga puja and Navratri.
3. The semal is also known as the Red Silk Cotton tree—'red' after its red flowers, and 'silk cotton' after the cotton-like filaments in its seed pods. The 'cotton' carries the seed, sailing buoyed in the wind. Some of the streets and parks of Delhi get coated

with a sea of these white fibres once the seed pods burst open. The fibre is collected and used to stuff mattresses and pillows. My mother got me one such pillow. It was perfect, because the stuffing was soft; it was also balanced, because the seeds nestled in the cotton rendered it with a firmness. Semal cotton thus carries seeds for the trees, and repose and dreams for us.

Forgotten Forests: The Central Ridge

1. The Delhi Ridge is part of the Aravalli hill range. Morphologically spread over 8,000 hectares, it has four main portions—the Northern Ridge, near Delhi University, the Central Ridge, the Southern Ridge (near Tughlaqabad) and the South-Central Ridge, near Sanjay Van. The British appeared unimpressed by portions of the Delhi Ridge and this might have led to their afforestation drive. The District Gazetteer of Delhi, 1883–84, describes the vegetation of the Ridge as follows: 'Their surface is generally bare supporting little or no vegetation save a stunted keekar (*Acacia nilotica*) or kareel (*Capparis decidua*) or the small bush beri (*Ziziphus nummularia*), which with its prickly thorn, is so inhospitable to the foot traveller.'
2. The aak, *Calotropis procera*, belongs to the milkweed family. It is a larval host plant for the Plain tiger and Striped tiger butterflies. The caterpillars of these butterflies feed on the leaves of the aak, and store the toxic compounds produced by the plant, which make emerging butterflies unpalatable to predators. And because tiger butterflies are toxic, the female Danaid eggfly butterfly mimics the Plain tiger butterfly to appear toxic. As they say, imitation is the sincerest form of flattery!
3. Pradip and his team recreated the 'Roee', the natural shrubland of the Thar desert (akin to the chaparrals of California) in the Kishan Bagh Sand Dune Park, located at the foot of the Nahargarh hill. For more, see: Krishen, P. 'Kishan Bagh Concept Note' (2021). Retrieved from https://era-india.org/resources/

kishan-bagh-concept-note-2021. For the Rao Jodha Desert Rock Park, see ERA-India. Retrieved from https://era-india.org/project/rao-jodha-desert-rock-park/#era_project_about_project

4. With its beautiful yellow, orange or red flowers, the roheda (*Tecomella undulata*), also called Marwar teak, is the state flower of Rajasthan. Overexploited for its timber and medicinal properties, it is listed as 'endangered' in the IUCN Red List of Threatened Species 2020. For more, see: Kalia, R.K., Rai, M.K., Sharma, R. and Bhatt, R. K. (2014). 'Understanding *Tecomella undulata*: an endangered pharmaceutically important timber species of hot arid regions'. *Genetic resources and crop evolution*, *61*, 1397–1421.
5. Pradip points out that between 1934–40, the British and the NDMC (New Delhi Municipal Corporation) hunted and killed hundreds of jackals in the Central Ridge because the howling of the jackals would disturb the Viceroy's sleep (the Viceroy House, now Rashtrapati Bhawan, is located at the edge of the Ridge). Even though the authorities tried to exterminate the jackals, the animals have held on, and a decent population exists in almost all parts of the Delhi Ridge, including the Central Ridge.
6. See the 'Firefly-light, Owl-light' chapter.
7. While vilayati kikar is a terrible invasive, a lookalike tree, *Prosopis cineraria*, the jand tree, also called khejri (from which the delicious sangri is derived) is indigenous to India and should be encouraged.

The Found City: Vallari's Delhi

1. In the years that I have studied the tree, I note there is always a feeding frenzy on a semal with open blossoms. Sometimes birds start their inspection even earlier, coming to see the buds before they open. The semal is also a tree that is cultivated and planted in the city for its large, showy flowers. Somewhat like the peepal and banyan, the semal manages to grow itself in unexpected places. Vallari notes the wind-dispersed semal is

a good colonizer of back-lanes, growing itself even with poor nutrients behind houses.

2. For more on this flower, please see the chapter, 'Found Places: Tughlaqabad'.
3. Lee, Jessica J. and Schlanger, Zoë. 'Learning the Language of Plants'. *Orion*. 7 May 2024: https://orionmagazine.org/article/plant-language-jessica-j-lee-zoe-schlanger/
4. Like the semal, the palash is another ornithophilous flower. It is a hardy native tree which is able to grow in many soil types. It can withstand frost, heat, drought, waterlogging and even salinity (*Trees of Delhi*, Pradip Krishen, 2006). It is a pioneer species of drier forests across India, and it comes up whenever a gap opens up in the forest. The Battle of Plassey (or Palashi) is named after the abundant palash of the area. Another name for the palash, apt for its licks of orange flowers, is 'flame of the forest'.
5. The palash attracts several nectarivorous birds. However, only the purple sunbird is considered to be an effective pollinator. For more on this, see: Tandon, R., Shivanna, K.R., and Mohan Ram, H.Y. (2003). 'Reproductive biology of *Butea monosperma (Fabaceae)*'. *Annals of Botany*, *92*(5), 715–723.
6. Flying foxes, *Pteropus giganteus*, are large frugivorous bats whose faces may remind you of puppies. In Delhi, they roost on Arjuna trees in Janpath and nearby areas, and also on large trees in Hauz Khas lake. Many bats need large bodies of water to drink from. Some are unable to sip water from shores. Instead, they have to dive down while flying to scoop up the water. You can see bats drinking at dusk in the lakes of Bhopal in Madhya Pradesh. For cities to sustain different kinds of bats, we need large ponds and lakes, as well as tall trees and undisturbed roosts like caves for smaller bats. In many parts of Delhi, undisturbed parts of old monuments serve as bat caves.

The Found City: Pankaj's Delhi

1. The Chandu-Budhera wetlands lie in agricultural areas on the outskirts of Gurugram. The area has a rich bird life, including

both residential and migratory species. Proximity to Sultanpur National Park, the Najafgarh jheel and the erstwhile Basai wetlands make this part of an important wetland complex. Chandu-Budhera is not a protected area and is constantly in flux, facing the pressure of agriculture and expanding urbanization.

2. Delhi is the second most bird-rich capital in the world, after Nairobi, Kenya. Partly, this is because the city lies on the Central Asian Flyway, a major migratory route taken by birds that breed in Siberia and Central Asia, and winter south of the Himalayas. The city also offers a variety of habitats in the form of the Delhi Ridge, the Yamuna and green spaces criss-crossing the built matrix. A total of 471 species have been recorded in the area since 1975, including both resident and migratory species, many of them breeding in the city. Vyas, S. (2023). *The Birds of the Delhi Area.* Juggernaut Books, New Delhi. Pp. 318.
3. Also see the chapter 'Sunil's Delhi'.

The Found City: Sunil's Delhi

1. See the 'Found Forests' section.
2. Every year between 2016–21, a pair of Brahminy mynas would nest in a nest box in my balcony in Delhi. They lined the nest with grass, but also with other things they found around them, including glimmering pieces of plastic.
3. Desert winds from the Thar desert area.

Found Forests: Aravalli

1. See 'Sunil's Delhi'.
2. Buzz pollination is a specialized method used by some bees, such as solitary bees and bumblebees, to dislodge pollen from the anthers of the flowers they visit. They do this by grabbing the flower and vibrating their flight muscles, causing the anther to vibrate and dislodge the pollen. While this helps in pollinating

the flowers, the bees do it because pollen is a primary protein food source for them, and they are able to get it from these flowers without much competition from other insects. Many of our common edible plants, such as eggplants and tomatoes, are pollinated this way. For more, see: Vallejo-Marín, M. (2019). 'Buzz pollination: studying bee vibrations on flowers'. *New Phytologist*, *224*(3), 1068–74.

3. See the section 'Forgotten Forests: Jaal'.
4. M.Z. Siddiqui, in a 2011 paper, writes about how Salai's frankincense was used as incense, for fumigation or as a multi-purpose aromatic.
5. Ecologists and restoration practitioners across India, like Vijay, have been experimenting with germinating and growing native plants for a couple of decades now. This information has been put together and is now available in the Seed Germination Database of ERA-India (Ecological Restoration Alliance). Find it here: https://era-india.org/seed-germination/
6. Siddiqui, M.Z. '*Boswellia serrata*, a potential anti-inflammatory agent: An overview'. *The Indian Journal of Pharmaceutical Sciences*. May 2011. 73(3):255-61. doi: 10.4103/0250-474X.93507. PMID: 22457547; PMCID: PMC3309643.
7. Crows have often taken me to Indian eagle-owls. The sound of three crows mobbing what seemed like the cliffside led us to find a rather sleepy looking eagle-owl, indignantly holding on to his perch in the face of the corvid onslaught in Gurugram's Aravallis.

Found Spaces: Tughlaqabad

1. *Lannea coromandelica*, also known as the Indian ash tree, or gurjan in Hindi.
2. This is the biogeographic region of the Earth that comprises all of Europe, Asia north of the Himalayas, and Africa north of the Sahara. Many migratory birds visit Delhi from the Palearctic.

Found Words: Bittern-Grass

1. Also see the chapter, 'Pankaj's Delhi'.
2. Black-breasted weaver bird nests are beautified by placing cow dung, clay or human excreta, yellow flowers or flower stamens in northern Tamil Nadu. Although several other wetland plants occur in the region, Black-breasted weavers choose only two nest-supporting species, sacrificial grass (*D. bipinnata)* and narrow leaf or cattail (*Typha angustifolia)*, observations by M. Pandian, in a 2023 paper in *Indian Birds*. Pandian, M., 2024. 'Nesting biology of the Black-breasted Weaver *Ploceus benghalensis* in Tamil Nadu, India'. *Indian Birds* 19 (4). Pp. 99–106; Prakash, D., Niangthianhoi, S.L., Kumar, R., and Khudsar, F.A. 2020. 'Nest construction process in Streaked Weaver'. *Indian Birds* 15 (6). Pp. 168–174; Pittie, A., Taher, S., Hash, C.T. 1999. 'Notes on the Breeding Plumage of the Male Black-breasted Weaverbird *Ploceus benghalensis* Near Hyderabad, Andhra Pradesh'. *JBHNS*, Vol. 96, No. 2.
3. Amur falcons are small raptors that migrate from Siberia to South Africa, stopping over in Northeast India to feed and fuel themselves for the long journey ahead. They make the longest migration for falcons. In 2012, we learned that thousands were slaughtered in villages in Nagaland for consumption and sale. I was part of a ten-year long successful campaign to protect Amur falcons. The villagers were moved after learning about falcon migrations. For more, see my book, *Wild and Wilful* (2021), and Sinha, N. (2023) 'When hunters turned protectors: The story of the Amur Falcon'. *The Mint Lounge*. Retrieved from https://www.livemint.com/mint-lounge/ideas/when-hunters-turned-protectors-111677768261913.html
4. The Yellow-footed green pigeon is a common bird of urban Delhi, although most people miss noticing them. They can be hard to spot as they are completely arboreal, and their green colour blends well with leaves. Unlike their cousins the Blue rock pigeons, these are frugivorous birds, feeding on figs and

other fruit. They can often be seen sunning themselves on the tops of trees early in the mornings, and have haunting, whistling calls which sound like a melodious wee-wao-ooo.

5. Conservation organizations such as ATREE (Ashoka Trust for Research in Ecology and the Environment) are advocating for the recognition of grasslands and scrublands as ONEs (Open Natural Ecosystems). These landscapes are important for soil carbon sequestration, to support rural livelihoods and harbour unique biodiversity. Unfortunately, most of them carry the colonial legacy of being called 'wastelands' and have historically been unrecognized.
6. Press Information Bureau, 5 November 2019. https://www.pib.gov.in/pressrelesedetailm.aspx?prid=1590395#:~:text=There%20is%20a%20net%20conversion%20of%200.84,and%20gullied%20and%20/%20or%20ravinous%20land.

Found Places: Firefly-light, Owl-light

1. This subspecies is *Otus bakkamoena gangeticus*. Though not as common as the Spotted owlet, I have seen them on many occasions, though most citizens remain unaware of their presence.
2. Dacke, Marie et al. 2013. 'Dung beetles use the Milky Way for orientation.' *Current Biology*, Vol. 23, Issue 4. Pp. 298–300.
3. The sound of jackals howling has contributed to eerie stories around Sanjay Van. Also see the chapter 'Forgotten Forests' on jackals being exterminated in Delhi by the British for howling.
4. This makes Sanjay Van and the Central Ridge Forest especially important because insect populations have crashed in many parts of the world, dubbed the 'insect apocalypse' by some. For more, see: Sánchez-Bayo, F., and Wyckhuys, K.A. (2019). 'Worldwide decline of the entomofauna: A review of its drivers'. *Biological Conservation*, *232*, 8–27. In Europe, butterflies have declined by a third (Warren et al., 2021),

and other parts of the world report similar crashes in bees, butterflies, ants and other insects. Also see the butterfly section: 'How to Become a Butterfly'.

5. 'Anang Tal declared monument of national importance.' *The Indian Express*, 25 August 2022. https://indianexpress.com/article/cities/delhi/anang-tal-lake-declared-monument-of-national-importance-8110070/
6. This is the *Chersonesometrus fulvipes*.
7. From the Gazetteer of the Delhi district. Part A, 1912, pp. 17.
8. Mole crickets are amazing insects. They are named after their large fore limbs, which resemble those of a mole, and which help them burrow with great efficiency. Males construct a special burrow just to project their mating song; the burrow is something like an acoustic horn.

The Found: How to Become a Butterfly

1. Both the meswak and jaal have recently been discovered to be larval host plants of the Pioneer butterfly. See: Chaudhary, R. (2024). '*Salvadora persica* (Family: Salvadoraceae) A New Larval Host Plant for Pioneer *Belenois aurota* (Lepidoptera: Pieridae) from India.' *Journal of the Bombay Natural History Society.* 121 (3). https://doi.org/10.17087/jbnhs/2024/v121/170673 and Chaudhary, R., and Dhasmana, V. (2025). '*Salvadora oleoides* (Family: Salvadoraceae): A New Larval Host Plant of Pioneer Butterfly *Belenois aurota* (Lepidoptera: Pieridae)'. *Journal of the Bombay Natural History Society.* 122 (2). https://doi.org/10.17087/jbnhs/2025/v122/170705
2. The term for mutualism with ants is myrmecophily, which translates to 'love of ants'. Apart from butterflies, plants also have myrmecophilous associations, and in return ants tend to the plants, pruning away parasites. In your garden, you might have observed 'aphid farming', in which ants protect aphids in return for sugary honeydew.

3. An exception is the *Hamadryas* genus of butterflies, which uses its wings to make clicking sounds when disturbed. This genus is found in Central and South America.
4. Several studies have found that butterflies are declining. The loss of habitats, rise in chemicals, and change in ranges due to global warming could be causes. Warren et al. (2021) note that butterfly numbers have fallen by 50 per cent in the United Kingdom and the Netherlands. Warren, M.S., Maes, D., van Swaay, C.A., Goffart, P., Van Dyck, H., Bourn, N.A., ... & Ellis, S. (2021). 'The decline of butterflies in Europe: Problems, significance, and possible solutions'. *Proceedings of the National Academy of Sciences*, *118*(2), e2002551117. https://doi.org/10.1073/pnas.2002551117
5. A butterfly proboscis is a long mouthpart which is like a tube or tongue; the insect uses this to take nectar.
6. Butterflies have specialized photoreceptor cells in their eyes that contain a UV-sensitive pigment called opsin. This allows them to perceive UV patterns on flowers and other butterflies, which are often used for communication and mate attraction.
7. References to dangerous 'black snakes' are also found in the Delhi Gazetteer. 'People adopt the simple classification of black (kala), yellow (pila), and spotted (chitkabri) which represents the superlative, comparative and positive degrees of banefulness. Of the poisonous [venomous] snakes the cobra is most common,' says the 1912 Delhi Gazetteer.
8. Unlike many other caterpillars, Red pierrot caterpillars bore into the leaf and consume the tissue between the upper and lower surface of the leaf, creating mine-like patterns along the way.
9. Red pierrot butterflies studied in India were infected by Wolbachia and the studied population had more females. Ankola, K., Brueckner, D., Puttaraju, H.P. 'Wolbachia endosymbiont infection in two Indian butterflies and female-

biased sex ratio in the Red Pierrot, *Talicada nyseus*'. *Journal of Biosciences*. December 2011; 36(5):845-50. doi: 10.1007/s12038-011-9149-3. PMID: 22116282.

10. A 2022 study delves into this phenomenon: Katsuma, S., Hirota, K., Matsuda-Imai, N. et al. 'A *Wolbachia* factor for male killing in lepidopteran insects'. *Nat Commun* **13**, 6764 (2022). https://doi.org/10.1038/s41467-022-34488-y
11. For more on this, see Arai et al., 2025. Hiroshi Arai, Arman Wijonarko, Susumu Katsuma, Hideshi Naka, Daisuke Kageyama, Emily A. Hornett, Gregory D.D. Hurst. 'Evolution of Wolbachia male-killing mechanism within a host species'. *Current Biology*, Volume 35, Issue 9.

Found Rivers

1. *Gyps* vultures—Whitc-rumped vultures, Slender-billed vultures and Long-billed vultures—have suffered a 99 per cent crash in India. This is attributed to the use of the veterinary painkiller diclofenac, which causes renal failure in vultures. *Gyps* vultures went locally extinct in Delhi around the beginning of the 2000s (mirroring national crashes), and so seeing nesting vultures in the city is the memory older generations have.
2. Betel nut. When chewed and spitted out, it gives off an orange colour.
3. In the present time, many puja samitis have rightly ended the practice of immersing idols into the Yamuna river.
4. The Indian skimmer, a striking bird with an orange bill in which the lower mandible is larger than the upper mandible, is a sympatric species with the Black-bellied tern. Skimmers get their name from their feeding behaviour—they scissor through water, skimming it for prey. Both Indian skimmers and Black-bellied terns nest on sandy islands or spits in rivers, and due to habitat loss, both are doing poorly. There are historic records of Indian skimmers in Najafgarh jheel. More recently, a few have also been coming to the Chandu-Budhera wetlands. Also see:

Vivek Menon and Tara Gandhi, 1992, 'Sighting of Skimmer at Najafgarh, Delhi'. *Newsletter for Birdwatchers* 32 (7–8). Pp. 17.

5. The Yamuna crossing 206 metres is the evacuation mark. For more on this, see: https://www.downtoearth.org.in/climate-change/north-india-deluge-2023-yamuna-crosses-evacuation-mark-in-delhi-highest-since-1978-90548
6. This has got to be one of the most delightfully surprising things I have read regarding the fauna of Delhi. Usha Ganguli's 1975 book, *A Guide to the Birds of the Delhi Area,* mentions that A.O. Hume recorded the Siberian crane in Najafgarh jheel. This is the same bird Colonel Pankaj Sharma thought he saw high up in the Himalayas, a rare, almost mythical bird. The Siberian crane visited only a handful of places in India (historically via Iran), until it went almost completely extinct from its migratory flyway, likely hunted to death. A single bird, Omid, migrated from Russia to Iran for the last fifteen years on the Western part of the flyway. However, his whereabouts are currently unknown and he is presumed dead.

Growing a City We Love

1. A vine with lovely white flowers. Interestingly, the Sanskrit word for vine is Vallari, and that is what my friend is named after!
2. To get started with birdwatching, invest in good bird identification books. There are apps that can help with identification, such as iNaturalist and Merlin. There are several bird and nature groups on Facebook and X. A few include Indian Birds (facebook), Indiaves (X), Trees of India (facebook).
3. Monroy, M., Keltner, D. 'Awe as a Pathway to Mental and Physical Health'. *Perspectives on Psychological Science*. March 2023; 18(2):309-320. doi: 10.1177/17456916221094856. Epub 2022 Aug 22. PMID: 35994778; PMCID: PMC10018061.
4. For more on this, see the chapter, 'Pankaj's Delhi'.

About the Author

Neha Sinha is a conservation biologist and an acclaimed author. With over a decade of wildlife conservation work under her belt, Neha is on a lifelong mission to make the joys and challenges of nature accessible to everyone, and re-look the ordinary through a new lens. Trained in conservation at Oxford University and in literature at St. Stephen's College in Delhi, Neha combines the rigours of conservation science with compelling literary flair. She is the author of *Wild and Wilful: Tales of 15 Iconic Indian Species*, published in 2021. She has received awards for both her conservation work as well as her writing, and is often found wandering in places looking for birds and the perfect words to describe the birds.

She lives in Delhi and is deeply partial to animals considered 'ugly'.

HarperCollins *Publishers* India

At HarperCollins India, we believe in telling the best stories and finding the widest readership for our books in every format possible. We started publishing in 1992; a great deal has changed since then, but what has remained constant is the passion with which our authors write their books, the love with which readers receive them, and the sheer joy and excitement that we as publishers feel in being a part of the publishing process.

Over the years, we've had the pleasure of publishing some of the finest writing from the subcontinent and around the world, including several award-winning titles and some of the biggest bestsellers in India's publishing history. But nothing has meant more to us than the fact that millions of people have read the books we published, and that somewhere, a book of ours might have made a difference.

As we look to the future, we go back to that one word—a word which has been a driving force for us all these years.

Read.

Harper Collins | Harper Sport | HARPER FICTION | HARPER NON-FICTION | हार्पर हिन्दी

HARPER LEARNING | HARPER VANTAGE | HCCB HARPERCOLLINS CHILDREN'S BOOKS | 4th | HARPER PERENNIAL

HARPER DESIGN | BOOKTOPUS | HARPER BUSINESS